TRAVELING THE TRAIL FOR PETE

TRAVELING THE TRAIL FOR PETE

Finding Belonging in a
Political Campaign

Sue Ann Rawlins

Minneapolis, Minnesota
2021

Traveling the Trail for Pete

ISBN: 978-0-578-96475-1

Trademarks used in the book are for identification purposes only.
Information about references to trademarked sources:

pgs. 70-71:
Information about the Myers Briggs Personality Type Indicator can be found on the Myers Briggs Foundation website (Myersbriggs.org).

Description of Merrick Rosen's Taking Flight with DISC Parrot Profile found on the meetingsnet.com website (https://www.meetingsnet.com/negotiation-insights/eagle-parrot-owl-dove-what-s-your-communication-style)

WOO personality strength
GALLUP CliftonStrengths website Quick Reference Card, (https://www.gallup.com/workplace/245090/cliftonstrengths-themes-quick-reference-card.aspx) 7/21/21

Direct quotations of Pete Buttigieg:

pg. 10: Pete Buttigieg, Presidential Campaign Announcement, April 14, 2019, C-SPAN. https://www.c-span.org/video/?459736-1/mayor-pete-buttigieg-officially-announces-presidential-candidacy

pg. 14: Pete Buttigieg, Campaign Fundraising Speech, Minneapolis Fine Line Café, May 2, 2019, from personal video.

pgs 118-119: Pete Buttigieg, South Bend Office Opening Speech, October 3, 2019, video posted on October 5, 2019 by Kelly Doak on YouTube. https://youtu.be/gMaGxNT00Kc

pg. 269: Pete Buttigieg, Iowa Caucus Results Speech, Des Moines, Iowa, February 3, 2020, C-SPAN. https://www.c-span.org/video/?468890-1/pete-buttigieg-addresses-supporters-des-moines-iowa

Dedication

To
Team Pete
far and wide

and

to
Pete

I'm sorry I had the audacity to call you "Pete" rather than "Mayor Pete" throughout the book, but it just felt like you were an old friend.

✈ Table of Contents

Photos can be found at travelingthetrailforpete.com

✈

Prologue

March came in like a lamb, which was a good thing because I was door knocking again. Not like that first time out with Wes in Council Bluffs, Iowa when my fingers had turned to icicles holding the clipboard. This time was easier. I barely needed to wear my Pete hat as I went door to door. It was the Sunday before Super Tuesday, and after many years as a caucus state, Minnesota would now be part of the big Super Tuesday brouhaha.

Knock, knock! "Are you voting in the Democratic primary on Tuesday? Have you decided who you're voting for? Is Pete Buttigieg one of your top three choices?"

My husband, Steve, and I had a turf in Minneapolis by Lake of the Isles. Most people weren't home. Still, I didn't mind walking door to door in the temperate slush and marking my results in the MiniVAN app on my phone. A few people answered their doors, which felt like success in itself. But since many of them were leaning towards Pete, I was able to use my personal brand of persuasion to seal the deal.

"I've met Pete. He's the real deal." Success. Just like my door knocking excursions in Iowa and New Hampshire, I felt like I'd made a difference, even if it was just a few people.

The canvassing operation was part of a big Minnesota for Pete day that started with a *Get Out the Vote* rally in St. Paul with special guests Sonal Shah, Policy Advisor for Pete for America, and Nan Whaley, Mayor of Dayton, Ohio, a surrogate for Pete. Excitement filled the air as we gathered to listen to the speeches. As I stood in the crowd, I looked around at the many familiar faces, faces I hadn't known before this started last summer. Faces I'd come to love. We'd journeyed so far together, and now this was it. Super Tuesday.

"Hello, Nan. Thank you for coming!" I said as I shook the mayor's hand after she spoke. "I'll be seeing you at the fundraiser tonight."

I'd gotten a lot braver about this sort of thing over the past six months. If you have the opportunity to meet someone, do it. It was easy to meet Pete in the rope line because that was expected, but just walking up to Nina Smith, his Traveling Press Secretary, or Mike Schmuhl, his Campaign Manager, to introduce myself took more courage. Each time, though, I was met with friendly appreciation, in keeping with the tone of Pete's campaign.

I was on the fundraising committee for the meet-and-greet cocktail party with Nan Whaley later that evening. I should say straight away that I'm not good at raising money. But at least I sold two tickets to the event. *Our* tickets. How did I ever get on the fundraising list, anyway? That's what happens when you max out with your personal contribution. Never before had I reached the $2800 FEC limit for a candidate. Not even close. Usually my donations were closer to $50. But Pete was different. Starting out with little name recognition meant that he needed the financial support more than any other candidate. And I desperately wanted him to win.

Finished with our MiniVAN canvassing list, Steve and I got in the car to go home. I was exhausted and ready for a cup of tea. Surprisingly, I wasn't looking forward to changing clothes for the fundraiser. Usually I loved dressing up, going to parties, but there was a tight turnaround, giving me no time to rest up. I had been door knocking the day before as well, and the cumulative effect was hitting me. *Why did I have to tell Nan Whaley I'd see her at the party?* I joked to myself. *Now she was expecting me.* Somehow, I'd be there with bells on.

I put the kettle on and settled down at the kitchen table to catch up on Twitter. I hadn't been able to check my feed all afternoon. One of the first posts I stumbled on was "It's too bad Pete Buttigieg dropped out of the race." I immediately thought it was a Bernie Bro with wishful thinking. They were always posting things like that. In fact, I replied, "You wish." It didn't take long for me to find out it was *real*. Pete really had dropped out of the race.

Heart pounding, I scrolled through my newsfeed in shock. Maybe Pete would have dropped out after Super Tuesday, but wasn't I just door knocking? *We don't even get to vote on Super Tuesday?* I wasn't prepared for this timing. *Wait a minute. Is the fundraiser still happening tonight?* My head was spinning.

Team Pete Twitter was awash with grief. So many friends I'd made in the past few months, many of whom I'd met in person, all upset beyond words. So many staffers also in shock. Some of the Minnesota for Pete folks were getting together at a bar to watch Pete's speech together, but I couldn't handle it. This social gal couldn't handle it. My energy and emotion had been devoted to the campaign since May. I'd met Pete and his husband, Chasten, several times; I'd even met Pete's mom, Anne. I'd met many of the staffers. I'd traveled to South Bend and many other cities meeting Pete supporters and interviewing them for my podcast *Twitter Travels for Pete.* The campaign and the people had become such an integral part of my identity—who was I without it?

1

Discovery

Susie Sunshine, full of naïve optimism, seeing the best in people. That's me. And that's exactly why I was deeply disturbed that the "best in people" didn't exist as much as I thought it did. I truly didn't understand how a man who had publicly belittled a disabled reporter, spoken crudely about women, and even criticized a Gold Star family had really been elected President of the United States. Donald Trump was who he was, but what about all the people around him? Was it suddenly acceptable to behave that way? I was continually shocked by his offensive tweets, even more so by the inaction of his party to censure him. It seemed he could do anything without consequence. Why would so many in the party just look away, put the blinders on?

What a lesson to learn so late in life—that the percentage of the population lacking moral character was much higher than I thought. I'm not sure I wanted to know that. When Trump was elected, I thought someone surely would speak up, that he'd be put in check and moderate his behavior, but instead, he seemed to only be emboldened. He said whatever he wanted to, whether it was true or not. As someone who is painfully honest, that was hard to take.

I didn't understand how his behavior was condoned, as it lowered the bar for acceptable conduct by the President of the United States. Instead of making even the smallest attempt to unite our country, he doubled down on dividing us. This was all contrary to my own core belief in community, working together and building consensus. What was happening to our country?

Before the 2016 election, Twitter was just another password I didn't want to set up. But now that Trump was tweeting every day, I joined the throngs of new accounts who wanted to read what he was tweeting. What I found on Twitter was so much more than Trump tweets, though. There were actually people trying to do something, trying to hold him accountable. I started by following well-known journalists and news outlets. And because of the platform's self-perpetuating algorithms, I quickly found other like-minded souls, other "resisters," and followed them.

As a Twitter neophyte, I discovered that the more I followed and interacted with accounts, the more followers I gained. And these people tended to be like me, all because of that Twitter algorithm. I checked my feed several times a day for some semblance of reason, fully aware I was living in a Twitter bubble. So what if I was only getting *my* side of the political divide? I wanted it that way. It was my retreat, a way of dealing with the new normal of the Trump presidency. But the news was still difficult, even inside the bubble. I started noticing the effect the political situation was having on my psyche. I didn't feel like my usual, upbeat self.

By 2019, at least we had the hope for a better future with the launch of the Democratic presidential primary. Twitter really heated up once candidates started entering the race. Finally, something uplifting to read in my news feed. In March, I stumbled on a random video clip from a CNN Town Hall that I had missed. Were these things happening already? November 2020 was still a long way off. Maybe it was the enthusiasm of the tweet, or maybe it was the glimpse of a new photogenic face, but in any case, I clicked on the video. There was no going back.

It was someone I had never seen before, a good-looking young man who reminded me of JFK. The question had been something related to immigration. I had never heard a politician, or anyone for that matter, answer the question this way: "Immigrants are part of our community. We have to take care of our communities."

My jaw dropped because this was reality. My reality, in fact. In my years of teaching English to adult immigrants, I had gotten to know many of my students personally. They wrote essays for me, took part in group discussions, and offered personal stories in casual conversation. I *knew* them as individuals. That's why I was so incensed by the constant stream of anti-immigrant rhetoric. I wondered if those critics actually knew any immigrants.

So Pete Buttigieg speaking on an issue near and dear to my heart in this way got my attention. *If he frames immigration this way, maybe he has a fresh perspective on other issues as well.* I then went down the proverbial rabbit hole searching for content on this new candidate. I found out he was the 37-year-old mayor of South Bend, Indiana, going by "Mayor Pete" since his last name was difficult to pronounce. "Buttigieg" was pronounced "Boot-edge-edge," and I quickly learned how to pronounce it correctly even though he would just be *Pete* to me.

In all the interview clips I caught of Pete, he answered questions brilliantly, befitting the Harvard - Oxford grad that he was. But it wasn't just his superior intellect that impressed me. It was his pleasing disposition as well. Pete was just so gosh darned nice! He was the smartest guy in the room but didn't act like it. He was such a refreshing change from the current occupant of the White House I wanted to listen to anything and everything he had to say.

Pete Buttigieg had a military background in Naval Intelligence and spoke seven languages, but at the forefront of his dossier was the fact that he was gay, the first openly gay candidate for the Democratic nomination for President of the United States. This made Pete an even more intriguing candidate in my mind, and his husband, Chasten, a teacher, added to the allure. I don't remember being so interested in a candidate's spouse at this early stage of a race. Chasten had charm and presence of his own and could draw a crowd on the trail speaking on LGBTQ and education issues. Pete and Chasten: a twofer.

"Have you seen that new candidate, Pete Buttigieg?" I said to my friends. "Take a look. He's impressive—a once-in-a-generation candidate." Most of them heard about Pete for the first time from me. But with over twenty candidates in the race, many of my acquaintances were intentionally distancing themselves from the Democratic primary this early on, waiting for the field to be winnowed out. Once Pete formally announced, though, he was on the radar.

Sunday, April 14, 2019 was appointment television for me. I could have streamed it on my phone, but with MSNBC covering it, I wanted to watch it on the big screen. I'd never scheduled my Sunday afternoon around a presidential campaign announcement before. The campaign had released a Spotify playlist called "Buttijams" for people to listen to while driving to the event, adding to the excitement of the day. I Buttijammed while doing the breakfast dishes. I hadn't had that much fun washing dishes in a long time.

It was a cold, rainy day in South Bend, but that didn't deter the throng lined up for blocks to get into the old Studebaker factory. Once inside, there was only partial respite in that old leaky building. No one seemed to care. The main venue was packed to capacity, with an overflow crowd outside. Some South Bend restaurants were posting on Twitter that they were welcoming those who couldn't get into the overflow. When a candidate can generate this kind of excitement, people notice.

I impatiently listened to the extensive lineup of warm-up speeches, wondering when Pete would finally appear. It was nearly an hour before Pete took the stage. Unbeknownst to me, he and Chasten, clad in rain gear, had first met with the overflow crowd outside, the right thing to do. Now as Pete addressed the main audience inside, I was there along with them, except warm and dry in my home. I was transfixed as Pete worked his rhetorical magic that I would come to know and love. His final words were galvanizing:

"My name is Pete Buttigieg. They call me Mayor Pete. I am a proud son of South Bend, Indiana. And I am running for President of the United States."

Creedence Clearwater Revival's "Up Around the Bend" started playing on the sound system and Chasten jumped up on stage to join his husband. The two embraced and then together faced the cheering crowd. Pete and Chasten, arm in arm. History in the making.

Before learning about Pete, I always thought I'd be supporting my home state senator, Amy Klobuchar, for the nomination. But that all went out the window that Sunday in April. Soon after the speech I went to PeteforAmerica.com and made my first donation: $100. That was a lot for me. It meant I was committed. I also signed up to be a volunteer and to be notified of future events. Knowing this was a historical campaign, I wanted to be involved from the start.

2

Pete at the Fine Line

I'd just snapped a photo of Picasso's "Courtesan with Hat" at the Cantor Museum when I saw the email notification on my phone. My California Twitter friend Jennifer and I were enjoying a marvelous afternoon in this Stanford University goldmine, so I was hesitant to divide my attention to check my email. But how could I not open the one from Pete for America?

I surreptitiously opened the email. Pete was coming to Minneapolis next week and did I want tickets? At this point I excused myself to Jennifer and took a seat on a nearby bench in the gallery. Next Thursday, May 2 at the Fine Line Music Cafe in Minneapolis, a smaller venue. I knew I was going, but who would be my date? I had no idea as I clicked on two tickets at the $50 level.

How early to get to the venue was the question. Was Pete so popular we needed to get there two hours early? Not yet. That would come later. My friend Laurie and I estimated a half an hour before door opening would suffice. We were right, because there were only about ten people in front of us lined up outside the Fine Line.

Extroverted by nature, I had no qualms about striking up conversations in line. One woman held an adorable, hand-painted orange sign, something tweet-worthy. It was a Team PETE 2020 sign with two dogs poking their heads over the top: Pete's and Chasten's dogs, Buddy and Truman.

"Can I take a photo of you with your sign?" I asked.

"Sure," the blonde woman replied, obviously used to being asked that question.

I asked for her Twitter handle and immediately posted the pic to Twitter. I soon discovered that the woman standing next to her was *Minneapolis for Pete* on Twitter, someone I had been following. What a coincidence! Katie was my first Pete person on social media and in real life, connecting my two Pete worlds.

Once the doors opened, Laurie and I made our way to the front to check in with the volunteer. The table inside the door was scattered with Mardi Gras beads and note cards with pens to write fishbowl questions for Pete. I had no questions; I was ready to hear whatever he had to say. Laurie and I donned our festive beads and made a beeline for a spot next to the stage. Not everyone was doing the same; some had stopped at the bar first, losing their opportunity for a prime spot. I was already savvy to Pete event strategy.

"I'll go get some drinks for us," I told Laurie, who would hold our place.

With no food available, those gin-and-tonics would hit hard if drunk too quickly. "No drinks on stage" was the sign facing me, tempting me even more to set my drink on the stage as a musician played the acoustic guitar for the warm-up. The room was filling up behind us, pushing us further to the front, squishing us all closer together. Somehow, I was not quite at the front anymore, but very close, especially when Laurie and I buddied up to the mother-daughter pair in front of us. I looked behind me and could see a balcony area filled with people as well.

Soon the introductory speeches started. As I listened, I couldn't help but notice a door to the left of the stage area that was ajar. Behind the door, someone was waiting, only a sliver of their head in view.

"Do you think that's Pete?" I motioned to Laurie. "I'll bet that's Pete."

"It must be," she whispered back.

Now that I knew Pete was standing there waiting for his cue, my eyes were glued to the door in anticipation of his entrance.

Former Minneapolis Mayor Betsy Hodges brought Pete on stage with a warm welcome. Old friends from her days as mayor, the two embraced to applause. Then Mayor Pete started his speech. I was curious to know if live-Pete was the same as TV-Pete and if I'd be able to detect any phoniness often ascribed to politicians on the trail. Up close and personal, Pete was authentic, with no pretense. To me, that was one of the remarkable things about him. The venue was intimate enough that instead of a stump speech; it seemed more like a conversation. Pete had this genuine, calming effect that comforted me.

As he was wrapping up his speech he said, "I get asked from time to time why I don't seem angrier. And I get that. Because there's a lot to be angry about right now. There's a lot to be upset about; there's a lot to be despondent about in the trajectory of this country. Patterns are setting in in the life of this country that have the darkest echoes in the history of our country and the history of civilization, but it was Dr. King who reminded us that darkness cannot drive out darkness, only light can do that."

Only *light* can do that. Decency and goodness. That's how I thought of it, anyway. Of all of Pete Buttigieg's attributes—superior intellect, education, and military background—it was his exemplary character that made me want to support him. He was the anti-Trump in every way, but it was the decency of character in a leader that I was starved for.

At the end of the speech, Pete bent down to shake hands with the people at the front of the stage. Believe it or not, a Norwegian was there, and his friends wanted Pete to speak Norwegian with him. This took valuable handshaking minutes, so by the time Pete got to my side of the stage, it was the quick hand-over-hand version. I thrust my hand forward to make sure one of the hands was mine. Pete made eye contact with each handshake, even my abrupt attempt. He was *kind*. At that moment, he reminded me of a minister, greeting parishioners after the sermon, listening intently to their concerns. And it was genuine. Could this be the rare servant-leader that this country needed?

Laurie and I stayed in our places watching Pete make his way up to the open balcony to greet people. Not wanting to miss anything, we stayed until he descended the stairs, where again he was met with a crowd who wanted to meet him. We couldn't get anywhere near him but made sure we got as close as possible to get some photos. Soon he disappeared out the back door.

"Wow," I said to Laurie. That's about all I could muster up since sentences wouldn't suffice.

"He's impressive," Laurie replied as she checked the pictures she'd taken on her phone. Although I had similar photos on my phone, Laurie was a better photographer, so I hoped she'd share.

The crowd had dwindled, so it was easy to make our way to the exit with hardly any elbowing. Easygoing chatter filled the air as the event wound down. The welcoming committee at the door had now become the "thank you for coming" committee. This gave me another chance for networking.

I started chatting with an especially enthusiastic volunteer named Darcy. "Join our Facebook group," she said.

"What?" I replied. "There's a Minnesota for Pete Facebook group?"

How had I missed that? Perhaps because I had forsaken Facebook in favor of Twitter. I could only concentrate on one social media platform at a time. Darcy extended a hearty welcome to join the group. Laurie was still undecided about which candidate to support, but I was ready to commit, especially after seeing Pete in person.

The Minnesota for Pete Facebook group. This was just what I needed—a way to get involved and meet other Pete supporters. I'm not sure I even waited until I got home to find the group on Facebook and click on "join."

3

Minnesota for Pete

Sixty was the perfect age for me to jump into a grassroots political campaign. It's that age before retirement where your foot is halfway out the door, and you're looking for new and exciting things to do. My part-time adult ESL teaching job gave me the flexibility that would come in handy. With both kids out of college and my husband Steve doing his own thing, I had time and social energy to burn. I couldn't wait to get involved in the Minnesota for Pete group.

Two weeks after the Fine Line event, Katie, who was *Minneapolis for Pete* on Twitter, posted an invite on the group's Facebook page for a house party to watch Pete's Fox News Town Hall. Pete had chosen to go on conservative-leaning Fox News when other candidates had refused, making it must-watch TV. I was so excited to be watching it at a party rather than by myself at home. This would be my first Minnesota for Pete event, so I offered to bring chili and cornbread. That would help make a good first impression in case I didn't.

I immediately felt at home in Katie and Kelly's house. The hand-painted sign Kelly had carried at the

Fine Line event landed a prime spot in their living room next to the fireplace. "Ah! The sign!" I exclaimed as I carried my offering to the food table. What a coincidence that the first two people I met at the Fine Line were the first two people to invite me to a Pete event. Or was it? I ladled out the chili, still hot enough to melt the shredded cheese sprinkled on top, and asked if anyone wanted a bowl. "There's cornbread too," I said.

Most of us had never met before, but we immediately bonded over our common interest: Pete Buttigieg for President. I sat comfortably on the sofa next to Kelly and relished every minute of the Fox Town Hall with Chris Wallace, cheering Pete on. I felt like a sports fan, watching an important game with my buddies, shouting out play-by-play commentary. "Good answer, Pete!" I had found my people.

Grassroots politics is exciting, but chaotic at the beginning when the group is trying to figure out how to organize themselves. With no official campaign staff in Minnesota yet, it was up to us to promote Pete. I wanted to make sure I attended all the planning meetings, not wanting to miss anything. I remembered my mantra from the day I first donated to Pete: *Get as involved as you can from the beginning. This is historic.* My mantra didn't mean I wanted to take on a leadership role, though. In fact, I felt like a fish out of water next to the seasoned campaign volunteers at that first meeting on Memorial Day weekend at Will's.

Darcy took notes on the flip chart as the group brainstormed committees and to-do lists. But to me, the most important thing on this day was meeting people. That's been my focus since elementary school when the teacher wrote, "Talks too much in class" on my report card. "Too social." Can I help it if that's where my skills lie? Surely this social butterfly could find a way to contribute. I wasn't good at chairing a committee, but I could show up, especially for the after-party on the swank rooftop bar next to Will and his husband's condominium. That's where I got to know two other extroverts—Stephanie, a first grade teacher, and Katie, a musician. Not to be confused with the Katie of *Kelly and Katie*, this Katie would later call herself *Irish Katie*, for her Irish brogue revealing her heritage.

A regular at the Ox Cart, Will showed us the circuitous route to the rooftop elevator. Once on the roof, we chose a large table for our group next to a couple with a fluffy dog. I noticed there were other dogs on the roof as well. *This must be the place to go if you want to have cocktails with your dog,* I thought. The longer we sat there, the more dogs arrived—Labradors, huskies, spaniels, terriers, pugs. Now I was starting to get suspicious. Was this a special *Dog* Happy Hour? Best in Show was more like it. Dogs make everything better in my opinion, but why here and now? We finally asked around and discovered that it was "Bring your dog to the game" night for the St. Paul Saints baseball game at the ballpark across the street. I'd have to put that on my calendar for next year.

The Ox Cart rooftop was soon bustling to capacity as the sound system was replaced with live music. It would have been fun to stay longer, but after many cocktails, burgers, and tater tots, we settled our tabs, giving multiple credit cards to our server. As usual, I would be one of the last to leave. Luckily, I kept on chatting with Stephanie even after she'd paid her bill because when I got mine, I noticed that it was actually *her* credit card number. She'd gotten mine.

"I'm so glad we noticed that!" she said.

"Now I don't feel so bad about making you late getting back to your family."

We both laughed and called our server to fix our bills, which took some time. Eventually the bills were straightened out, and I finally let Stephanie go.

"Are you going to the potluck at Darcy's?" Stephanie asked as she got up to leave.

"Yes, I am. I'll see you there!"

The potluck get-together at Darcy's house in mid-June was a major event that attracted many new Pete supporters. I'm not sure how many attended, but the potluck table was already overflowing when I arrived with my mandarin salad. I took a spot at the crowded kitchen counter to assemble my salad, jockeying for position as others unwrapped dishes too. Stephanie bumped shoulders with me, and Kelly stopped by the refrigerator to get her dish as Darcy played the perfect hostess. The open kitchen and family room echoed with a cacophony of chatter. The guests spread out all over the house and deck with their plates of food. So many new people to meet.

During the business meeting, we discussed how to get Pete's name out there. Saren, who managed the Minnesota for Pete Facebook account, reported that our numbers were growing. We had more than enough people who would be interested in the volunteer training session scheduled for mid-July. Since we would have many new supporters to welcome, we decided to schedule regular "Pete-ups" at coffee shops. At the end, Lisa passed out the Minnesota for Pete info cards she had made for us to use for our Pete conversations at home or away, and Will announced a debate watch party for the first debate, location to be determined. Wherever it was, I would be there.

On debate night, I drove over to Lush, a gay restaurant and bar in Minneapolis where our group had a large presence in the main restaurant. As I entered, I soon saw Irish Katie and Stephanie and joined them with some others in a cushy seating area with white leather couches. I ordered the signature burger and a gin and tonic and got comfy. Watching Pete in a debate was entertaining on its own merits, but with cocktails and new friends? *That* was the way to do it.

Showing expert debate skills, Pete did not disappoint. Far from it. We all left feeling even more assured in our choice of candidate. Since it was a weeknight, most people started leaving during the post-debate analysis, wanting to get home before it got too late. But there are always hard-core partiers in the bunch, and with a drag show starting soon in the next room, why would I want to go home when Irish Katie invited me to join her? It was FUN. I was having so much fun with Minnesota for Pete I almost forgot we had a primary to win.

I planned my Saturdays around the Pete-ups at Caffe Bene in St. Paul. Each Saturday for several weekends in a row we welcomed new people interested in Minnesota for Pete. Time-challenged, especially in the morning, I missed the introductions the first Saturday. I soon realized that this was an actual meeting rather than just chatting. *Next time I need to allow extra time to order my latte . . .* Each week, I met more and more Pete people at Caffe Bene. A core group was forming in our Minnesota for Pete community, with many taking on leadership roles through their own initiative, which is what grassroots organizing is all about. I was happy to be a worker bee in the hive.

Nearly everyone was sporting Pete 2020 T-shirts at this point, except me. This was partly because I hadn't gotten around to ordering any yet, but also because T-shirts weren't my style since they tended to run straight and I was curvy. I preferred flowery, flowing tops. This would soon change as I got caught up in the excitement of the campaign. Ordering merchandise from the Pete for America store counted as a donation, so why not place a big order? Buttons and stickers? Yes. The basic blue PETE 2020 shirt, for sure. The orange Pete &

Chasten & Buddy & Truman shirt? Absolutely. As new T-shirt designs came out, I ordered them.

Irish Katie spearheaded the effort to get our own Minnesota for Pete T-shirts made. They would be dark blue with heartland yellow lettering, using Pete for America's design toolkit. I ordered a large, which should have been big enough, but these ran small, which I discovered too late by trying on a sample large. No problem. I kept the large for my husband and ordered an extra-large for me in the next round. In the meantime, those blue Minnesota for Pete T-shirts were being worn more and more, becoming the team uniform. Feeling left out, I couldn't wait to get mine.

"Sure, Wes. I can help with the refreshments," I replied on Facebook messenger. Saturday's volunteer training was coming together with the planning committee tying up loose ends. I'd met Wes at another Katie and Kelly party, and now we were headed to a much bigger party. "I'll bring lemonade, iced tea, and a jug of ice water," I added.

I wish I could just slap something together and dash off to an event feeling like it was good enough. But no. Preparing for an event was a major production for me. *We need iced tea and lemonade so people can make Arnie Palmers,* I thought. *And the iced tea has to be freshly brewed.* OK. That was going to take a while.

I pulled into the Hennepin Avenue Methodist parking lot that morning and backed my car up to the side door to unload. Two five-gallon beverage coolers and a glass iced tea urn made it safely to the meeting room with Wes's help.

"I can't believe you're leaving us and going to Omaha!" I said to Wes.

"I know. I'm sad too, but it's a teaching position I can't refuse. It will be nice to be back home."

With Facebook and Twitter, I knew I wasn't really saying goodbye to Wes.

Eric, one of the organizers, welcomed volunteers as they came in. I hobnobbed near the refreshment table, meeting new people and reconnecting with my buddies. With nearly 100 people there, I was glad for name tags. I was also glad I'd brought freshly brewed iced tea because people noticed.

Back-to-back presentations packed the morning's schedule, a different presenter for each. The topics covered were Pete's policies, political organizing, planning events, and how to talk to people about the issues. We then broke out into interest groups for information gathering and further planning — visibility at festivals, debate watch parties, honk-and-waves, and service projects honoring Pete's National Service Plan to start. The big unknown was the Minnesota State Fair in late August. Would we be able to get Pete and Chasten to make an appearance? Would we be able to get our own booth? With only five weeks to go, we'd have to settle that soon.

I helped with the cleanup and loaded the beverage coolers back into my car with Wes's help again.

"Are you going to Punch Bowl Social?" I asked.

"No. I wish I could, but I'm supposed to be moving this weekend," Wes replied.

Too bad because Wes was fun at parties. I asked around and found that several people were headed over to the restaurant for food and libations. Not ready to end my Minnesota for Pete day, I was soon on my way to join them.

I hadn't told anyone of my idea to visit Pete's hometown of South Bend yet. Partially this was because I wondered if it was audacious. And if so, I didn't want to brag about it. But still, if I was going, I should make a plan. As I walked to my car, I stopped to chat with Eric in the parking lot.

"Hi Eric! I'm thinking about taking a trip to South Bend next week. Do you need me to deliver anything to the campaign office?" He didn't have anything business related, but together we started thinking about a Minnesota gift I could bring. Ideas were swirling around in my head.

"Let's think about it and touch base later," he said.

It occurred to me that I had an extra Minnesota for Pete T-shirt—the one earmarked for my husband. That would be a nice gift for Pete, especially if he came to the State Fair. But what about Chasten? What if he came too? I asked Irish Katie if there were any extra shirts, but she said no. It was Sunday before a Thursday departure. No time to order a new one. Before I could message Eric about my idea, he sent me a message suggesting the same thing: T-shirts for a gift. What serendipity, especially since Eric also had an extra T-shirt. Score! He'd bring it to the service project we were both attending the next day and then I'd have *two*.

Now I had to think of a charming way to wrap the T-shirts. The pressure was on because the gifts were for Pete and Chasten. *Pete and Chasten.* Plus, I was representing our Minnesota group. Even though in my heart the gifts were from me, the card would say *Minnesota for Pete.* How to wrap? Wrapping paper? Gift bag? That didn't seem right. I was shopping for Minnesota themed items, trying to get ideas, when the Minnesota Map dish towels struck me. Hey! I could use those towels to wrap the T-shirts. And that cool Minnesota tote bag to carry them.

"Would you like these gift wrapped?" The store clerk asked.

"No, thank you. I'm using the towels as gift wrap. But I would like some ribbon to take with me if that's OK." Colorful grosgrain ribbon with stars. Those packages were definitely going to be charming.

When I got home I set everything out on my dining room table to wrap. I carefully folded the T-shirts and then strategically wrapped them in the dish towels so that the featured design was centered. Then I tied them closed with the ribbon and tucked Minnesota post cards underneath which were written in my neatest handwriting, "To Pete —from Minnesota for Pete. Just in case you come to the Minnesota State Fair— Something for you to wear!" And one addressed to Chasten, of course.

4

South Bend

"D elta flight 3599 to South Bend will begin boarding in ten minutes," the gate agent announced. No stranger to the Minneapolis St. Paul airport routine, I had passed through TSA with flying colors and arrived at my gate in plenty of time that morning. I stared at the monitor, waiting for it to flip to the "Waiting for seat assignment" screen. There it was: *S Rawlins*, along with some other names. The most important notation was "Seats available" at the bottom. There still were seats available.

It's a strange way to travel, never knowing if you're going to get on a flight, never knowing if you'll actually make it to your destination. But I was used to it. It was actually *fun*. The Delta flight benefit through my husband's former job allowed me to travel at a moment's notice, if there were empty seats. Sure, I'd been stranded; it was the risk of flying as a non-revenue passenger, but it was free. So given that reality, why wouldn't I travel to South Bend? Why not add the SBN airport code to my repertoire?

As a candidate, much of Pete Buttigieg's record was as the two-term Mayor of South Bend, Indiana. I knew South Bend would come up when talking to voters, so I wanted to be able to tell them firsthand, what the city was like. *Shortest Way Home*, Pete's memoir, was heavily focused on his hometown of South Bend, and it was written with such affection for the city that I was drawn to it. I was curious. *What was South Bend like?*

Once I got my seat assignment, I scanned my boarding pass and walked down the jetway to the small aircraft. I stowed my carry-on bag in the storage bin above and crammed my tote under the seat in front of me. All part of the routine I could do in my sleep. But my emotions were far from routine. I was *nervous*. Why was that? Perhaps because this was a momentous pilgrimage to my candidate's hometown, the city where he was serving as Mayor. Perhaps it was because I had gifts to deliver and I wasn't exactly sure how I was going to do that. But even more so, my plans to meet up with some new Twitter friends had been freshly made and still felt perilously tentative. Would I end up spending all of my time alone? A scary thought for an extrovert.

With an on-time departure, the plane left the gate and taxied to the runway for takeoff. I sat back, closed my eyes, and gave myself my usual pep talk: *You can handle whatever happens. Make the most of it.* I worked out a Plan B and even a Plan C so I'd be prepared. Flexibility with confidence. A short flight later, my reverie was interrupted by the flight attendant's announcement,

"Welcome to South Bend, Indiana. The time is . . . "
Eastern Time. Time to change my watch from Central.

South Bend Airport was the smallest airport I'd ever experienced, and I loved it. Compared to MSP, SBN was the anti-stress airport. One eating and drinking establishment graced the gate area for all your refreshment needs—coffee, food, cocktails. The South Bend Chocolate Cafe had you covered from morning until night. Since it was still morning, I ordered a latte and wondered if anyone could tell that I was fangirling already.

The Marriott Courtyard downtown by the river was the perfect location for the pedestrian traveler that I was. Another time I'd rent a car and drive around, but for a one-night stay, I'd be on foot. As a Marriott Rewards member, I was allowed to check in early. Thank God I could freshen up and get organized. Once in my room, I dumped out the contents of my tote bag on the bed, surveying my inventory. I set my suitcase on the luggage stand and opened it making sure not to miss anything. *There's my black Minnesota bike T-shirt. Time to put that on.* My plan was to wear that over my black sundress while I was making my deliveries, so as to play the Minnesota Goodwill Ambassador. That was easier than just being Sue Ann, a crazy Pete supporter from Minnesota. Instead, I'd be Sue Ann representing Minnesota for Pete as she delivered a gift bag to the campaign office.

The Minnesota Goodwill Ambassador also had another delivery to make. To the mayor's office. This was a last-minute idea I had. *Hey, I should give something to the Pete for America staffers—how about a box of chocolates? Made in Minnesota. And wouldn't it also be cool to give a box of chocolates to the mayor's office?* Maybe that was the delivery that made me the most nervous.

First up, though, was the delivery to the campaign office—the Minnesota for Pete T-shirts for Pete and Chasten, neatly tied up in Minnesota dish towels with ribbons, packed in a Minnesota tote bag along with two boxes of deluxe Abdallah chocolates for the staff. I packed the mayor's office box of chocolates in my personal tote bag and headed out the door.

Except I didn't know where I was going. I didn't know the exact location for the campaign office. I had done my pitiful Google search and found an article in the South Bend Tribune which said the PFA office was in the Jefferson Centre Building just down from my hotel. I would go in the lobby and check for the listing, of course. Except there was no listing. I was embarrassed that I hadn't done more research before coming. I'd asked Eric from the Minnesota group if he knew the address, but he didn't. What was I going to do? Who could I call? I had made the trip; I didn't want to bring these gifts back home.

What to do next? In any case, I needed to get some lunch first, and Chicory was right next door to the Jefferson Centre building. In a daze, I walked a few steps down the sidewalk and in the door to the Chicory Cafe. There was a line. Immediately, I saw someone who looked familiar. Our eyes locked. He knew me too.

"Stefan!"

"Hey, Sue Ann!" he warmly replied.

"I can't believe I'm running into you like this!" Stefan was a Pete for America staffer I'd gotten to know on Twitter and in fact, was someone I'd wanted to meet. We'd tried to set up something for this trip, but he was swamped with a policy rollout, so I wasn't expecting to see him. In fact, he and his colleague Carrie were just getting takeout and had to get back to the office, so this was true serendipity.

"We have to get a picture," I said.

I don't know what was wrong with my phone at that very moment, but their food was ready and they had to get back to the office, so Carrie took the photo on her phone.

"I have gifts for Pete and Chasten from the Minnesota for Pete group," I said, showing the tote bag. "But I don't know where the campaign office is."

"That's a secret. We've just moved to another location," he replied. Apparently, Pete was a real contender because now they had to worry about infiltrators.

"Could you please take it for me? I also have some chocolates in there for the staffers."

"Sure," he agreed. "Security will probably have to unwrap the gifts, though. Protocol." It made me a little sad to think that no one would see my adorable wrapping effort. Even sadder to think that Pete had to worry about nefarious deliveries.

"Enjoy the chocolates!" I called out as he and Carrie walked out the door.

Wow. That was lucky. What if I hadn't run into Stefan? They had a new office at an undisclosed location. I never would have been able to deliver my Pete gifts. Sometimes chance meetings are meant to be.

My muffuletta sandwich was ready, and I was ready to devour it. Seated at a table, I unwrapped the sandwich and lifted the roll to check for the mass of chopped olives. Yum. That's what makes a muffuletta a muffuletta. I wolfed the sandwich down, thinking of my next delivery. Then I realized I didn't have a card. I had nothing saying the box of chocolates for the mayor's office were from Minnesota for Pete! I took the box of Downtowner chocolates out of my tote bag to see if it would be possible to write on the box itself, but only a Sharpie would have worked. No luck. Why wasn't I more prepared?

Just then, I noticed a display of artist-made greeting cards near the register. What luck! One of these cards just had to fit the occasion. It just had to. Or I would make it. This is the one I settled on: personified root vegetables with smiling faces saying, "We're rooting for you!" Perfect. I returned to my table and wrote out the card. This one would be addressed to Laura O'Sullivan, Pete's Chief of Staff. And even though I signed it as being from Minnesota for Pete, I also added my own name and Twitter handle since I knew Laura on Twitter. Before sealing the envelope, I slipped in a decorative Minneapolis magnet. In my mind, Minneapolis and

South Bend were sister cities in some way. Now I just had to find the mayor's office.

Again, I was lacking in the preparation department on this too. I was usually more organized than this. For some strange reason on this trip, though, I trusted things would turn out, that I'd be able to find out once I got there. But with an early start to my day, I was tired and fuzzy headed at this point. I eventually found the County City Building through a highly inefficient route involving unnecessary detours. Let's just say the walk back to my hotel was a straight line.

When I walked into the County City Building, I was struck by its proportions. Not so much that it was small, but that it was as if a larger office building had been shrunk down, keeping all the proportions the same. I loved how it felt different to me. Not lesser by any means, just different. I was immediately met with a metal detector and two guards.

"I have two knees," I declared, pointing to both knees before I walked through the detector.

"I do too," said one of the guards.

"I have two *titanium* knees," I clarified.

I was fairly certain that the mayor's office was on the top floor, but I surreptitiously checked the directory to make sure, pretending to have actual business there. I was an interloper from Minneapolis, not a South Bend resident, and I preferred not to blow my cover. Yes, I was right. The fourteenth floor.

After riding up the elevator with residents who had actual business on other floors, I finally dropped my poker face when I reached the top floor. I was now the Goodwill Ambassador from Minnesota. As I stepped out of the elevator, I could clearly see the glass door marked "Office of the Mayor—Pete Buttigieg—Mayor." Now was the moment of truth. What was I going to say? Even though I knew the mayor himself was on the campaign trail, I lost all courage for conversation as soon as I entered the office.

"May I help you?" the intern at the front desk asked.

I set the card and box of candy on the counter and said, "This is for Laura O'Sullivan." Then I made a quick retreat. Mission accomplished, I ducked in the ladies room for my other essential business and then took the elevator back to the main floor. On the way down, I mulled over my brief time in the mayor's office. I was disappointed in myself. *I didn't even ask to talk to Laura. What a chicken.*

Deliveries completed, I walked back to my hotel to rest up before meeting my Twitter friends. How fortuitous that South Bend Chocolate Company was practically annexed to the Marriott Courtyard, providing a welcome shortcut back to my room. Chocolate, chocolate, everywhere. I was immediately drawn to the display of beautifully decorated gift baskets filled with a decadent array of milk and dark chocolate. *These are so pretty!* I thought. *I think I'll buy two.* Never did it occur to me that they wouldn't fit in my carry on. *I should buy something to pass around at Caffe Bene on Saturday too.* Salted caramels and chocolate-covered pretzels would do the trick.

Once back in my room, I kicked off my sandals and plopped down on the bed to check Twitter. Direct message alerts always made me happy. That's just how it is with us extroverts. I had a few. One was from Laura O'Sullivan, thanking me for the chocolates. The touching gesture surprised me, but it shouldn't have. I responded with the usual, "You're welcome!" but then asked if she had gotten the magnet too, just in case it had fallen out of the envelope. The next message included a photo of the very magnet on her desk lamp. Minneapolis was now represented.

Before making the final arrangements with my South Bend Twitter friends, I had another trick up my sleeve. Why eat breakfast alone the next day when you can meet your Regional Director? So what if that Regional Director was also from Minneapolis, but just happened to be in South Bend for staff training? Just a couple of days before I left on my trip, Kyrstin sent out an email to our Minnesota for Pete group introducing herself. We were excited to finally have someone from the campaign working with our grassroots group. I wanted to meet her. We were both in South Bend. And we both needed to eat breakfast. Why not ask? I was a little nervous sending that DM. Was it presumptuous of me to ask? Apparently not, because soon I got a reply - Yes! We would be meeting at PEGGS in the morning before I had to head back to Minneapolis.

Time was flying. Soon I'd be meeting my three new Twitter friends, Lety, Joy, and AJ, so there was no time for a much-needed nap. Freshening up would have to do. Lety was *Good Guy Pete*, a popular account on Twitter devoted to promoting Mayor Pete from the South Bend perspective. Joy called herself *Everyone's Mom* on Twitter, and that's how I first bonded with her. AJ was a new acquaintance, and I almost didn't contact her because I thought she'd wonder who I was. At the last minute, I thought, *why not?* I'm so glad because she was game.

Joy was the first one to become available and offered to meet me early at our meeting point, the Chocolate Cafe, right next to my hotel. Would I recognize her? Would she recognize me? I had just made it to the barista counter when a blonde woman with a cane walked up to greet me. That's what threw me. I didn't know Joy was recovering from foot surgery. "Hi Sue Ann," she said. This was obviously Joy. We each got something to drink and chose a table on the sunny patio to wait for Lety and AJ.

Joy, a hairdresser and salon manager, was naturally friendly. As we waited for the others, she told me about how she and Lety had known each other for years, having met through common acquaintances. Soon Lety herself arrived, followed by AJ. AJ seemed to know Lety and Joy already, but I wasn't sure how. It might have just been the South Bend effect. Compared to the Minneapolis/St. Paul metro, South Bend felt like a small town where everyone knew each other. I liked that feeling.

Lety worked in Social Services, and AJ had a job in higher education administration, so together with Joy, I was getting a variety of perspectives on life in South Bend. They seemed happy to represent South Bend and answer all my questions. I always say you can't get to know a place if you don't get to know the people. I absolutely loved listening to it all, feeling a part of it somehow as a Pete supporter, an honorary South Bender in the making.

I had no expectations beyond this Chocolate Cafe meeting because Lety had said she didn't have much time. She had to pack for a trip the next day. Because of this, I didn't want to be presumptuous about extending our social gathering beyond it. My schedule was free, though.

"Want to go get something to eat?" Lety asked.

"Sure!" I said, pleasantly surprised.

"I'm up for that. Where should we go?" said AJ.

"We should go to Fiddler's," Joy said.

Fiddler's Hearth was the Irish pub where Pete and Chasten had their first date, so definitely a Pete tourist attraction and why Joy suggested it. She had assumed the role of tour guide before I even knew it. I never would have asked her to do it. Again, I lucked out.

I got in Joy's van and Lety and AJ followed us over to Fiddler's in their cars. It was a five-minute drive, or less, and I was reminded again of how condensed South Bend was compared to Minneapolis. Traffic was less stressful; parking was less stressful. Perhaps South Bend would be my new vacation getaway.

Upon entering Fiddler's on this bright summer day, my eyes had to adjust to the darker pub feel. The heat of the sun, though, was replaced by the warmth of soft wood—the wooden tables and chairs, the substantial bar—inviting me in. The walls were laden with Irish photos, prints, and curiosities to keep you entertained while waiting for your brew. And the performance area was set up for the next musical gig, dare I say *fiddlers*? Pubs had the kind of ambiance that invited you in and made you want to stay.

As it was early for dinner, the pub was quiet, so we had our choice of seating. We sat at a large communal table with bench seating against the wall. I could easily picture what Fiddler's was like on a Friday night with live music, full to capacity.

"I'll have the fish and chips," I said to the waitress taking our order.

"You should get a Scotch egg," Joy prompted, not wanting me to miss ordering what Pete and Chasten had on their first date. I did as she said and ordered a Scotch egg as well. Little did I know that the total amount of food would be impossible for me to finish.

We all ordered food except for Lety, who had to get home to her wife to pack for their trip. She finished her soda and said it was time for her to go. *Already?* I quickly retrieved the little gifts from my tote bag. Yes, I had bought Minnesota gifts for them too. I gave them each a tiny snow globe featuring Paul Bunyan and Babe, his blue ox and a Minnesota dish towel.

"We need a picture!" I said, as Lety got up to leave. We called the waitress over to our table and asked her to take one. Three South Benders and one Minneapolitan together because of Pete.

After Lety left, AJ, Joy and I chatted over our pub fare, getting to know each other better. I felt so comfortable, I could have stayed another hour, but soon it was AJ who had to leave.

"Would you like to see some of South Bend? I'd be happy to drive you around and show you the sites," Joy offered.

"That would be fantastic!" I replied, grateful for her offer.

Joy took me to the old Studebaker factory where Pete made his announcement speech.

"That's where I was standing in line for the announcement," she pointed out.

"In the rain?" I replied.

"Yes, but not for long. It was only a few weeks after my foot surgery, so I was in line on my wheely cart with a plastic bag over my cast. A staffer noticed me and invited me to go in early and sit in the ADA section. That's when I knew this campaign was special."

After seeing how far away that spot in the line was from the entrance, I was relieved for her.

Joy stopped in the parking lot of the Studebaker factory, and even though I was only seeing the exterior, I was able to connect my TV viewing experience with the live event in some way. It was silly, but it was like I was there on that day with the crowd. It's amazing how the mind can do tricks like that.

Nearby was the ballpark where the South Bend Cubs played, and coincidentally, also part of Pete and Chasten's first date. There was no game scheduled, or it would have been bustling instead of deserted as it was. Joy then drove through the beautiful Notre Dame campus, which deserved its own separate tour. We then went along the river and saw the East Race, a man-made canal now used for whitewater rafting. To finish up, we stopped at the "I *heart* SB" sculpture for the requisite photo op, making my pilgrimage official.

Now it was time for Joy to get back to her family. She dropped me off at my hotel and we hugged goodbye. It wasn't really goodbye because I'd see her on Twitter. As I watched her drive away, I was struck by her kindness. Until today, she didn't really know much about me. I was some Pete supporter from Twitter suddenly showing up in South Bend without an invitation. But Joy showed me what South Bend hospitality was like. Something I also felt with Lety and AJ. Something I felt when Laura O'Sullivan sent me the direct message. Was that hospitality part of small city life, or was it the Pete effect?

The evening was still young, so I decided to take a walk along the river. From the bridge nearest my hotel, I had a clear view of the Jefferson Avenue bridge up-river, the bridge that was used in designing the Pete for America logo. As darkness fell, the lights under the bridge came on in a light show of sequencing, multicolored lights. The light installation was something Mayor Pete had worked on as part of South Bend's sesquicentennial celebration in 2015. It was a stunning display. I walked along the river to get a closer view for a video. On that warm summer evening on the St. Joseph River, I felt magic. Funny how lights can do that to you.

My biggest fear when traveling is oversleeping, so I always use an alarm *and* a hotel wake-up call. I had a breakfast date with the Midwest Regional Organizing Director for Pete for America. I didn't want to be late. As it turned out, I got to PEGGS a little early, and Kyrstin was running a little late. It was a beautiful summer morning, so I grabbed a table outside for us. Kyrstin, a Nordic-looking woman, befitting her Minnesota heritage, soon joined me. She had a winning personality that I'm sure worked in her favor when interviewing for the job, but it was her extensive experience in Minnesota Democratic politics that probably sealed the deal. Kyrstin had such confidence I found myself forgetting that she was more than thirty years younger than I was.

"Tell me what the Minnesota for Pete group is doing," Kyrstin asked in between bites of French toast.

"Mostly visibility at this point. We're trying to show up at events and festivals with signs wearing Pete gear. We've also made our own info cards to pass out," I replied, wishing I had one of those cards with me to show her. "We had a volunteer training session that was very well-attended. Oh, and there are Pete-ups at coffee shops."

"Impressive," she said, genuinely.

I wasn't sure how our Minnesota grassroots efforts compared to the other eight states she had under her wing, but since she was just starting her job, she probably didn't know at this point either.

We talked Minnesota politics and what we liked about Pete as a candidate. The conversation could have gone on past lunchtime, but Kyrstin had to get to her meeting with her boss, the PFA Marathon States Organizing Director, Samantha Steelman. Kyrstin would be in South Bend a few weeks for training and then be on the road visiting her states. Eventually she'd be back in Minnesota and meeting our team. But the Minnesota/PFA relationship had already started at PEGGS in South Bend.

As I was standing in line at the register to pay for my meal of eggs, hash browns, and bacon, I noticed some T-shirts on display: PEGGS for PETE Buttigieg 2020. I just had to get one to wear to Caffe Bene on Saturday. Then I had a lightbulb moment. *Hey—I should get a few of these PEGGS shirts and use them for fundraising.* I'd offer a shirt to anyone who donated at least $30 to Pete for America, while supplies last.

"I'd like to buy some of those Pete T-shirts," I said at the register. "I'd like two of each size, please."

The Pete shirts were easier to pack in my carry on than the two South Bend Chocolate gift baskets, which I had to partially disassemble and redistribute between my tote bag and carry on. As I made my way back to the airport, I thought about how lucky I was that my trip all worked out despite my tentative planning—the gift deliveries, meeting Joy, Lety, and AJ, a guided tour, breakfast with Kyrstin. I guess it was meant to be.

5

The Iowa State Fair

Minnesotans have a distinct advantage during a Presidential primary because of our geographic proximity to Iowa, the first state to vote. Aside from those who actually live in Iowa, it means that we have the easiest access to campaign events large and small—if you don't mind driving a few hours.

"Pete's going to be speaking on August 13 at the Iowa State Fair," Katie posted in the Minnesota for Pete Facebook group. "Anyone want to go down for it?"

The Iowa State Fair was a big deal for primary candidates, who each had a speaking slot at the *Soapbox* sometime during the run of the fair. I was intrigued by the idea, but didn't know if I wanted to drive for almost four hours to Des Moines, walk around the fair all day, and then drive back home another four hours. I don't think I was quite getting the *Pete* part of the equation. I responded that I might be interested. Katie and Kelly were making a trip of it and staying in an Airbnb, so I couldn't go with them. I wasn't going to go down by myself. Not many people were able to go since it was a weekday, so I was starting to give up on the idea.

"Anyone interested in carpooling to the Iowa State Fair?" Tricia posted on our Slack channel.

"Sue Ann might be," Katie replied.

I met Tricia, a creative director for an advertising agency, at the volunteer training session in July and had gotten to know her a little at our Saturday Caffe Bene sessions. We connected the next Saturday and started making plans for the Iowa State Fair. Who would drive? What time should we leave? As the days wore on, and we thought more about it, we knew we'd enjoy the fair more if we drove to Des Moines the day before and stayed in a hotel. That was a good call because it felt like a very long drive even with a talkative companion.

Tricia was about fifteen years younger than I was, but looked younger, just like I did, so the relative difference in age was preserved as we presented ourselves at the Iowa State Fair. Unlike the Minnesota State Fair, which involved remote parking and shuttle buses, we were able to casually drive to the gates of the fair and into the parking area on the grass. The parking guide motioned us to our spot using airport hand signals, and Tricia obediently parked her Mini Cooper Countryman in line. As we got out of the car, she stopped to take note of its location in the sea of cars.

It was sunny and already hot, and I knew I had to pace myself. I was one hundred percent sure that Tricia was in better shape than I was. I sighed as I could see the entrance to the fair was still a long walk ahead. But then we saw people waiting for a shuttle. There were little golf carts ferrying people to the entrance. What a godsend. Tricia and I got in line and soon had a Shriners golf cart to ourselves with an amiable driver. It was free, but donations were welcome, and we obliged.

As planned, we got to the fair early and had some time to kill. First up, find the Soapbox. It's funny how at your own state fair, you have a routine set in stone, but at another state fair, you don't even know where the restrooms are and you feel like you don't belong. It was impossible not to compare layout, food vendors, and exhibits with the Minnesota State Fair, but the main difference was size. Thank God the Iowa State Fair was smaller.

We followed the map to the Soapbox to get our bearings. It wasn't a soapbox at all, but a small stage surrounded by straw bales. There was a small grassy area where I presumed the audience would be standing. One of the media outlets was starting to set up already, two hours ahead of time, but no one else was there. Tricia started talking to the cameraman. She, like me, wasn't shy about talking to strangers.

"I'm going to start saving a place for us," I told Tricia. The thing about events where people arrive early to get a place is that you never know when the first person is going to get there. If I walked around the fair for twenty minutes and came back, things could change. At least now I knew I was the first person camped out at the front of the stage. At one point, someone asked if I was with C-SPAN. They must not have noticed my bright white *PEGGS for PETE Buttigieg 2020* T-shirt.

There was absolutely no shade where I was standing. I could feel the sunburn in progress even with sunscreen, but I didn't care. I had a prime spot to see Pete. Eventually Katie and Kelly arrived, Kelly with the iconic orange dog sign in hand. More people arrived to stake out their place on the grass, and when the fair staff brought out chairs to be set out, we helped. Chairs. The immediate audience would be seated, not standing. Thank God. But helping with the chairs lost me a spot. Tricia had to sit behind me with Katie and Kelly in the second row. I was in the center, next to the seat reserved for the timer. Of course Pete didn't need a timer.

Soon various photographers emerged and lined themselves up along the stage in front of me, kneeling with their cameras, bumping my knees at times. A Pete campaign videographer was chatting with people in the first row, trying to get some interviews on Pete's newly released rural policy. Pablo asked me a few questions, but I knew there wasn't much he'd be able to use since I was an urbanite from Minnesota.

By the time Pete took the stage in the full sun, my face was glowing with sunburn and the sleeves of my PEGGS shirt were rolled up James Dean style. No need for a spotlight for Pete this time. I turned around to see how many people had shown up for Pete. I couldn't see how far the crowd behind the chairs extended, but the standing-room-only spilled out to the side as well. My second time seeing Pete in person was as equally impressive as the first. The Iowa State Fair version of his stump speech, complete with blue jeans, had the same core values and charm.

After a fun Q&A session involving a child asking if he'd go on the giant slide with him, Pete ended his speech to a standing ovation. The feeling I had when Pete walked off the stage was one of disappointment. It was over already. Now there was nothing to look forward to except another four-hour drive. I turned around to talk to Katie and Kelly. They were going to head home. Tricia and I looked at each other. What should we do?

"Let's follow him," Tricia suggested.

Pete had gone back behind the building next to us for interviews, and an entourage was forming.

"OK," I replied, not sure this sort of thing was allowed.

Unlike other Soapbox days of the fair, Pete was the only candidate speaking that day, so C-SPAN kept filming. They followed Pete from the initial interview as he walked the fair. Tricia and I became part of the entourage, a smash of people. I would later tell prospective voters that I could vouch for Pete's fitness level. Even though he was constantly talking to people, he kept a fast walking pace. It was hard to keep up with him.

"I'm going to try to get a selfie," Tricia said. She then disappeared into the throng of people ahead.

A few minutes later, she found me again.

"I got one!" she said, showing me the photo. "You should try to get a selfie."

"Really?" I replied. "I don't know if I should." For some reason I was shy about barging to the front, elbowing my way to Pete to get a selfie.

"Go ahead. You should do it."

I started my journey of weaving in and out of people in the crowd walking with Pete, mostly fans, but some reporters. In front of Pete was the C-SPAN camera crew walking backwards, complete with boom microphone held high above Pete's head. I mentally said *excuse me, excuse me* as I bumped my way to get to Pete. Once at my destination there was no other way to talk to him except to just butt in and assertively take my turn.

"Hi Pete!" I said. "I'm from Minneapolis and I traveled to South Bend, and . . . "

"Hey—PEGGS! That's a good place," he interrupted, noticing the T-shirt I purposely wore for this very moment.

Pete knew the drill. Now it was time for the selfie. Smile!

"I have a flight benefit so I can travel easily," I added, which seemed to impress him, but it was hard to tell because he was already being pushed by his people to keep moving. "There are three flights a day from Minneapolis to South Bend . . . " I continued, thinking I could have a real conversation. Then he was abruptly pulled away by someone else wanting to talk to him. Dang. I wanted to tell him that I loved South Bend.

That was the shortest conversation I'd ever had. It was maybe fifteen seconds at most. But I got my selfie. Pete and I look like old friends in the picture. Were we old friends? It's not like he recognized me from the Fine Line in Minneapolis. That's just how Pete made you feel. Later on I'd be able to find that selfie moment in the C-SPAN video of the event. Talk about an out-of-body experience.

Tricia and I continued walking with the entourage as Pete alternated between interviews by local officials and sampling fair foods. First off, he voted in the corn poll, where fairgoers put a corn kernel in their preferred candidate's jar. Pete put a kernel in the Pete jar, one of the jars that was filling up. We then followed him into the Agriculture Building to see the famous butter cow sculpture, which luckily was in a refrigerated display area, a welcome relief from the heat.

We were far enough behind in the entourage that we couldn't always see exactly what Pete was doing, but his voracious eating at the Iowa State Fair would become the subject of memes, the most famous being the pork chop on a stick, which he tore into. I may not have seen him eat that pork chop, but I followed him to the Pork Tent where it all happened.

We'd been walking for a while at that point and truly felt a part of the festivities. I had a lot of time to observe the staffers in the entourage. I recognized Lis Smith, his Senior Communications Advisor and Nina Smith, his Traveling Press Secretary, from Twitter, but I was too timid to talk to them. At one point, I noticed a ginger haired man who had fallen to the back of the crowd and I thought I recognized him. By that time, I'd developed some courage.

"Are you Mike Schmuhl?" I asked, thinking he was Pete's Campaign Manager.

"No, I'm Pete's friend from college," the man replied.

The entourage had stopped so Pete could do his Pork Tent interview, and Tricia and I found ourselves hanging out with Pete's friend.

Tricia broke the awkward silence that followed my botched conversation starter. "We drove down from Minneapolis," she said.

"Oh? We were there last night," Pete's friend said. "We ate at the Spoon and Stable."

"That's by my house!" Tricia exclaimed.

Unbelievable. Tricia and I were driving from Minneapolis down to Des Moines while Pete and his friend were in Minneapolis eating at a restaurant by Tricia's house. Then I remembered the best way to fly to Des Moines is through Minneapolis and thus an opportunity for a layover if need be.

We slowly followed the group to a spot where we could watch Pete grill pork shops on the giant grill. This was tradition for all the candidates. Pete was surrounded by cameras and reporters, so it was hard to see what was happening. I was standing next to Pete's friend. Was this Nate from Harvard? Of course I was too afraid to embarrass myself again and ask. Still, extroverts can't stand silence, so I said something I wanted him to hear.

"You know, you can tell a lot about a person who keeps lifelong friends," I said, looking at Pete.

The entourage was on the move again at that moment, so we started walking, cutting any chance of a conversation short. Still, my comment seemed to resonate. I hoped that he'd relay it to Pete.

Pete went into a building for some interviews and his followers waited outside. That was the perfect opportunity to try a pork chop on a stick ourselves. Tricia and I backtracked to the Pork Tent and sidled up to the counter. The order was simple because that's all that was offered: pork chops on a stick. At first glance I wondered if the chop was cooked enough because it lacked the golden-brown tone I was used to in a chop. This was rather gray, and frankly, unappetizing. I wondered what the big attraction was. But then I ate it. So tender and delicious. I don't know what their secret was. Was it brining?

Having finished his interviews, Pete emerged from the building and started walking the fair again, the entourage falling in step behind. Tricia and I hesitated. After two hours of walking around the fair with Pete, I was exhausted. *How long was he going to do this?* I wondered. I really wanted to stick around to see if he was going to go down the giant slide with that little boy. But I just couldn't. Plus, we had a long drive ahead of us. Later when I saw the photos on Twitter of the giant slide moment, I was sad I'd missed it. All in all, Pete walked around the fair for three hours, eating and talking to people, demonstrating that youthful vigor is advantageous in presidential politics.

Tricia and I exited the fairgrounds and followed the signs to the shuttle pick-up area. I thought I was grateful for a shuttle before. That was a convenience. This was a necessity. My legs felt like rubber, my skin burned, and my throat was parched. I found myself actually looking forward to the four-hour drive home. Again, we had a friendly Shriners volunteer ferry us to the parking area, going beyond the call of duty to find the exact parking spot.

On the drive home, Tricia and I had much to debrief, break down, and analyze. We'd both had the same surreal experience but had little chance to discuss while it was happening.

"Thank you for encouraging me to get a selfie," I told Tricia. "I can't believe I would have missed that."

"I'm glad you did," Tricia replied in a supportive tone.

"It was so fun walking around the fair with Pete," I added. "I wish we could have stayed until he left, but I was exhausted."

"Oh, me too. I was ready to go," Tricia reassured me.

Looking back on the experience, I could see that none of it would have happened without Tricia. She was the one who was looking for someone to carpool. I don't think I would have gone at all otherwise. She was the one who urged me to get a selfie and was game to walk around the fair with Pete for two hours. Tricia was the perfect travel buddy, and there would be many more opportunities.

We made it to Minneapolis just before sunset and Tricia dropped me off at my house. My husband came out to meet her. "How did it go?" Steve asked.

"It was great!" Tricia said, getting my luggage out of her car.

Steve took my larger bag. "You're sunburned," he said looking at my face.

"I know. And I was wearing sunscreen!" I replied.

After waving goodbye to Tricia, Steve and I walked into the house. I set down my tote bag and checked the mail. There was something for me. The hand-addressed personal card stood out among the junk mail. *Pete for America?* That was the return address. What was this?

Letter opener in hand, I plopped down on a comfy chair and carefully opened the card. My eyes scanned the handwritten note to the signature line. Anne Montgomery. It was from Pete's mom. My heart started racing as I read her words.

Anne was thanking me for my support for Pete. Not my donation, but my support. I thought for a moment. This must be about the card I sent Pete back in June after the officer-involved shooting of a Black man in South Bend. His city taking priority, the mayor cancelled his campaign visits and immediately returned to South Bend and was met with protesters. It was a very difficult time for South Bend and for Pete as both mayor and candidate. Some of us on Twitter decided to send cards of support to Pete. Many sent postcards, but I sent a full note card with my return address on the envelope. That must be why I got a thank you.

"I got a card from Pete's mom!" I shouted to the universe, waving the card.

All other thoughts left my mind as I relished the magnitude of this moment. *Pete's mom.* I actually clutched the note to my heart.

I should write back to her, I thought. Most people would never think of doing that, but it was very me. I can't help but try to build a relationship whenever the opportunity strikes. To me, this was an opportunity. But really, what was I thinking? You can't make friends with a high-profile presidential candidate's mom. There's something charmingly naïve about me that drives me to do these things. What harm is there in writing back? Especially when Anne signed her card with, "I hope to see you on the trail!"

In my stash of note cards, I found a beautiful art card of Minnehaha Falls in Minneapolis and wrote probably one of the best thank you for a thank-you I've ever written. Knowing Anne was a retired linguistics professor, I wove linguistics into my profession as an ESL teacher into Pete's policy on immigration. I sealed the envelope and addressed the card to the Pete for America PO box since I had no other address.

Linguistics was one of my favorite classes when I was studying for my master's in ESL. I loved learning about the structure of different types of languages as well as the functional commonalities. In the classroom, I could see how a student's first language affected acquisition of English. And many times I'd tell the class that an aspect of grammar was universal to all languages. I really wanted to discuss this with Anne. I imagined that she'd dust off her professor's cap, and we'd have a tutorial. I thought she'd be interested in my class of adult learners and the languages represented.

I was sure Anne would write back to me, either just a brief note by mail or an email. I made a mental note of the date I sent my card so I could calculate when to expect a reply. And then I was on the lookout. In my imagination, Pete's mom and I were going to be friends chatting about linguistics. But that's where I was delusional. Writing to Anne was one thing, but expecting a reply from the mother of a presidential candidate was another. I remember asking my good friend Maureen, "Do you think I'm delusional?" But Maureen, being a supportive friend, always answered this question with, "No. I don't think you are." Which left open the possibility.

6

The Minnesota State Fair

On the heels of the Iowa State Fair was the much larger Minnesota State Fair, the largest in the nation when measured by average daily attendance. Minnesota for Pete desperately wanted a Pete Buttigieg 2020 booth at the fair. With over two million people expected to visit the Minnesota State Fair during the twelve-day run, a booth would be an ideal opportunity to reach people. Except it almost didn't happen.

The Caffe Bene meeting that next Saturday was devoted to State Fair planning. I had been out of the loop, so I didn't know what was going on—did we have a booth or not? I should back up and say this was due to some confusion based on communication with the State Fair and multiple parties involved. It was Lisa who championed the effort now, and she did not give up even though multiple roadblocks popped up along the way.

Lisa reported that the Fair had finally accepted our application and had assigned us a spot on Underwood Street near the corner of Dan Patch Avenue. But we needed to have a professional architect draw plans for the booth. First roadblock. We had less than two weeks to find an architect, get a design, and build a booth. Then there was the cost. How would we pay for it? Sure, we could all donate, but those donations in total might inadvertently create a funded political organization that would have reporting requirements we weren't prepared to meet.

We plowed ahead, knowing that we would make the finances work somehow. It was too important. How to find an architect? Darin, a St. Paul native now living in D.C., had been vicariously following the State Fair saga on Twitter and wanted to help.

"I wonder if there's an Architects for Pete account on Twitter?" he tweeted.

That got Lisa checking, and behold! She found *Architects for Pete* and asked if he could help us with a design. Architect Kyle said he could help and soon produced a beautiful design Lisa could submit to the Fair. Team Pete had come through! What a relief. Now we could get to the task of purchasing building materials.

But then another roadblock appeared. The Fair said we needed to have the construction of our booth supervised by a licensed contractor. With about a week to go, how were we going to find a licensed builder? Unfortunately, the two contacts we found fell through with one week to go. This time it was Gina who saved the day. I had met Gina back in July at the volunteer training realizing that I'd also seen her at Darcy's potluck. She had taken on a leadership role in our group. Gina had the kind of mind I didn't have. The kind that can investigate and stick with a mission until accomplished. The kind of mind that can keep lots of details straight. In this case, she searched an online database for Twin Cities contractors and then looked their names up on Facebook. Many of the Facebook profiles had the company name listed under the "works at" section. She then looked through the page likes and groups of each. It only took a handful of names before she stumbled upon one who belonged to a Pete group, just not the Minnesota for Pete one. She found Timothy in the nick of time.

Now it was on to purchasing building materials. This was all down to the wire, and Lisa remained project manager on our behalf. I'm not sure she got much sleep during this stressful time of running against the clock. Fortunately, the question of how to pay for the booth was resolved by our PFA Regional Director, Kyrstin. She was able to arrange for a donation link that would be earmarked for the Minnesota State Fair booth. We were able to raise enough money from our Minnesota for Pete group to pay for all that we needed. When we added some banners for the sides of the booth, some of us volunteered to buy them and take them home with us after the fair.

With the fair starting on Thursday, August 22, the weekend before was open for exhibitors to start setting up, and since we were building our booth from scratch rather than moving in an existing structure, we had to make use of every minute. I realize I'm using the pronoun *we* to refer to *Minnesota for Pete*, but I can hardly be included in the *we* at this point. Construction of all kind was beyond me. I couldn't even hold a discussion on two-by-fours. And physically speaking, I literally wasn't a heavy lifter. I knew I would just be in the way if I signed up to help build, so I waited for the painting phase.

Booth Building Weekend was well-documented on our Slack channel and the Minnesota for Pete Facebook page. Our contractor Timothy was on site to supervise, and those with large vehicles, and spouses to help, transported the building materials. Stephanie and her husband were crucial in this effort as well as Lisa and her husband. Katie and Kelly were there as well as many others including Saren, our Facebook moderator, and her husband. As problems came up, they were solved just as quickly. When the site map incorrectly placed the booth by a few feet, and the Fair inspector tagged us on it, the team moved it over. Melani, who was *Minnesota for Pete* on Twitter, had set up a camera to capture the long day on a time lapse video, which made it all look so easy.

Sunday and Monday were scheduled for priming and painting, respectively. I found my painting clothes in the very depths of my closet, hoping they still fit.

"Have you seen my old tennis shoes, the ones I use for painting?" I asked my husband. "I can't find them."

"I'm sorry, honey. I got rid of them," Steve answered. "I was trying to clear up clutter." To be fair. I didn't use them that often. He probably thought I'd never be using them again. That should tell you something about my painting skills.

How hard is it to paint? That's what I thought, but then once on site, I felt like I was all thumbs—opening paint cans, pouring the velvety paint in the pan, choosing the correct tool for the paint area. Then there was always the added aspect of speed, or lack of. In an effort to be thorough, I accomplished my section of painting area in twice the amount of time as the other painters. I hated that feeling of incompetence. But I swallowed my pride because I wanted to be part of the process. I wanted to be *there*.

I loved the camaraderie of painting together. The Monday paint crew included Kelly, Gina, Lisa, Stephanie, and Therese. While Stephanie and Kelly were inside painting the ceiling dark gray, Lisa did the white trim outside, Gina and I painted the yellow posts around the booth, and Therese worked on the sides in blue and yellow. The counter was one of the last areas to paint, which I did in the medium blue color. The colors had been chosen in keeping with the campaign's toolkit of colors, as best we could anyway.

Even with the painting pros, the process was taking longer than planned, and we were still there well past dinnertime.

"I'm starving. Anyone want a submarine sandwich?" Stephanie asked, offering to go pick it up.

When Stephanie returned with the subs, we stopped painting just long enough to wolf them down.

"We really need a Pete sign on the roof," Stephanie said, as she stepped out into the street to get a full view of the booth. "With the crowds, no one is going to see the signs on the side."

"We need to check with the fair to see what is allowed," Lisa said. "I think there is a height restriction."

"I'm sure it will be OK," Stephanie replied "This might be a time to ask for forgiveness rather than permission. They probably won't even notice." She would check out possibilities.

"We're so lucky to be right next to the Butterfly House," Kelly said, opening up another can of paint.

"Yeah, parents are going to be standing around here with their kids as they watch the butterflies, and we can talk to them about Pete!" said Gina.

"The butterfly guy is so friendly! He talked to us when we were building," said Lisa.

I learned that the butterfly exhibit was taken very seriously by the State of Minnesota Department of Natural Resources. I'd never thought of butterflies as an invasive species before. Once the butterflies were delivered, the manager of the exhibit had to remain onsite with the butterflies, making sure none escaped. As a result, Dave, the butterfly guy, had small sleeping quarters in the back of the exhibit.

As it got dark that evening, and we had trouble seeing what we were doing, Dave approached the booth.

"Would you like me to put my lights on for you?" he asked.

"Really?" Lisa answered. "That would be great!"

"Thank you!" we all added in chorus.

"I can't wait until we get the lights figured out for our booth," Lisa said, noticing how dark it was in the booth.

"But there's no electricity access," said Gina.

This would be something to figure out in the next two days. Maybe battery powered?

We were winding down, and now it was Therese with an idea. "What about curtains? I think they would look great. Plus, we could close them if it was raining."

Hmm . . . curtains? I'd never seen curtains in a political booth at the fair. But a grassroots idea is a grassroots idea, especially if someone is willing to do the work. Therese was going fabric shopping the next day for dark blue, water-repellent fabric.

We sealed up the paints and washed the brushes and rollers in the ladies restroom across the street. The supplies were stored discreetly inside the booth in case we needed them for touch-ups. There was still some more cleaning to do, but I had to say goodbye and head home.

"There's only one way out of the fair this late," Lisa warned me. "It's the exit down by the animal barns."

I knew where the animal barns were. But everything looked different in the dark. To be fair, I wasn't used to driving on those streets. I was used to walking down them with thousands of other people. I kept driving around, hitting dead ends. The exit I thought it was, wasn't. Terrified, I was just about to give up and go ask for help when I stumbled on a well-concealed exit . . . *by the animal barns.* It was so small I was sure it was only used for people bringing in show animals, which explained why I didn't know of its existence.

On Tuesday the floor was painted and Stephanie had indeed found a way to get a sign made. Wednesday, the night before the fair opened, was the big wrap-up. Everything had to be ready. I headed to the fair to deliver the volunteer binders I'd put together for Gina and the sign-up sheets for fair visitors wanting more information on Pete. I was glad to have an excuse to show up on opening eve. I wanted to be part of the final touches, even if I probably wouldn't be of much use.

One last time I drove to the exhibitor's entrance, passed the security check, and drove into the fairgrounds. Tomorrow that would all be closed to traffic—only hordes of pedestrians would be allowed. Again, I was able to park near our booth. I immediately saw Stephanie's sign installed on the roof and let out a small squeal of delight. PETE BUTTIGIEG 2020. She had been right. We *needed* this. The thought of not having a sign there was inconceivable. It just goes to show how important successful grassroots efforts are when you let creativity have free rein.

The second thing I noticed right away was that Therese had pulled her car right next to the booth and was sewing curtains right there out of the back of her small SUV.

"Curtains!" I said as I approached.

"This seemed like the most convenient way to do it," Therese said with a smile. She was obviously excited about the project.

There was an assembly line in action with Tricia handing each finished panel up to Gina, who was standing up on the booth counter threading the finished product on the curtain rods.

Melani was there figuring out the lighting. She hadn't been able to make any of the Saturday meetings, so I was just getting to know her. At that moment she was intent on detangling Kelly's string of lights while her fiancée Alexis was testing the battery, the solution to the electricity problem. The lights would be plugged into their boat battery, which would be set on the floor inside the booth. The last challenge was how to charge the battery every night.

"Steve from the Midtown Men's Club said we could charge our battery in their booth every night," Stephanie told us, coming back from the food booth across the street. Stephanie proved her resourcefulness once again.

"Really? That's so nice!" I said. Throughout the entire process, we had people helping us in some way, big or small.

I stayed late enough to see the lights up and curtains installed. My goodness. It was the coziest political booth in the history of the Minnesota State Fair.

Our grassroots Pete 2020 booth was welcoming and inviting, evoking *Belonging,* from Pete's Rules of the Road.

Twelve days of the fair, four shifts each day, a minimum of two volunteers each shift. I'll let you do the math, but that's quite a lot of slots to fill. Thank God Gina took leadership on that project. I signed up for three shifts, but for my first visit, I wanted to be a regular fairgoer and see the booth as the public saw it.

"We have to go to the Pete booth first thing," I told Mary, my Fair buddy, a friend from college.

There was a small crowd around the booth as we approached. Someone was having their picture taken with *Flat Pete,* the nearly life-size stand-up photo of Pete. I'd forgotten Flat Pete was going to be there. A few people were voting in the bean poll, putting their bean in the jar labeled with the issue most important to them. I hoped they would also be going to the DFL booth nearby and voting for Pete in the Democratic primary bean poll there. I know I was planning to do that.

"How's it going?" I asked the crew of three working the booth.

"Great!" Stephanie said. "We're getting lots of people interested in Pete."

"The sign looks fantastic, Stephanie. Thank you so much for doing that," I said with sincere appreciation.

We had a true grassroots booth, a collaborative effort made and funded by volunteers from Minnesota for Pete. It had been noticed by the campaign and we were famous on Twitter. I felt such pride standing there admiring it. But not because I did the work. No, I was proud of our group. It wasn't a straight line to get here, but we made it, thanks to the efforts of many, but especially Lisa who wouldn't give up.

Caitlin was my volunteer buddy two of the three times I signed up to work the booth. When surveying the open shifts, I saw her name with an open slot and thought, *Caitlin is an engineer, she'll be the concrete sequential to my abstract random.* I know it sounds silly, but that's the kind of thing I think of to make up for my shortcomings. I also wanted to get to know Caitlin better.

Caitlin was wearing her "Introverts for Pete" T-shirt. These Pete introverts had a slogan: You know it's Pete when the introverts show up. As an extrovert, this was an important first step in understanding introverts. You mean, it's actually hard for them to attend events? Get involved? But introverts bring so many skills to the table. They are needed. In fact, I envied their ability to get work done. I was constantly distracted by social activity. That's why I felt better taking on the responsibility of a booth shift with Caitlin. She would make sure we plugged in the battery and followed instructions. I could talk to people.

Back when we were painting the booth, I had complimented Kelly on her skills, knowing that she had been on the build team as well.

"You seem to know how to do everything," I said with envy. "I'm not good at doing things." I always said that to my family, not so tongue-in-cheek.

"You're social," Kelly replied kindly. "A social butterfly." At that she tipped her head towards the butterfly exhibit.

Yes, that was me. A social butterfly.

I wasn't good with details like Katie, Lisa, Gina, and Caitlin. I couldn't build and paint like Kelly or sew like Therese. I didn't have Stephanie's energy. What could I do? I mentally checked Pete's Rules of the Road to see what I had to offer the campaign.

Respect—naturally
Belonging—my ace skill
Truth—to a fault
Teamwork—my preference
Boldness—socially, yes
Responsibility—not always
Substance—on the light side
Discipline—not my strength
Excellence—near retirement
Joy—let's party

Responsibility, Substance, and Discipline, in stark terms, scared me. I was well aware of my weaknesses. I preferred to think of my strengths. I was especially in tune with my Myers Briggs Personality Type, which was

ENFJ. I was an extroverted, intuitive, feeling, planning sort of person. Interacting with people was what got me up in the morning. I was people oriented, not task oriented. In Merrick Rosenberg's Bird analogy for personality style, I was a *Parrot*: "Interactive, optimistic, enthusiastic, group-oriented, energetic, humorous." Clearly a social butterfly, like Kelly said. Instead of downplaying that in some sort of shame, why not build on that strength?

Back when I was a Toastmasters division director, I did Tom Rath's StrengthsFinder assessment with my division team to see what each member could bring to the table. It was surprising to me that there was little overlap in strengths. With the key strengths covered, we were sure to do well as a team. My strength shouldn't have been a surprise. It was just that I'd never seen it articulated so decisively as something that was valued as a strength.

WOO. I was woo, or I *had* woo. My strength was *Winning Others Over*. This is the shortened description of WOO from StrengthsFinder: "People exceptionally talented in the Woo theme love the challenge of meeting new people and winning them over. They derive satisfaction from breaking the ice and making a connection with someone." The longer description in the book fits me so well, it's almost spooky.

If I was an ENFJ Parrot who could WOO, how could I find a place in the campaign? As far as I knew, there wasn't a job title with that description. For now, I could still be a part of the team, following the direction of leaders like Gina and Katie. But at least I could feel confident that not everyone was like me and that I could bring my personality style and social skills to events to welcome people and connect them with others.

7

Lis Smith in D.C.

My Twitter bubble had now evolved into primarily Team Pete people. It was my happy place. It was also my preference over Facebook because once you get used to the pace of Twitter, Facebook seems frustratingly slow. I'd see news reports posted by friends on Facebook that had been on Twitter hours before. But it wasn't just the speed; it was the broad range of people posting. And for Team Pete, this meant supporters all over the country and even the world. In true Parrot fashion, I loved getting to know so many new people, people who shared my values.

Facebook would remain my go-to for Minnesota for Pete news, but beyond that, I just wasn't keeping up my account. This was a disadvantage for building up relationships in the Minnesota group because I noticed some of them were very actively following each other on their regular accounts and building friendships. Since I personally wasn't able to keep up both Twitter and Facebook, I made a conscious choice to be a part of the broad Team Pete world in lieu of just Minnesota for Pete.

At the end of August when the State Fair was winding down, and I was ramping up for the new school year, I saw a Tweet announcing a Pete for America fundraising event—*Drinks and Conversation with Lis Smith in Washington, D.C.* Lis Smith, Pete's Senior Communications Advisor, had achieved the rank of goddess among Team Pete because of her successful *go-everywhere* media strategy. Of course I wanted to see Lis. I could use my flight benefit to fly to D.C. But I didn't know whom I would go with, or even if I could go at all, since it would be only the second week of teaching for me. How could I take a personal day so soon in the school year? Not knowing if I could attend, I paused a moment but then clicked on two tickets. I told myself that if I couldn't go, the money would still be going to Pete's campaign, so no real loss.

The more I thought about it, the more I knew I was going to go. I was entitled to my two personal days, and this was personal. My husband wouldn't be going with me, which left me with an extra ticket. Again, what to do with an extra ticket? I didn't know right away who it would be, but I knew it wouldn't go to waste. For the time being that was filed away in the back of my mind in the file labeled: *It will work out somehow.*

I noticed some Twitter chatter about the Lis event and took note of the people talking about going. Of course they already had tickets. They didn't need mine. But now I had an idea. The lowest ticket level was sold out, and only the higher-priced tickets were available. So I decided the first person to mention that they wanted to go but couldn't afford it would be offered my extra ticket. I loved doing random acts of kindness whenever I could. Once I made the decision, I kept an eagle eye on my news feed for anyone wishing to see Lis Smith. It didn't take long. Less than twenty-four hours passed before this person surfaced. It was *Gingers for Pete*, someone I'd exchanged comments with as a fellow South Bend tourist.

"I have a guest tic for Lis Smith," I wrote in a direct message to Gingers. "I would be very happy if you would be the one to take it!"

I'd obviously caught him by surprise because he replied with, "OMG. Are you serious? I am so grateful. AW! I don't know what to say."

Gingers was really Christopher, a ginger from Maryland, slightly younger than I was. Christopher and I shifted to email to make plans for meeting up on the day of the event. But because I suggested we try to get acquainted a little beforehand, our emails were also packed full of information on our personal lives. Once at the event, there would be little time for us to get to know each other. Lis would be much too distracting.

By this time I had been talking about the Lis Smith event on Twitter, about how I was going to fly from Minneapolis to D.C. I was touched when a couple of women from the Northern Virginia group reached out to me. Both Kristi and Patti sent me direct messages asking me about my flight plans, where I was staying, and if I had any questions about finding the venue for the event. Darin, a Minnesota native now living in D.C., also reached out in tweets. The three of them were my personal welcome wagon. With Christopher, Kristi, Patti, and Darin, I no longer felt like I would be alone.

Making sure I would be in Washington in time for the Lis Smith event, I arrived the night before. With no guarantee of a seat on a plane, I always had to have Plan A, B, and C for getting to my destination, padding the schedule, especially if I *had* to get there. The same was true for the trip back if I *had* to get home, which meant very early flights. This is why I chose a hotel close to the airport rather than near the event venue. In fact, it would be an hour Metro ride to the Smith Public Trust restaurant in Brookland.

I had the whole day to play tourist in D.C. before *Cocktails and Conversation with Lis Smith* at 7 PM. Once I left the hotel I wouldn't be back, so I had to choose my outfit, swankier than a Pete T-shirt, guessing what the weather would do. My shoes were what I wore when teaching. They were fashionable, yet comfortable sandals, but as I would soon discover, not good for long hikes. I don't know why I always forgot how grueling it was walking around big cities, even with mass transit options.

My tourist plans were to go to the National Mall and see what fancied me once I got there. I got off the Metro at the Smithsonian station, walked up the stairs to the street level, and stopped by the tourist information board to get my bearings. I looked down the iconic mall and thought, *I'm in Washington, D.C. again! I'm really here.*

Since I'd already been to Washington many times, there was no pressure to see multiple tourist sites. I was content just to be there. But first, I needed my Starbucks latte, and that took me on an unfortunate detour. That was the first hint that my sandals weren't good for walking.

While sipping my latte at Starbucks, I researched tourist options on the mall and decided two things. One, I would visit the National Museum of African American History and Culture, a new museum that didn't exist the last time I was in Washington. And second, I was definitely taking an Uber. My driver dropped me at the museum, and as soon as I got out, the gleaming Washington Monument came into view, stretching into the sky. The perfect photo op to prove I was in D.C. I decided to take a photo for Twitter and tag Lis.

For a frame of reference, a quick detour back to the Iowa State Fair is needed. As I've said, I was too shy to talk to Lis when I saw her among Pete's entourage as we walked the fair. But I wasn't too shy to tweet a photo I'd taken of her with, "Saw the Queen, Lis Smith, yesterday at the Iowa State Fair . . ." I was surprised when she replied. "You should have said hi!" she wrote. Gulp. Really? It would have been OK for me to say hi? Well then. I was set for the fundraiser now that I knew I could talk to her.

Standing on the Mall, I posted a photo of myself with the Washington Monument in the background and tweeted, "Watch out @Lis_Smith, Minnesota will be represented tonight! Can't wait to meet Patti, Kristi,

Darin, and other Twitter Pete Pals!" I pushed *tweet* and walked into the museum. My phone soon dinged with an alert. Lis had liked my tweet. Now she knew I'd be there. With a sudden spring in my step, I bought my museum ticket and started wandering.

The African American History and Culture Museum was expansive, but the highlight was the timeline of African American history in the history galleries down three levels. Visitors took the elevator down to the bottom level and then walked the timeline up to the street level—present day. There was a notice that once you started the self-guided tour there was no going backwards, only forwards. You were asked to be as quiet as possible as you walked the timeline. After reading those instructions, I decided that maybe I needed to eat lunch first at the Sweet Home Cafe.

A "Celebration of African American Cooking," this cafeteria was the absolute best museum cafeteria I've ever experienced. I didn't know what the food offerings would be like at the Smith Public Trust, so this would be my main meal. It was hard to choose, but I knew I wanted something hearty. I took my full tray through the cashier line and found a table for one among the sea of visitors. There I sat gnawing delicious barbecued ribs with sauce dripping down my chin, not a care in the world. It was probably a good thing I was dining alone.

Riding the elevator down to the beginning of the exhibit in complete silence was a strange experience. Normally, families and couples would chat, but everyone respected the museum's request. It was important to set the tone for the serious and often sobering nature of the exhibits to come. There was so much to see, so much to read, but I couldn't do it justice because of all of the walking and standing. I just wanted to sit down. It wasn't fair for my sandals to take all the blame; I just wasn't used to walking so much.

With a promise to come back again someday, I moved quickly through the exhibit, taking some of the marked shortcuts until I got to the decades leading up to present day, covering events during my lifetime. I lingered as I tried to connect my memories to the reality of what I hadn't understood at the time. The last section was on Obama, *President Barack Obama*. I stood stock still with tears in my eyes, yearning for those days again, feeling the loss. We could have compassion, decency, and brilliance in a leader again. We could have Pete Buttigieg as our president.

At the gift shop, I checked my watch and did a rough calculation on when to start making my way to Brookland for the fundraiser. What if I cut it too close? What if I took the wrong train, in the wrong direction? I couldn't be late. In fact, I had to be early. I was meeting Christopher there. He was depending on me for the guest ticket. I was so nervous I decided to head to the Metro right away. I could find a coffee shop where I could kill those extra two hours before I had to meet Christopher.

It was a fifteen-minute walk to the Metro Center station, where I easily found the Red line headed in the direction of Glenmont. I was on the right train, going in the right direction to Brookland-CUA. As the train got closer to the Catholic University of America, more and more students got on. There was a decidedly different feel to the city now as tourism gave way to real life.

As I exited the station, I looked around for a coffee shop, but there was nothing in the immediate vicinity. This is when I made a decision that took me further away from my ultimate destination. But when you're unfamiliar with a city and you're too tired to think clearly, you simply Google *Starbucks near me*. Starbucks was near Catholic University, but essentially I couldn't get there from here. I'm sure the students knew a shortcut, but I ended up with a highly inefficient twenty-minute walk.

Starbucks was my oasis. I got a cup of hot tea and settled into a comfy seat among students studying for exams. I pulled out my phone and saw that there was a text from Christopher. Probably just confirming plans. But no. It was his husband texting me. He said Christopher had taken ill and wouldn't be able to join me at the Lis Smith event. He assured me Christopher would be fine but felt really bad about leaving me without a companion. That didn't bother me; I was just sad that he had to miss it.

"Christopher will try to find someone else to take the guest ticket," his husband added in the next text.

After a few minutes another text came through with the name of my new Lis Smith event buddy. "He found someone from the Maryland group who wants to go. Her name is Raezel. Her number is __."

It felt like a blind date, but I knew anyone on Team Pete was a future friend to me. Raezel and I briefly exchanged texts. "I'll meet you at the door at 6 PM," Raezel texted. Now I couldn't be late to meet Raezel, so I calculated how much time I'd need to get to the Smith Public Trust restaurant, which wasn't nearby at all because of my botched coffee shop plan.

I thought I could walk it, but it became obvious that I just couldn't handle it. Again, I had to call an Uber. Except that I'd forgotten all about charging my phone. Immediately after ordering my Uber, my phone went dead. I felt a wave of panic sweep over me. I felt very vulnerable. Not only could I not check on my Uber, I had no access to Google maps. I couldn't believe I'd let this happen. I obviously had been distracted by the Christopher/Raezel switch. I had planned to charge my phone at Starbucks, but that idea evaporated.

I had no choice but to patiently stand outside of the gas station where I'd called for my Uber. I had to stay put. I estimated how much time it would take for my car to come and tried to think of my Plan B. Just then, my driver arrived. It was only a five-minute drive to Smith Public Trust. Finally, I was there. I couldn't believe I had made things so difficult for myself. But I had the ability to rise to the occasion, and all was forgotten once I opened the door to the restaurant and saw Raezel standing there.

"Hi Sue Ann!" the woman in a leopard print blouse said as soon as I stepped over the threshold.

"You must be Raezel!" I replied.

"Name?" asked the event organizer, pulling up the app on her phone.

"Sue Ann Rawlins. And this is my guest." I replied pointing to Raezel.

"Thank you so much for the ticket," Raezel said, as we walked further into the restaurant. "I thought I was going to be out of town, so I didn't get a ticket. But here I am!"

Raezel was just under 30 years old and seemed to know a lot of people there. Gregarious in nature, she immediately made me feel at ease.

Smith Public Trust had a tavern-like feel and was reserved exclusively for this event. One hour before showtime, it was already crowded with D.C. area Pete people. A Korean-American woman was bustling about with a clipboard. *Kristi.* I knew it was Kristi because she had tweeted about getting signatures for the ballot initiative. In Virginia, presidential candidates had to receive a minimum number of signatures to get on the primary ballot, unlike Minnesota where all official candidates are automatically put on the ballot.

"You must be Kristi," I said as she buzzed by me. "You are amazing, doing all of this ballot work."

"Hi Sue Ann!" she replied. "Welcome to D.C. It's so cool that you could come for this."

Then I recognized Patti, who approached me with a hug. "Hi Sue Ann! It's so fun to meet you!"

"Thank you for reaching out to me, Patti. It made me feel very welcomed." I replied.

All my Twitter pals must have been standing in a group together because as I turned around, there was Darin, my fellow Minnesotan, and Lee, a familiar face from Twitter, welcoming me as well. I recognized *Virginia for Pete* from Twitter and introduced myself. Kyle, in his late twenties, was one of the chief grassroots organizers for the Northern Virginia group.

"You're Virginia for Pete!" I said.

"I feel like I'm talking to a celebrity," he said, having overheard the preceding conversations. That's how I felt about meeting him.

Patti took me under her wing and gave me a menu in case I wanted to order something. I ordered a gin and tonic at the bar and nibbles from the menu. Raezel saw that I was well taken care of and hobnobbed about the room talking to Maryland for Pete people.

I felt totally at home sitting among my Pete Twitter pals. What a respite from my exhausting journey there. In my mind the welcome I received was remarkable, much more than I was expecting. Was this the *belonging* Pete talked about?

We were all watching the clock—and the door—as 7:00 neared. She was running late, coming from another event. But soon I saw the iconic black bob come through the door. Lis looked into the crowd and waved. I looked behind me to see who she was waving at, and then I realized she was waving at *me*. The featured speaker, Lis

Smith—the goddess—was waving at me. I might have blushed.

Instead of the skinny jeans and cowboy boots she so often wore on the trail, Lis took the stage in a silky flowered dress with stiletto heeled sandals.

"I want this to be more of a conversation than a speech," she said at the start, setting the tone for the evening.

Lis talked in general terms about the campaign, divulging no secrets, and about the state of politics. During her speech Lis introduced her mother, who was visiting from New York. Then it was time for the Q&A. In this informal setting, it was fairly easy to get your question answered, but my mind was blank. I couldn't think of one question.

When Lis ended her speech, she left the stage area to greet people near the door. Some people just thanked her as they left the restaurant, but a line soon formed of those wanting selfies. I watched Lis with the people at the front of the line. She was taking her time, not rushing, giving everyone her full attention. To me this was remarkable.

As I was getting in line, I ran into a familiar face from Twitter.

"Are you Crimson?" I asked, referring to her Twitter handle.

"Yes," she said with a knowing smile. "Hi Sue Ann. My name is Nicole."

She had recognized me too.

At last, it was my turn to meet Lis Smith.

"Hi Sue Ann," she said with a warm hug.

I was floored. This was not what I was expecting from a top campaign staffer. I was discovering that *belonging* applied to the staff as well as volunteers.

Lis and I posed for pics together, a staffer taking the photos. Lis had perfected her selfie pose, the angle and tip of the head, so she looked fantastic in each picture. We talked briefly about the Iowa State Fair and I told her about my flight benefit, explaining how I could fly to Washington for the fundraiser.

"You're one of those people who can fly anywhere you want for free?" she exclaimed. "I'm so jealous."

Jealous? I was jealous that she got to fly all over the country with Pete.

Speaking of flying to Washington just for this event, I wasn't going to leave the Smith Public Trust while there were still people there to talk to. In fact, I wasn't leaving as long as Lis was still there. Raezel had the same idea. My other friends gradually left as the crowd thinned.

Lis was not in a hurry to leave, the advantage of this being the last thing on her schedule for the day. As she chatted with people, I noticed that her mother was sitting alone at the bar eating a burger. *I should go and talk to her*, I thought. *She shouldn't be sitting alone*. I walked up to the bar and started talking to Lis's mom. I don't know exactly what I said. I probably introduced myself and told her about how I'd come from Minneapolis. But once the ice was broken, Lis's mom, who was no shrinking violet, took control of the conversation. I thoroughly enjoyed myself.

At some point she had a question for the bartender. "How do I get to the Metro station from here?" she asked.

"Just turn right as you leave the building and it's just a couple of blocks down the hill to the station. You can't miss it," he replied.

No. She wasn't going to take the Metro. Lis Smith's mother wasn't going to take the Metro by herself at night. I knew this wasn't going to happen.

"I'm sure Lis will get you an Uber," I told her.

"Oh, that's not necessary, I can take the Metro," she said.

Raezel and I decided to stay until the end of the event just in case Lis's mom really was going to take the Metro, and then we'd go with her.

The event was truly winding down now, and we could see that Lis had corralled her mom and was arranging an Uber. Raezel and I could leave now.

"Bye! Good luck on the trail!" I said to Lis as I left.

"Thanks for talking to my mom," Lis said in earnest.

Hey, I could be the official mom-whisperer of the campaign, I thought. And I imagined myself sitting with Pete's mom, Anne, at a rally. I could totally handle that.

Raezel walked with me to the station and rode with me on the Red Line for a while until I had to transfer to the Blue Line.

"Can you believe Lis's mom was going to take the Metro back to her hotel by herself?" Raezel said.

"Well, we know where Lis gets it!" I said.

It was quite late by the time I got back to my hotel. Now I had to worry about getting on my flight the next morning. Getting on a flight out of Reagan National Airport on a Friday was especially difficult for non-revenue passengers, like me. I had to start with the very first flight so I'd have time in the day for Plans B, C, and D. And I *had* to get home on Friday because Saturday was the Steak Fry. Our Minnesota group had rented a tour bus to go down to Des Moines to see Pete. I wasn't going to miss that.

It was midnight, and I set my alarm for 4 AM so I could catch the 4:30 AM hotel shuttle. Four hours of sleep wasn't a night's sleep. It was a nap. So for the first time ever, I decided not to take off my makeup and to sleep in my traveling clothes. As I drifted off to sleep, I thought about the fundraiser. Scenes of meeting Lis and my Twitter friends played through my mind. They made me feel like I belonged.

8

The Steak Fry

Back at the Iowa State Fair while we were waiting to hear Pete speak, I overheard Katie and Kelly chatting with a woman from Iowa named Carma.

"You're from Minnesota?" she asked.

"Yes! We drove down just to see Pete speak," Katie replied.

Carma then conspiratorially lowered her voice and drew us all in for her secret, "You have to come down for the Polk County Steak Fry in September," she said. "All the candidates come and speak. It's a big deal, and we're going to need a lot of Pete people to show up for it."

I could see Katie's mind already working on the logistics.

A few days after the fair, Katie messaged me, "Do you think we could get enough people interested in the Steak Fry to pay for our own bus?"

"I don't know. How many would we need?" I said, feeling out of my league already. "I'll go for sure and I can get my husband to go too."

"I'll call some bus companies and run the numbers," Katie replied.

As a church youth leader, Katie knew which bus companies to call and how to plan something like this. But in order to plan, she needed to know how many would come. We spread the word on Facebook, but people were slow to commit. We kept talking about the Steak Fry, the Steak Fry. Who's going down to Des Moines for the Steak Fry? And eventually we had forty-two people for the bus on Saturday, September 21.

It was raining that morning, and as Steve and I loaded our lawn chairs in the trunk, I made sure to include umbrellas. The forecast was for rain on and off all day. I prayed it would mostly be off. Windshield wipers going, Steve drove down the empty streets of Minneapolis in the predawn light to the church where we were meeting the bus. No matter how hard I tried that morning to be ready in time, I was still running late. I blamed it on my early wake-up in Washington the day before.

"Oh no!" I said in a panic, looking at the clock in the car. "It's 6:00 AM right now, and that's when the bus is supposed to leave!"

Knowing there was nothing to say that would calm me down, Steve kept on our path and soon we were pulling in the church parking lot at the same moment the tour bus was arriving. The bus was late. I couldn't believe how lucky we were. In fact, we were able to simply park, load up our lawn chairs in the luggage compartment below, and get on the bus. None of that pesky waiting. That was a close one.

Katie walked up and down the aisle checking her list to make sure everyone was there and everyone had paid. She was definitely in charge and definitely *fun*. I could see the youth group leader in action. But this was no work trip. This was more like taking a bus to see our team play an away game. Yes. That's what it was like. We were the Pep Squad traveling to Des Moines to cheer on Team Pete playing in a tournament.

Katie stood at the front of the bus and turned around and said, "Ok. Let's go! Des Moines or Bust!"

Cheers of "Whoo hoo!" and "Go Pete!" echoed through the bus as the driver pulled out of the parking lot to begin our journey.

The cheers faded as the bus headed south on I-35 for its four-hour journey to the Steak Fry. It was still dark outside, so most people went to sleep or talked quietly with their seat partners. It's funny how the absence of daylight changes behavior to mimic that of nighttime rather than early morning. Steve and I were seated in different seats, across the aisle from each other and we both chatted with our seatmates. I loved getting to know Sarah, a new face for me. She was in her late twenties, studying for a master's in public health, and soon to be married. Talking about plans for her wedding made the time fly by.

It was no longer raining, and as the sun rose over the cornfields of Iowa, more and more people were awake and chatting. The excitement grew as the fields gave way to urban development, and we got closer to Des Moines. On a trip back to the restroom to powder my nose, I discovered that the back of the bus was where the action was, just like in high school. Stephanie and Irish Katie had brought lots of snacks and were chatting away with the others in the back. My kind of fun.

The bus was a little behind schedule, but we would just make it in time for the 10:00 AM pre-rally with Pete. As the driver took the freeway exit in Des Moines, still miles from the Water Works Park, we could already see a backup. Was this just Saturday morning traffic—people out and about doing errands? Oh. Road construction. One lane was closed up ahead. Really? Now everyone was craning their necks, trying to see what was causing the slowdown. At this point, we were traveling at a snail's pace.

"What's going on?" I called up to Katie.

"There's a backup getting into the park," she replied.

"We're going to miss Pete!" shouted someone from the back of the bus.

The Minnesota for Pete cheerleaders were not happy. Four hours riding in a bus and we miss the pre-event rally with Pete? Sure, he'd be speaking later, but the pre-rally and march was when we'd really be able to show our support. The collective mood of the bus instantly deflated, and you could feel it.

I noticed Katie talking to the driver and checking her phone. Soon, she stood up in the aisle to make an announcement. "Don't worry. They're behind schedule. Pete isn't going to speak until 11:00."

"Thank God," uttered a few under their breath.

Finally, the bus made it to the entrance of Water Works Park. Hooray! Except that now we were essentially at a standstill. This time as we craned our necks we could see the long line of cars and buses curving through the 1500-acre park to who knows where because it was impossible to see our destination. The bus inched along and now it was nearly 11:00. I had already resigned myself to the very real possibility that we were going to miss Pete.

Steve and I chatted with the people sitting in the seats near us. It seemed like the Polk County Democrats were unprepared for the hordes of people who would try to get into the Water Works Park at the same time, thousands of people. With seventeen candidates, of course there would be a huge turnout. Some of my friends were downright angry that plans hadn't been made to alleviate the inevitable traffic jam.

As we made our slow progress on the park road, we could see that some people had decided to pull off, park their cars on the grass, and then do the rest on foot. There were many people walking along the park road, carrying their lawn chairs through the sea of candidate lawn signs that seemed to stretch for miles.

"Can we get out and walk?" someone called up to Katie.

After conferring with the driver, Katie announced, "For those of you who want to get out and walk, the driver is going to pull over up ahead to let people out," Katie announced. "You'll be able to get your chairs out of the luggage compartment."

Steve and I looked at each other. After thirty-three years of marriage, he knew to defer to me on all decisions that required walking great distances. He was hearty; I was a wimp. But this wimp wanted to see Pete at all costs. I would just grin and bear it, not knowing what I was getting into.

The bus stopped, and several of us got out to walk. Steve carried both lawn chairs, and we joined the pedestrian traffic on the grass along the road. At first we were moving faster than the bus, but eventually, the bus passed us, and it was at that point that I realized we might have made the wrong decision. It was impossible to stay together with the other Minnesota for Pete walkers in the crowd, and soon it was just Steve and I walking on our own.

After twenty minutes of walking, I still couldn't see our destination, but at least I could hear cheering and noisemakers. It was a relief to see the first pep squad encampment—for Beto—as we reached the outer ring of the event map. Beto organizers lined the road, holding signs and cheering for Beto. We passed the Biden area, complete with bouncy house, the Amy Klobuchar spot, Warren's territory, Kamala's K-Hive. It was a cacophony of chants and cheers as we walked by each candidate's holding pen.

"Do you know where the Pete group is?" I asked someone wearing a Pete T-shirt.

"Over there," he pointed. "Just keep walking."

Eventually we were met along the road by Iowa Pete organizers doing their cheer—a hand jive that would later become the High Hopes Dance. Just ahead was an arch of yellow and blue balloons marking the entrance to the Pete encampment, where two hours after arriving in Des Moines, we finally reached our destination. I could see the Minnesota bus already safely parked, engine cooled. The riders beat us by twenty minutes. *If only we had stayed on the bus . . .*

Beyond the balloon arch was a sea of yellow Iowa for Pete T-shirts. I couldn't wait to get mine, so we quickly walked to the registration table to get our wristbands and shirts, XL for me so I could put it over my jacket.

"Did Pete speak yet?" I asked the volunteer.

"No. He's supposed to be speaking at 1:00," he replied.

That was a lot later than the original 10:00 time. I guess they were waiting for that line of cars and buses to get into the park. Thank God.

"Where?" I asked, trying to get my bearings.

"Over there by the Buttibus," he pointed.

I looked where he was pointing and could see a crowd already in place ready to listen to Pete. A stage was set up right outside of Pete's tour bus, affectionately known as the *Buttibus*. This was the official launch of the Buttibus. Pete would be leaving directly from the Steak Fry for a three-day press tour.

Steve and I found a place in the crowd and set up our lawn chairs, which until now, had been a huge inconvenience. I looked through the crowd of 1300 Pete supporters for Minnesota people and could only see a few scattered here and there. We were now part of the larger community of supporters from all over. I wasn't a Minnesotan anymore.

Soon the warm-up speakers took the stage with the last one introducing Pete. The door to the bus opened, and Pete, wearing jeans and his iconic white shirt, climbed down the bus steps to the stage and took the microphone. At this point, the lawn chairs became redundant as we stood up to cheer for Pete. Steve and I were towards the back, making it hard to see through the crowd. Those who brought their children had them up on their shoulders for a better view. I couldn't ask Steve to do that. I stood on tiptoe and peeked between bodies. The pre-rally speech was different from his regular stump speech because he didn't need to sell us on his candidacy. We were already with him 100%. The prime purpose was to rally us, energize us to help him win the nomination. If only I had pom-poms with me. They would have been perfect.

"Are you ready to win Iowa?" he called out at the end of this speech to cheers.

Then, like the Pied Piper, Pete left the stage and led us down the road to the Steak Fry. We all followed him in march formation carrying signs on sticks, chanting: I-O-W-A, Mayor Pete ALL THE WAY! I-O-W-A, Mayor Pete ALL THE WAY! Was this what being in high school marching band was like? Steve and I were towards the back of the group, unable to see Pete at the front, but photos would later show someone carrying a sign with a giant Pete head and someone in a T-Rex costume.

The Pete Pep Squad, the largest group at the Steak Fry, was making headlines as we ushered Pete to the central venue where the main stage and food tents were set up. Pete would have his turn flipping steaks on the giant grill, just like he did at the Iowa State Fair with pork chops.

I was both excited and surprised by the number of people at the Steak Fry. I would find out later that 11,000 were in attendance. I never imagined it would be this big, this many people. Now I was playing catch-up in my mind, adapting to the situation. *Oh, I get it! This is going to be a crowd crush all day. OK. I'll try not to lose Steve.*

"Let's stake out a place to watch the speeches," I said to Steve.

"Is this alright?" Steve asked, planting our lawn chairs in a central position. I nodded, hoping that we would be able to find them again in the sea of chairs.

The smell of steaks grilling made my mouth water. I could see the food tent, but I couldn't see where the line was. To me, it looked like a slowly moving mob. *How are they going to feed all of these people?* I wondered. Just then, someone tapped me on the shoulder. It was Wes.

"Hi there!" said Wes.

"Wes!" I replied, hugging him. "It's so good to see you again!"

"Where is the Minnesota group?" he asked.

"I don't know where everyone is. We got separated."

Wes from Minnesota, now living in Nebraska, was at the Steak Fry in Iowa with some fellow Nebraskans. I recognized Jana from Twitter.

"Are you Jana?" I asked the blonde woman with Wes.

"Yes. You're Sue Ann, right?" she replied.

Thank God for Twitter making it easy to spot Team Pete friends. We took a selfie for posterity, but soon were separated as we tried to keep up with our companions.

At last, Steve and I found a food line and patiently stood in the slowly moving queue until we could finally give our steak ticket to the nice lady at the end of the table. The line moved faster now as we got our baked beans, potato salad, and dinner roll. Then we got our steaks, fresh from the grill. When I first heard of this event, I wondered if they were really going to serve steaks. Maybe it would be burgers. But no. They were really going to serve people steaks—with chicken and vegetarian options as well. They were really going to feed 11,000 people. I had to hand it to the Polk County Democrats.

As we looked for a place to sit down, Steve and I passed a few Minnesota for Pete friends sitting on the ground,

"Hi! Finally I see some Minnesota people," I joked. "I'm not going to join you, though. I need to sit at a table. See you later!"

Surprisingly, the dining tent had lots of open spaces for eating, and it was a relief to finally sit down for our dinner date. I was glad to be a carnivore because that steak was delicious. Steve and I struck up casual conversation with those sitting next to us at the communal table and found that many were still undecided on which candidate to support. They came to the Steak Fry to hear the candidates speak. They knew who we supported by our yellow Iowa for Pete shirts.

It was almost time for the program to start, so after stopping by the porta potties, we went in search of our lawn chairs. Pete would be the eighth speaker, when we would really show our team spirit. Until then, we would enjoy the privilege of listening to the other candidates' speeches in person. I'd seen some of them milling about in the crowd beforehand—Joe Biden, Kamala Harris, Tim Ryan, Cory Booker—but not close enough to talk to them.

Beto started off the program, followed by Kamala Harris and Cory Booker. Elizabeth Warren and Bernie Sanders, the two anointed progressives, came next with unconventional Andrew Yang following. Joe Biden, Pete Buttigieg, and Amy Klobuchar were scheduled next to each other as the perceived moderates. There would be eight more candidates to go. What a marathon.

When Biden took the stage, that was our cue to get in place for cheering on Pete, the next one to speak. Steve preferred to stay put, but I walked around to the side, moving as close to the stage as I could, near the press bleachers. If our goal was to show that Pete Buttigieg already had a lot of support, we exceeded the goal because Pete took the stage to deafening screams and cheers. I hoped we weren't overdoing it. It started to rain as Pete spoke, but the audience, mesmerized by Pete, stayed put. I didn't care that I was getting wet as I listened to Pete's uplifting message. The ten-minute speech was over in no time, and we again showed our support with uproarious cheers as Pete left the stage.

It was over. Everything had led to this moment, and now Pete's speech was over. Pete would soon be leaving on his bus tour. But rather than feeling anticlimactic, it felt triumphant. I turned around and wove my way back to Steve, feeling the satisfaction of a job well done.

Next to speak was our own senator, Amy Klobuchar. It wasn't that we didn't like Amy. It was just that Pete was a remarkable, once-in-a-generation candidate. After Amy's speech, I didn't know if I could sit there and listen to the other candidates, even if the rain was more of a drizzle. Having already listened to all the major candidates, the audience was thinning out; people carrying chairs and umbrellas, headed for their cars. Our bus wouldn't be leaving for two more hours, so we'd just have to kill time.

Steve had more listening stamina than I did, so I left him to get a couple of beers for us. It felt so good to be off the clock and on my own as I wandered over to the food truck area. The rain had mysteriously stopped. On my way, I came across Irish Katie and Jeff, one of the regulars I'd gotten to know on Saturdays at Caffe Bene, sitting on the ground having beers with some of the others.

"Wasn't that fantastic?" Irish Katie asked, referring to Pete's speech.

"Amazing."

"We're celebrating," Irish Katie said, holding up her beer.

"I'm headed that way too," I replied.

"What did your husband think of Pete?" Jeff asked.

"I think he was impressed," I said.

When I got back with the beers, Julián Castro was just starting his speech. I know Steve had been waiting to listen to him. During the next speech, though, I convinced Steve to pack it in. There was no way I could sit there for five more speeches. So with lawn chairs under arm, we walked back to the food truck area to try to find our group. Maybe our bus would leave earlier if we were all there.

It was a relief to see Katie and Kelly standing in the long line for the ice cream truck.

"Hi, you two!" I said. "I'm exhausted. When are we supposed to be on the bus?"

"We're leaving at 6:00 sharp, but you can get on before that," Katie answered. "You know where it's parked, right?"

I nodded and continued to walk around talking to people with Steve. I looked at my watch, eager for departure time. Maybe we'd get on the bus early. At least we'd have a place to sit down. Our decision was made easier once it started raining again. We were going to the bus early. On our walk to the bus, our pace quickened as it rained harder, and just as we got to the bus, the skies opened, and it absolutely poured. Pity the last speaker on stage.

We waited until every last person was accounted for—some diehards had stayed for the last speaker—and then the driver pulled out of his parking spot and started the long trek out of the Water Works Park. Katie and Kelly walked down the aisle handing out treat bags full of candy. What a fun and welcome surprise to end the day. I wondered if it would take just as long to get out of the park as it had taken to get in, but since many people had left already, it really wasn't that bad, and soon we were back on I-35, but headed north.

It continued to pour as we made our way out of the Des Moines metro area, which made darkness come even sooner. At first the bus was lively with chatter about the day. I walked to the back of the bus to talk to Stephanie and found that I had completely missed cocktails. Stephanie and Irish Katie had brought margarita makings for the back of the bus crowd, and they were just finishing them up. I lamented not being on Facebook because I would have known about this party ahead of time.

Two hours of dark cornfields would pass before we got to the Minnesota border, so Katie put in a video for us to watch on the tiny monitors scattered down the rows. In keeping with the Iowa theme, Katie had brought *The Music Man*. Having played the part of *Marian the Librarian* in a community theatre production,

I knew all the songs and had even started talking about the song, *Iowa Stubborn*. Meredith Willson didn't mince words in his stereotype of Iowans, and I joked that we should be prepared for that stubbornness when we're door knocking.

This wasn't the time to launch my Music Man Appreciation Club, though. Those tiny TV monitors and matching tiny sound system made it nearly impossible to really watch the musical. Most people were talking quietly or snoozing—the bookend to the beginning of the trip. I noticed my attention wandering and had to admit that even I didn't want to watch my favorite musical. Instead, I took the opportunity to shut my eyes and reflect on the day.

On the surface, only hyperbolic language could describe the experience of joining 1300 Pete Buttigieg supporters in a crowd of 11,000 to cheer our candidate as he spoke alongside sixteen other Democratic primary candidates. *Once-in-a-lifetime, monumental, amazing*. But at my core, the day affected me more deeply than that. What was it exactly? I couldn't put my finger on it. It was *profound, surreal, magical*. But why? I think it was the sense of community I felt, not just with Minnesota for Pete, but with the other Pete supporters, Team Pete. I loved standing in that sea of yellow T-shirts, being a part of it all, showing by our numbers that Pete Buttigieg was a serious contender for the nomination, that he shared our values. In the middle of my reverie, I drifted off to sleep, finally succumbing to exhaustion.

I woke up as the bus pulled into the church parking lot at 11:00 PM. It was hard to believe we were all the same people who left this parking lot at 6:00 AM. Steve and I groggily gathered our belongings from the seats and got off the bus to get our lawn chairs out of the luggage compartment below. Miraculously, they had made the trip without getting lost along the way.

"Thanks for planning this, Katie," Steve said as we were getting ready to leave.

"Yes, thank you!" I added. "It wouldn't have happened without you."

"I'm so glad it all worked out," she replied.

It had indeed all worked out. I had a feeling this wouldn't be our last trip to Iowa.

9

The South Bend Office Opening

I looked forward to our weekly call with Kyrstin, our PFA Regional Director, eager to know what was going on with the campaign. We had shifted to organizing ourselves by congressional district, and the two Katies were spearheading ours, CD5. There was a slightly different feel to our group now that we were both branching out by congressional district and broadening the total group. I enjoyed hearing what was happening up in northern Minnesota as well as down south. Kyrstin told us that for now we were to focus on three main goals: Pete-ups to attract more volunteers, relational organizing (talking to everyone you know about Pete), and a monthly service project in keeping with Pete's message on service.

Carrots. Pallets of cargo boxes full of bright orange carrots. Our service project at Second Harvest Heartland was to pack up 40-pound cartons of carrots and slide them down the conveyor belt to the truck. They would go to where they were needed. Carrots, carrots everywhere, which made us all giggle. Steve was especially charming holding up a prize-winning carrot next to the cargo box. The bright orange was eye-catching on photos that would end up on the Pete Mosaic, a compilation of Team Pete photos from all over the country that together made up an image of Pete.

In campaign news, Kyrstin had told us about the South Bend field office opening. It wouldn't be advertised on social media until later, but she kept us updated on the status of the planning. Finally, on one of our weekly calls, Kyrstin had a date for us: Thursday, October 3. Another no-brainer for me. I was definitely going even though I would have to take my second and last personal day, only four weeks into the school year. With the historic nature of this campaign, I had promised myself that I would attend any event possible during the primary cycle.

This may sound to some like an obsession, or perhaps stalkerish, but in reality, there were two reasons. One, each time I saw Pete speak in person and met those around him, I was able to tell voters that yes, he was the real deal. And two, attending events was a way of showing support for my candidate, of adding to the numbers. But if I were to be completely honest with myself, I'd have to admit it was all one huge party I wanted to attend while I could. I knew it wouldn't last forever.

I had to allow an extra day to get to South Bend just in case I had trouble getting on a flight. It was a good thing I did because I got there on my Plan D. The direct flight to South Bend was full, so I tried two Detroit flights before I got a seat, and then I didn't get on the connecting flight to South Bend, so I had to stay over in Detroit. Luckily I got on that first flight in the morning to South Bend. Thank God the Marriott Courtyard waived my first night charges and let me check in early. It pays to be a *Rewards* member.

My morning plans had to be shifted slightly because of my late arrival. I had planned to meet up in the morning with Michael Yoder, the producer of the *Good Guy Pete* podcast, a popular show aimed at covering Mayor Pete from the South Bend perspective. South Benders Michael, Lety (my Twitter friend), and Ryan hosted the show and interviewed various guests about Pete's record in South Bend. I loved the show because it gave me insight and actual facts that I could use when talking to people about Pete as Mayor.

The idea of doing a podcast myself was something on my back burner, and I wanted to talk to Michael about how he would structure working with me, how much it would cost, the logistics of recording. My idea was to incorporate a podcast somehow into my Susie Young at Heart website and blog devoted to the topic of friendship. I'd done YouTube interviews with friends for my website. Maybe I could transition to doing podcast interviews. But I didn't know the first thing about it.

Since I wouldn't arrive in time for the originally scheduled morning meeting, Michael and I had to reschedule for early afternoon. That meant I had time to grab a late breakfast at PEGGS. What's a trip to South Bend without a stop at PEGGS?

"Table for one?" the hostess confirmed as she showed me to my table.

As I walked through the restaurant, I noticed Laura O'Sullivan just settling in at a table with a business associate. I couldn't believe it. What were the odds? I suppose she had meetings there often, but the exact timing was fortuitous because I wanted to meet her. Still, I wasn't going to interrupt her meeting. In fact, I tried not to even look in that direction while I was eating my order of Fred's Home Plate. She would definitely recognize me from my Twitter profile picture. I thought about how I could introduce myself to her. Maybe later, on my way to the restroom.

I finished my meal and got up to pay at the register and there was Laura O'Sullivan at the door saying goodbye to her companion. I held back, suddenly shy. As soon as her appointment had left, Laura approached me with outstretched hand,

"Hi Sue Ann," she said, recognizing me.

"It's nice to meet you, Laura!" I replied, shaking her hand.

She definitely had her Mayor's Chief of Staff hat on, which I respected, so there was no time for chitchat. She went on her way, and I walked to the register to pay my bill. As chance meetings go in crowded restaurants, it was perfect.

It was now on to my appointment with Michael Yoder. A little early, I walked across the street to the Chicory Cafe and placed my latte order. Chicory Cafe, with its charming nod to New Orleans, invited me in and made me want to stay. Last time, it was a muffuletta sandwich after meeting Stefan. Today, a latte to talk about podcasting with Michael. I took a table with a good view of the door and checked Twitter, the number one thing to do while waiting.

There was much talk about that evening's event on Team Pete Twitter. It wasn't clear who would be the featured speakers, though. Neither Pete nor Chasten had been mentioned as being there. But conversely, no one ever said they *weren't* going to be there. Was it assumed? Surely Pete would try to be at the South Bend field office opening if at all possible, right? Still, I knew his schedule had to be kept flexible in case he had to dash off for a media appearance, so I kept a guarded sense of optimism. I had decided it would be OK with me if only campaign staffers were there. I wanted to meet them too and be a part of the celebration.

I messaged Joy that I made it to South Bend and was excited about seeing her again. She was already at the campaign office, busy getting everything ready with the other volunteers.

"How early do you think I need to come and get in line?" I asked her.

"Come at 5:00," she replied. That was one hour before the posted start time.

I glanced up from my phone to see Michael coming through the door. I stood up to shake his hand, but as he approached me, he opened his arms and said, "I'm a hugger." *South Bend is for Huggers*, I guess, and that's fine by me. Already caffeinated enough, Michael opted out of coffee and sat down right away, ready to get down to business. But that still needed to be defined. From his perspective, he didn't know what to expect from me as a potential client.

"What are your ideas for a podcast?" he asked me.

"I'm not sure. But I have a theatre and speaking background, so it sounds like a good fit. It sounds fun. Right now, I'm thinking of it as a future possibility for my website Susie Young at Heart."

I told him about my hobby of making friends online and then traveling to meet them in person. Michael showed genuine interest as I explained my flight benefit and my penchant for making Twitter friends.

"Maybe you could interview them for a podcast," Michael suggested. "You can use portable recording equipment and take it on the road with you."

"Really?" I replied, the wheels turning in my mind. I'd never thought of this before, and the idea was exciting. I loved traveling and talking to people. Why not make it official and record it?

I asked him about his company, Truth Work Media, and what production services he provided. He made it sound easy—he would guide me through anything I needed to do on my end, and then he'd handle the rest on the production end. The pricing structure seemed reasonable to me. But more importantly, Michael was so warm and friendly I knew I would enjoy working with him.

"How sure are you that this is something you want to do?" he asked me.

"Well . . . I'm very sure I want to do it, but I don't know when. I've taken a break from my Susie Young at Heart website while I've been volunteering on Pete's campaign," I explained. "I can let you know for sure in a week or two." We wrapped up the meeting with an action item for me.

As Michael got up to leave, I asked him if he'd be at the office opening, and he said he would be, that he'd be volunteering.

"Do you know if Pete and Chasten are going to be there?" I asked.

"No one knows," he said. "I'll let you know if I hear anything."

"That would be great," I said getting up to toss my cup in the trash. "I'll see you there!"

Thank God I had some time to rest before then. I was starting to feel the effects of that early wake-up call in Detroit that morning. I walked around the corner to my hotel and headed up to my room for a nap. I thought through my timing and checked Google maps. The office was at 218 Sycamore, just across the river from the Marriott, so I could easily walk it. *I'd better allow a half an hour, just in case,* I thought. I was a slow walker. Before then, I'd have to change into my Pete gear.

Refreshed from my nap, I rifled through my suitcase to find my blue and gray Pete 2020 baseball tee. I checked my jean jacket to make sure the various Pete buttons were still firmly pinned on. As I was heading to the bathroom to touch up my makeup, my phone dinged with an alert. It was a message from Michael—*Both Pete and Chasten would be there*. Beaming, I put down my phone, and proceeded to create a selfie-ready face.

I gathered up my tote bag and carefully slid my copy of *Shortest Way Home* inside, hoping to get it signed. Clad in my Team Pete uniform, I checked the mirror before leaving. *Not bad for an old lady*, I thought. I was ready to celebrate. I walked out of the hotel into a fall day perfect for an outdoor event—not too hot and not too cold, with no threat of rain. From the Marriott, it was a two-block walk up Dr. Martin Luther King Drive to the Colfax Avenue bridge across the St. Joseph River. With such a beautiful view, my pace across the bridge slowed to a stroll so I could take it all in. As I reached the crest of the bridge, a small white event tent came into view. Since I knew that was where the line started, my pace quickened.

As I neared Sycamore, I could see that the street was blocked off for the event. Authorized vehicles only. I checked in at the white tent and got in line. Only two people were ahead of me. Others were starting to arrive, and the lineup behind me gradually stretched down Colfax Avenue. In this festive setting, we all started chatting to pass the time. The woman in front of me was on Twitter, so we traded handles. She had driven from another town in Indiana. The retired couple behind me had traveled from California. I had wondered if this was just a South Bend party I was crashing, but now I knew there were many supporters coming from all over. And the South Benders were welcoming us. Literally.

Out of the blue, a beautiful Asian woman wearing a Mayor Pete dress ran up to me and hugged me.

"Hey, Sue Ann!" she cried. I knew it was *Musicians for Pete* from Twitter, someone I was hoping to meet. Her hug attack was one of the biggest compliments I could ask for.

"Musicians for Pete!" I said. "I love your dress!"

"I'm so glad you could make it!" she said with an enthusiastic smile. Jackie showed positive exuberance online, and now I could see that was how she was in real life too. It was contagious.

"Are you volunteering?" I asked.

Jackie nodded

"How's it going?"

"It's going to be so cool," she answered. "I have to get back and help. See you later!" And then she vanished.

A little later, I saw AJ walk up to talk to the volunteers working check-in. I knew right away the symbolism of her stylish sweater dress.

"AJ—the South Bend flag!" I cried, looking at her yellow and blue color-block dress.

"When I saw it, I just had to get it," she replied, as she hugged me. "Thanks for coming!"

Jackie and AJ looked so festive in their frocks that I started to feel underdressed. But then looking at the others in line, I fit right in wearing blue jeans.

I was relieved to be welcomed back by AJ, someone I'd met on my July trip. I don't know why I was worried about that. Probably because we hadn't gotten to know each other that well yet. I thought of everyone I'd come in contact with that day—Laura, Joy, Michael, Jackie, and now AJ. I was starting to feel the welcoming South Bend effect.

The field office was just a few doors down Sycamore from the check-in tent, and as I chatted with people in line, I made sure to keep an eye down the sidewalk for clues that it would soon be time to go in. Finally, a volunteer came to open up the line. As I walked down the sidewalk, I could see a group of volunteers on parking duty across the closed-off street, and one of them waved at me. It was Michael. Just more South Bend friendliness.

Pete's speech would take place outside the office in a grassy area between buildings. The stage backed up to the outside of the office where a mural of the South Bend flag was painted, forming the perfect backdrop. To the left was the ADA (Americans with Disabilities Act) seating section, and stanchions marked a large area in the center for the audience to stand. Strategy is important if you want to stand along the rope line at an event like this, so given the option of going into the field office for a tour or staking out a spot in the audience, you need to go directly to the rope line. I had counseled the couple from California on this strategy, and together we walked to the front of the stage while most of the people in line behind us went inside for the tour.

But now I was in a quandary. I wanted to see the office and nibble on the appetizers. I wanted to meet other South Bend volunteers and maybe even Pete's mom if she was there. If only I had a clone. I must have been thinking aloud because my new friend from California urged me to go inside and that he'd save my spot. Grateful, I took him up on his offer and walked over to the building.

Inside the door was a bustle of activity in the small campaign store devoted to selling Pete 2020 merchandise. I recognized one of the volunteers from Twitter—*Grandmas for Pete*, Lauren, who had driven down from Illinois to help. She was swamped, so I couldn't really talk to her, but I made sure to catch her attention and wave. I walked further into the front room, a small space with murals on each wall, most notably the iconic Pete 2020 Jefferson Avenue Bridge with "South Bend" over it. Selfie central for everyone, including me. A small kitchen connected the L-shaped floor plan, where a large celebratory sheet cake was placed on a table to enjoy later. The main room beyond was where the action was. It was full of people. I scoped out the lay of the land—photos, displays, appetizers—before going on my search for people to meet.

It's easy to spot Anne Montgomery's gorgeous head of white curls in a crowd. She was there. I made a beeline to that side of the room and waited eagle-eyed for my turn to talk to her. She was standing with Julia Chismar, Pete's high school teacher who helped on his campaigns. At last, I saw my moment.

"Hello, Anne," I said, extending my hand for a handshake.

"Hello," she replied graciously, not knowing who I was or what I was going to say.

"My name is Sue Ann Rawlins," I said getting right to the point. "You sent me a thank you note, and I wrote back to you about linguistics . . ."

"Oh... I think I remember that—"

Our conversation was then cut short as someone pulled her away for an introduction. I couldn't believe it. I actually got to the point of talking to Pete's mom about our pen pal relationship and wasn't able to even finish the conversation. It was incredibly frustrating because she obviously remembered. We could have made a connection. I hung around a bit to see if there would be a way to continue our conversation, but at that point, she was ushered away to talk to people.

I turned to talk to Julia Chismar, who we affectionally referred to as "Mrs. Chismar" on Twitter. Julia and I had communicated recently on the subject of fundraising. She made the plea for us to all donate whatever we could for the end of the quarter. I asked her if I should donate to the maximum allowable amount now or space it out over the primary. *Do it now,* she wrote. So for the first time ever in my life, I added a donation to my current level and reached the $2800 maximum for a political candidate.

"Hello, Mrs. Chismar," I said as I approached.

"Hello," she said, recognizing me from Twitter. *Ah, the advantage of using a real photo for my profile picture.*

"Thank you for your fundraising advice," I said, hoping to link this conversation to our Twitter exchange. "I donated to the max."

"Oh, that's great! They can really use the money."

"Thank you for everything you're doing for the campaign," I said.

"Well, you know what he's like . . . " she said with a cocked head and knowing look. The subtext being— *Pete's so extremely gifted. How can I not help?* I couldn't have agreed more.

The crowd inside was filtering out and taking their place outside for the program soon to start. That was my cue to get back to my California friends. I wove my way through the crowd to my saved spot up front, a much smaller space now that the crowd was pushing as close to the stage as possible.

There were many speeches before Pete came on stage. The program began with speeches from South Bend faith leaders representing the major world religions, led by the campaign's Faith Engagement Director, Reverend Shawna Foster. Arielle Brandy, the newly hired Indiana State Director spoke followed by South Bend Organizer Breana Nicole Micou who introduced Chasten.

This was my first time seeing Chasten in person, and his charisma added spark impossible to see in a photo. Chasten began his short speech with a heartfelt greeting to South Bend, his now hometown. I could see that he was happy and relaxed, that it really was home.

I started to feel like this was a private party I had the honor of attending.

When Chasten introduced Pete, Pete came on stage and they embraced so tenderly I almost felt the need to look away. If anyone dared to wonder about their relationship, I could tell them unequivocally it was real. Then Pete took his place on center stage to address the crowd for a speech that wasn't the Iowa State Fair. Nor was it the Fine Line Music Cafe in Minneapolis. This was for South Bend.

"Not bad for an office opening, huh?" he said to the opening applause.

Conscious of the effect his presidential campaign had on the city of South Bend, he graciously thanked the community.

"I'm so thankful to everybody who is a South Bend native for the way you have embraced members of our team and folks who have come through by way of the campaign."

Although the speech focused on South Bend's success story, on the power of community, I imagined that the same thing could happen in any city, given the right tools and the support of the community. South Bend represented the potential of all cities and towns, something Pete had talked about on the trail. The potential of *people*. In my mind, Pete Buttigieg was the only candidate focusing on real people in their communities, and that message resonated with me. He was talking about something so basic perhaps the others missed it—he was talking about real life.

Pete finished off his speech with a thank you.

"Thank you for believing in me. Thank you for everything we're going to ask you to do. Let's go win this thing beginning right here in South Bend."

He had thanked South Bend for believing in him. With a lump in my throat, I felt like I had just witnessed a very private moment between the city and its mayor-turned-presidential-candidate. This was for South Bend, but South Bend and the campaign welcomed me. So did that mean I was part of it? Was I part of it all despite being from Minneapolis?

I watched Pete descend the stage to start greeting supporters along the rope line, starting with the ADA section. Soon he would be getting to me, and I had already decided what I was going to say to him. Knowing I'd have less than a minute to talk to him, I wanted to get right to the point of telling him my thoughts on his book, *Shortest Way Home*, as he signed my copy. I decided against trying to get a selfie as well, especially since Pete had said in an interview that he wished there weren't so many selfies, that he could just talk to people.

When I read Pete's book, I experienced it like many people did. I cherished his literary turn of phrase; I marveled at his accomplishments; I swooned at the story of his romance with Chasten; and I loved the South Bend comeback story. But I also was struck by Pete's earnestness, which I thought unusual for a political memoir. I felt like there was no pretense, only genuine thoughts and emotions, freely given to us, the reader. He made himself vulnerable in a way that said—this is who I am. I valued his authenticity and wanted to let him know that someone had noticed.

You can mentally prepare yourself for the moment when Pete Buttigieg is standing right in front of you, in close proximity, waiting to hear what you have to say, but in reality, your heart races as you adjust to the in-person version of Pete, knowing that you'd better strike up enough nerve to say what you want to say, or the opportunity will have passed.

Saralena, Pete's body-woman, was shadowing Pete, helping with selfies and moving him along. Seeing I had my book and pen out, she opened the book and positioned it for Pete to sign. And then Pete was there with his warm smile.

"Hello," said Pete, as he took up the pen to sign the page.

"Pete," I said. "I can see your soul in this book."

He was clearly caught off guard by my comment, taken aback for a moment. I'm not sure anyone had said something like this to him before.

"Thank you." he said, graciously. "That's what we tried to do."

And then Saralena ushered Pete to the next person in line. Of course I had more to say but wasn't the least bit surprised he couldn't stay to chat. I closed my book and stepped back to make room for others. Beaming inside and out, I wandered around musing about what had just happened. *I told him.* I really told him I saw his soul in his book. And he seemed to know what I meant.

Then I realized something. Chasten was following Pete down the line, and had I stayed put, I would have been able to talk to him too. Dang! I was kicking myself for getting out of line. But then I remembered that he would be coming to Minneapolis in less than two weeks for a small fundraiser. I would see him then.

As I mingled in the crowd on my way back to the building, one of the volunteers tapped me on the shoulder.

"Someone wants to talk to you. I'm supposed to bring you over," he said, pulling me through the crowd.

"OK . . . " I said, curious to know what was going on.

He took me over to the end of the rope line where Joy was waiting to talk to Pete and Chasten.

"Joy!" I said, hugging her. "You got him to bring me over!"

"I didn't want to lose my place in line."

"Thanks for telling me what time to get here. I got a good spot up front," I said. "Pete signed my book!"

Joy introduced me to her school-aged child, and we talked a little more while they stood in line. I asked her where Lety was. She told me it was Lety's wedding anniversary, and she was out with her wife. She hated missing the big event.

"I'm going to see if I can get a piece of cake," I said, taking my leave.

Back in the office, cake was being served, and selfies were being taken everywhere. I met Breana, the South Bend Organizer and discovered that she was AJ's sister. Then I met Amanda, one of the South Benders from Twitter. She was a super volunteer.

As I was taking pictures of the murals, a woman approached me.

"Hey—I got some good pictures of you with Pete," she said.

"Really?"

"You were standing a few people down from me, and I was taking pictures of Pete as he came down the line."

She then showed me the pictures on her phone. They were perfect. The three photos captured my short conversation with Pete in succession. I could tell what was being said in each one. This was a real gift. To have that moment authentically captured was so much better than a selfie. How lucky I was.

The woman was Beth, who went by *Independents for Pete* on Twitter. I gave her my cell number, and she sent me the pictures.

"Thank you so much," I said emphatically. "This means a lot to me."

I felt eternally grateful to her. What a kind thing to do, track me down to give me the photos. The one time I purposely decided not to get a selfie with Pete was captured, anyway.

I stayed around for a while as the event wound down, not wanting the night to end, but it became clear that it really was over. By now it was dark, and I started my lonely walk back to my hotel. As I got to the bridge, the stunning river lights under the Jefferson Avenue

Bridge made me stop in my tracks. I had to take a picture to match my picture from July.

I stood there for a while thinking. I'd heard the South Bend volunteers were going to a bar to celebrate. Why hadn't I asked them if I could join them? I was kicking myself for this. I could be with Joy, AJ, and Jackie. Now I was on my own. Then I realized that no, this night was for them. Sure, they would have welcomed me, but I hadn't helped out. I wasn't a volunteer. I wasn't a South Bender, but I was on my way to becoming one.

10

The Birth of a Podcast

When I met Chasten the first time, I was hopped up on benzos as I staggered to shake his hand. Steve had to take my arm and guide me because I couldn't really feel my feet. With swollen jaw, I proudly announced, "Hi Chasten. I'm on drugs from oral surgery." Chasten sympathetically acknowledged my condition as we got in place for our selfie. I'm sure I made a memorable impression.

Kyrstin had arranged for Chasten to meet up with Minnesota for Pete volunteers in the afternoon before he headed to a small fundraiser in Minneapolis. Lake Monster Brewing Company in St. Paul was the perfect location, and I desperately wanted to be there with my Minnesota friends, especially since I missed meeting Chasten in South Bend two weeks before. Never mind that I had a dental procedure right before the event that couldn't be rescheduled. I would just have to arrive in a compromised condition. I wasn't going to miss it.

I enlisted Steve to help make this possible.

"We have to head right to Lake Monster immediately after my appointment," I said on the way to the dentist's office. "If we have to go to the pharmacy, we can do that after."

He nodded. He usually knew that it was best to follow my advice when it came to getting places on time.

My appointment went well, but since I had taken two triazolam doses—one before and one during the procedure—I couldn't walk to the car without the assistance of both Steve and the nurse. He was now hesitant to go straight to Lake Monster Brewery. Instead, he drove to Walgreens and parked the car.

"Nooooo!" I cried. "We have to go right to Lake Monster! I'm going to miss Chasten!"

Steve took my protestation with a grain of salt, knowing that I was still under the influence of a sedative, and went into the pharmacy to get my prescription. I was fuming. How could he do this? I had distinctly told him we had to go to the venue first.

By the time we got to Lake Monster, Chasten was in the middle of his speech. I had missed the group photo, but at least I hadn't missed the selfie line that followed his speech. I was mad at Steve for making me miss the first part of the event. We could have made it in time had we not squandered away valuable minutes at Walgreens.

"I'm sorry, Sue Ann, but you were in no condition to go to an event. You couldn't even walk. I thought you needed a little more time for the drugs to wear off," he explained later in the car driving home.

Eventually, I came to terms with his reasoning. It was bad enough meeting Chasten in that condition; I wonder what the group photo would have been like, had I come even earlier. My eyes might have been crossed. Two weeks later in Des Moines, I reminded Chasten of our meeting at Lake Monster.

"Hi Chasten," I said. "I met you when you came to Minneapolis. I was the one who had just come from oral surgery."

"I remember that," he said.

I knew I had made an impression!

Meeting Chasten had been on my to-do list from my South Bend trip. Check. But the biggest to-do had been making a decision on doing a podcast with Michael Yoder. I was torn. I really wanted to do a podcast; the performer in me was champing at the bit. But I knew I wasn't going to revive my Susie Young at Heart friendship interviews anytime soon. My heart, pun intended, wasn't in it. I was much too distracted by the primary race and helping Pete get the nomination.

It's funny how ideas just come to you out of nowhere. Sometimes it's in the shower, or while you're washing dishes. It seems like it's usually when your mind is free from working on a task that requires concentration. My idea came to me when I was driving a well-known route to a local coffee shop. My mind was swirling around the idea of traveling to interview online friends in person—Michael had said I could use portable equipment. *Wait. I was already traveling around to meet Team Pete friends from Twitter. Why don't I interview them?* I could easily do that, but what would be the purpose? Then I had my next brainstorm—*If I could capture the grassroots energy on the ground for Pete, maybe that could help the campaign.*

This was my chance to help Pete's campaign by using my strengths. My unique skill set was perfect for this kind of podcast. After all, I was an ENFJ, Parrot, WOO with a flight benefit. One week after meeting Michael Yoder in South Bend, I accepted his business proposal. I was going to be a podcaster.

The primary had a finite life span, with the first big test being the Iowa caucus at the beginning of February. If I wanted to make some sort of difference, I had to get the podcast up sooner rather than later. I felt the fire under me as I worked with Michael to do all that needed to be done to launch my podcast. But this fire felt *good*. I had a purpose.

The preparation was two-fold. One was the tech side—ordering the equipment and learning how to use it. The other was setting up the show itself. I had to make many creative decisions from naming the show—*Twitter Travels for Pete*—to choosing music and recording my intro and outro clips. For the artwork, I chose my Pete selfie from the Iowa State Fair, which captured the celebratory energy I wanted for my show.

Next was planning interviews. Who was I going to interview? The clock was running because I knew that I wanted to record interviews at the big Liberty and Justice event in Des Moines on November 1, just two weeks away. The group *Barnstormers for Pete* had organized a thousand volunteers from across the country to attend the event. I definitely had to capture *that* energy. But that shouldn't be my first interview, especially for technical reasons. Something so high stakes shouldn't be the first time I use my portable recording equipment. It shouldn't be the first time I publish an episode. Plus, in terms of building a show, I needed to start with my home base first. I needed to talk about Minnesota for Pete.

I was excited about the idea of interviewing my Minnesota for Pete friends. There was so much we could talk about, especially our State Fair booth. I assumed that everyone would be game to participate in the episode, but as it turns out, the very people who make things happen in an organization are also the ones least likely to want to talk about it. To an introvert, the idea of being interviewed for a podcast was terrifying. I don't know why that surprised me so much, but it's more evidence of the difference in personality and how we often get caught up in our own perspective. I was so happy that Melani, *Minnesota for Pete* on Twitter, and Gina agreed to participate.

Wanting a lively discussion, I set out to recruit a couple more people via our Facebook group. In doing so, I was able to broaden my Minnesota for Pete acquaintance. The two women who expressed interest were new to me. Mary and Laura were onboard to join Gina and Melani for a recording session on Sunday, October 27. I sent everyone the show format in advance and practiced with my Zoom Handy H6 portable recorder and plug-in microphones.

As I wrote the show prep, I vacillated between *I know exactly what I'm doing* and *I have no idea what I'm doing.* My confidence was at war with my doubts on this since I had never done a podcast before. I knew what content I wanted, but organizing it into an episode was trickier than I thought it would be. Maybe starting with four guests wasn't the easiest way to do it, but I wanted rich content. *Well, I've done my best to plan a good episode. Whatever happens once we start recording will have to be OK.*

The night before the recording session, Laura messaged me that she was sick and wouldn't be able to participate. She was disappointed that she wouldn't be able to do it. I understood. But in my mind, I needed four people, and I scrambled to find a replacement. Steve. My husband could do it. He was part of Minnesota for Pete. He was a talker and definitely not shy about being on a podcast. You may wonder why I didn't include him from the start. That was because when my podcast launched, I didn't want anyone to think, *who is this lady? Can't she find enough people to interview so her husband doesn't have to do it?* I'm sure that was just my own insecurity getting the best of me.

That first recording session was nerve-wracking for me. I'd made all this effort to set it up; what if I was a tech fail? What if I failed at guiding the conversation? All of that confidence I had when imagining this moment two weeks ago went out the window. I was especially conscious of the person new to our group, Mary. I wanted her to feel like taking time out of her day for a podcast interview was worth it. I was very glad to have her participate because now we'd have the perspective of someone new to the Minnesota for Pete group. She came on board after the State Fair.

The five of us sat around my dining room table, with me and my H6 Zoom recorder at the head. There were four tracks, four microphones. Michael had told me that to avoid confusion, I should always be track one. Gina had track two, Melani three, and Mary and Steve would share track four. Each person had brought headphones or earphones to plug into my splitter and once that was done we were ready to start.

"First, I have to check everyone's mic level," I told the group.

One at a time, they each spoke into their mic as I set the sound level, the gain, for that track. Michael had taught me the difference between gain and volume, which made me feel like a pro.

I'd made copies of the show format for everyone so we all knew what would be coming next. The plan was to go chronologically, with each person covering a specific event or aspect of Minnesota for Pete. But most importantly, I wanted everyone's *Why Pete?* story—why they thought Pete was the best candidate for the nomination.

I pushed Record.

"For this first episode, I'd like to talk about my home base, Minnesota. Minnesota for Pete, in particular," I said in my best radio voice.

Then we were off to the races. Melani started us off with her story of starting the Minnesota for Pete Twitter account. Gina was next with the trials and tribulations—and successes—of our Minnesota State Fair booth. Then Steve followed with tales of the Steak Fry. Mary wrapped up the first round as our newbie. The second round included upcoming events and relational organizing (talking to friends and family about Pete). One of my last questions was whether anyone had talked to any Republicans who were considering Pete. The answer was yes. Pete was the candidate who could win the crossover vote.

The first wonderful lesson of being a podcast host is that not only do you learn new things, you learn about the people you're interviewing. No matter how much you prepare in advance, or how well you know the individuals, you can't possibly predict what they will say. And that is the beauty of it all. I thought I already knew the basic answers to the *Why Pete?* question, but the four of them surprised me in their unique answers; even Steve surprised me. *I think I'm on to something here.*

After nearly an hour of Pete conversation, I pushed the button to stop recording. There was an immediate sense of relief as we were no longer under pressure to say something witty. The nervous energy was released in giggles as we chatted about how we thought the episode went. I played back the first part of the episode so they could all hear what it sounded like through the headphones—amazing sound quality. Everyone was excited for the finished product to be published.

Showing them to the door, I thanked Melani, Gina, and Mary for participating in the recording. When the last one was gone, I essentially did a Doris Day after a date with Rock Hudson—leaned back on the door with a swoon. *It was a success.* I had done my first episode! What a relief. But the show still had to be produced. Michael and I still had work to do.

I headed straight back to the dining room table to work on my show edits. Two hours later I was still working on them. As I listened to the 50-minute show a couple of times, I noted the exact timing of anything that needed to be cut. Luckily there wasn't much because that much detail usually made me go into my unhappy place. I also wasn't used to dealing with SD cards, so I was all thumbs as I removed the tiny card from the portable recorder and put it into my laptop for the transfer. With the sound file in Dropbox, I emailed Michael with the edits.

A few loose ends needed to be tied up before the show could be published. The album artwork had to be finalized, and Michael was still in the process of getting the show set up on Podbean. Considering that it had been just over two weeks since Michael and I started this adventure together, we were moving at breakneck speed. But in my mind, we were already behind schedule because I wanted to get this first episode out before the big Barnstormers event in Iowa on Friday, only a few days away.

Barnstormers for Pete was spearheaded by four women from the New York group as a way to organize Pete supporters to attend the Liberty and Justice Dinner in Des Moines on Friday, November 1. Similar to the

Steak Fry, this high-profile event featured each candidate speaking, but in a more formal, much larger setting—the Wells Fargo Arena. Barnstormers for Pete wanted to get as many Pete supporters in the audience as possible cheering for Pete, with every state represented. As the date drew closer, more and more excitement was building. The Barnstormers weekend was the talk of Twitter, and I'm assuming, Facebook, for all of October. "Are you going to Barnstormers?" "Who is going to Des Moines?" were the most often asked questions. Not only were we going to the Barnstormers weekend, we were *Barnstormers* ourselves and we were an army.

11

The Liberty and Justice Dinner

Y ou may have already figured out that November 1 is preceded by October 31. Halloween. Anyone making the trip to Des Moines would be traveling on Halloween. It was the best reason ever to miss handing out candy to trick-or-treaters in my mind, but those with younger kids at home would never be forgiven for opting out of this well-loved holiday.

I distractedly taught my regular morning ESL class that day without much holiday fanfare except for the Halloween candy at break time. My spirit was already in Des Moines, but now I had to get my body there. Steve was taking a half day off work so we could leave in the early afternoon. I quickly submitted my attendance, straightened up my classroom, and rushed out the door. On my drive home, my mind was preoccupied with podcast plans for the big weekend. I'd decided to do a compilation of interviews including the women who started Barnstormers for Pete. At the traffic light two blocks from home, I decided to check my phone for messages. My phone. *Where was my phone?*

My phone was secured safely in my center desk drawer at school. No pockets that day meant my phone went in my desk. I couldn't believe it. It was the worst timing. I turned around at the gas station and headed straight back to school, scolding myself the whole way. This would put us behind schedule at least an hour. Now we wouldn't get to Des Moines before dark. But at least I'd still have time for my interview with *Grandmas for Pete* at the Hilton.

The Honda Accord was loaded up and ready for the journey south on I-35 to Des Moines. Steve was in the driver's seat so I could catch up on Twitter, which was *all atwitter* with Barnstormer posts. So many people were posting selfies en route that I wanted to do the same. We used Steve's much longer arm to take a cute selfie of the two of us clad in Pete gear sitting in the front seat of our car ready to take off. Des Moines or bust.

I was waiting to see when Episode 1 of *Twitter Travels for Pete* would go live. All week, Michael and I had been scurrying to get everything ready for the launch, which was to be today. Hallelujah! An hour into the trip I got a message from Michael which read, "Congratulations! Your show is now live." I looked on Podbean to see the photo of me with Pete at the Iowa State Fair on my show page. "Episode 1—*Home Base—Minnesota for Pete*" was there with a running time of 51 minutes 39 seconds. I was an official podcaster now. My heart beat a little faster with nervous excitement as I knew people would be listening.

My internet signal had been good until we got deep into the cornfields of Iowa, but now that I wanted to promote my show far and wide on social media, it was spotty. How frustrating. Steve probably was glad that I had to get off my phone since I was using up time on the cellular network rather than free Wi-Fi. I would just have to wait until I got to the hotel. I forced myself to relax, but knew I'd be checking for Wi-Fi at the rest stop.

We stopped for a break at the Dows rest stop along southbound I-35. Yes. They had Wi-Fi. As I checked my phone for prime Twitter activity, a text message came through from Tricia. I knew that she and her partner David would be Barnstorming this weekend too and staying in the same hotel as we were. David, a guitar builder, had set up some sales appointments in the Des Moines area, killing two birds.

"Can you call me?" the text read. This concerned me.

I immediately called her, but the call didn't go through. The cellular network was letting me down again. I found Steve reading the Visitors Information board and told him about the text from Tricia. Once we got on the road, I'd try calling again.

"Hi Tricia," I said, finally connecting. "What's up?"

"Are you still on your way to Des Moines?" she asked.

"Yes. We got a late start." I answered. "We just stopped at a rest stop in Dows."

"We hit a deer."

"What?" I cried. "Are you all right?"

"We're fine, but the car is totaled," she said with a shaky voice. "I think you're still north of us. Would you be able to pick us up?"

"Absolutely. Just text me the exact location. I'm so sorry, Tricia!"

I ended the call and updated Steve with what had happened. Of course we were going to help them. Then I had the realization that if I hadn't left my phone at school, we would have already been in Des Moines and not in such an easy position to help them. The serendipity of the timing now was that we were only 25 minutes away from rescuing them. Was there a higher power delaying my departure today? Something that had infuriated me earlier in the day was a blessing in disguise.

Tricia texted me the meeting spot—Love's Travel Stop in Ellsworth, exit 133. When we pulled into Love's parking lot, I could see the forlorn couple waiting by the side of the building with their luggage and gear on the sidewalk. I felt so bad for them. Tricia loved her Mini Cooper Countryman. I thought of our trip down the same stretch of freeway last August in that car and sighed. Tricia had been driving the car when a deer came out of nowhere and jumped in front of her car. She was understandably still shaken by the experience. I've always been terrified of the possibility of hitting a deer.

Adding two people's luggage to our own in the Honda Accord trunk would usually be fine, but this was more complicated because of the guitars. They couldn't be squished in. But they fit perfectly on Tricia's and

David's laps in the back seat of the car. Although the circumstances were regrettable, I enjoyed having travel companions for the remainder of our drive. We were all cozy and safe together. The four of us had done some text banking together at our house a couple of weeks earlier, so the guys knew each other. With constant conversation, the time flew by. We'd made it through the cornfields into the Des Moines metro, and soon we were pulling up to the AC Hotel in the East Village.

"I think I'll take an Uber to the airport and pick up a rental car there," David said as we loaded our respective luggage on the bellman's carts.

"I'm happy to drive you," Steve offered.

"No. You've already helped us so much. It's no problem for me to Uber."

Once Steve and I got to our room, I finally had a moment to reassess my podcast plans for the evening. We were much later than planned. I didn't see how I was going to be able to interview *Grandmas for Pete*—Lauren, who was staying at the Hilton. Steve and I still had to have dinner. I sent a message to Lauren letting her know the status. Since she had been a little reticent about being interviewed in the first place, she wasn't exactly disappointed. Still, I hoped that somehow we could fit in an interview. Steve and I would stop by the Hilton after our late dinner.

I scoped out the hotel dining options while Steve was stretched out on the bed, recovering from three and a half hours in the driver's seat. The hotel bar and restaurant, *The Republic on Grand*, was on the sixth floor, and although open to the public, had a private feel to it. As I strolled through the restaurant, I ran into Tricia and David who were just leaving.

"Wow. You were fast!" I said, incredulous that they had managed to get through dinner already.

"We were starving, so we had to eat right away," Tricia said. "The food is good."

I took a look at the menu, already deciding what I was going to order when I came back with Steve. Before Tricia left, she pulled me aside, and said. "I saw Saralena. She was picking up food for Pete. They're staying in our hotel!"

I didn't know how I could sleep knowing Pete and company were staying in the same hotel as I was.

The Barnstormers Base Camp was at the Hilton, and from what I could see on Twitter, it was swarming with Pete supporters. Lauren and I had already decided against an interview, but why not get together for a cocktail?

There were still lots of people milling about when Steve and I finally walked into the Hilton lobby at 10:30 PM, but it was easy to spot Lauren sitting by the window with some other women in Pete shirts.

"Sue Ann," Lauren called to me. "Join us for a drink."

"Looks like we have some catching up to do," I said, noticing their empty glasses.

I looked straight at the blonde woman with gorgeous blue nails and said, "You're Paula, aren't you?"

"Yes," she answered.

"I'm Sue Ann," I said introducing myself. "Nice manicure!"

"Thank you. I just had to get blue for Pete."

I had recently gotten to know Paula on Twitter and knew it was her as soon as I saw those nails. Earlier in the week, she had posted photos of her manicure in preparation for her exciting lead up to Barnstormers weekend—a Chasten meet-and-greet in San Francisco on Tuesday followed by a performance of *Hamilton* with Chasten, the next day. Definitely worth a special manicure!

A beer for Steve and a Scotch for me, we settled in for a late-night conversation with Lauren, Paula, and Carol, the third woman in the group. The three of them had met on Twitter, and this was their first time meeting in person. An easy-going conversationalist, Steve held his own with four Pete fanatics. He also loved meeting people from all over the country. The Barnstormers for Pete organizers had said that all fifty states would be represented at the LJ, so we were curious about where everyone was from. I knew Lauren was from Illinois and that Paula was with the huge California contingent. Carol was from New Hampshire.

"Whoa," I said looking at my watch. "It's so late! We have our state meet-ups tomorrow morning."

"We're probably going to take over the entire Scenic Route Bakery," said Paula of her California group.

"Minnesota is meeting at Mars Sidebar," I said. "I have no idea where that is. I'd also like to find where the Virginia group is meeting."

Barnstormers for Pete had assigned a location for each state to meet together in the morning to get organized for the rally later that day. Some states would take over entire coffee shops, but some states with a smaller showing would be combined. In any case, Pete Buttigieg supporters would have a dominant presence in Des Moines coffee shops in the morning. I pitied the other candidates.

As an old married couple, Steve and I knew our routine when traveling—he wanted to walk everywhere, and I didn't. But since I had my own agenda that Friday morning before the Minnesota meet up, we would be separate anyway. No negotiation needed. I would simply take the free hotel shuttle bus across the river to meet Pam, *Hope4Pete*, at her hotel for breakfast.

Pam and I had bonded on Twitter over Pete's memoir *Shortest Way Home*. It was uncanny how similar our minds were. We both experienced Pete's book in a similar, intuitive way and felt equally emotional when reading certain passages. If you're doing Twitter right, the algorithm will eventually lead you to a kindred spirit like Pam. And if your kindred spirit is in Des Moines with a thousand other Pete supporters, you'd better make sure you find her and meet her in person.

There was barely enough time to meet Pam before the state meet-ups at 10:00 AM, but I still wanted to try since my late arrival the night before had prevented us from meeting then. At 9:15 I breezed through the Renaissance Savery Hotel lobby and quickly made my way to the executive lounge where Pam was waiting for me.

"I've already eaten," she said after greeting me. "But you can be my guest. Have something to eat."

"Thank you so much," I replied, heading to the buffet for something quick and easy to eat.

Knowing that we only had about fifteen minutes to talk together, I delicately tried to talk while shoving food in my mouth. We obviously couldn't discuss anything in depth, so we stuck to the basics. Pam talked about how she was looking forward to her upcoming retirement from her university job in southwestern Virginia, and I told her about my new podcast. Pam was keeping track of the time better than I was and soon started gathering up her things to leave.

"I'm going to the Northern Virginia meet-up at Java Joes," Pam said.

"Where is that?" I replied, remembering my plan to fit in one more thing before heading to Mars Sidebar.

"It's just down the street," she said.

"I'll go with you. I want to try to catch some of my Virginia friends and say hi."

I guzzled my tea while putting on my coat and wrapped the rest of my bagel in a napkin and threw it in my tote bag along with the apple I'd taken from the buffet.

Java Joes Coffee House was a charming place with a long and narrow seating area opposite the espresso bar. At first I wondered how there would be room for all of Virginia and Maryland Pete supporters, but then I soon came upon the adjacent music venue with a small stage and audience area. That's where everyone was gathering.

I had a not-so-hidden agenda for briefly crashing the Virginia meet-up. If I'd only wanted to say hello to my friends from the Lis Smith event in September, I could have waited to run into them. But I had business to attend to.

"Patti!" I said as I saw her ordering her coffee.

"Hi Sue Ann!" she said. "Isn't this fun?"

"So much fun. I have to get to my Minnesota meeting now, but I wanted to plant an idea with you."

Patti nodded and gave me her full attention.

"I just started a podcast—*Twitter Travels for Pete*—and I want to come back to D.C. and interview you and some of the others about your grassroots organizing. Would you be up for that?"

"That sounds awesome. I'd love to do it!" she said, grabbing her coffee. "The only trick will be scheduling."

"I'll send you an email. Fingers crossed we can make it work!"

Mission accomplished, I rushed out the door and down the street to the Minnesota meeting at Mars Sidebar for my first interview in my Barnstormers podcast compilation.

The Barnstormers event organizers were true geniuses in their idea for individual state meet-ups. To make it work, though, there had to be a captain for each state group to streamline the flow of information and to run the meeting. Our captain was Karen. I admired Karen for her attention to detail and her take-charge, no nonsense approach to tasks, something I was lacking, but fitting for her profession as a nurse. She was the perfect captain.

"Hi Captain!" I said as soon as I saw her. "Ready for this?"

"As ready as I'll ever be!" she said, jokingly. "We're going to wait a little bit to get started since some people are just getting to Des Moines now."

Steve arrived soon after I did, and we briefly compared notes on our respective breakfasts.

"I went to the place by our hotel, but it was full of Pete supporters," said Steve. "I think it was California."

"Whoa. At least you can have something to eat here," I said, eyeing the menu.

"I saw Chasten, and Pete's mom in the hotel lobby," Steve said.

"Really?" Anne Montgomery was staying in our hotel too, which made sense since Pete was. The wheels in my head were turning. There was still time for me to run into her. I hoped the universe would put her in my path so we could finish our conversation on linguistics.

I ordered my latte and found a place in the middle of the tables pushed together for our group. My tote bag was packed with my recording equipment, and as soon as I sat down at the table, I set it up. Instead of individual microphones, I had decided to use the microphone capsule which attached to the top of the recorder. That way, I could pick up the ambient sound and energy of the room in addition to anyone I was interviewing. My recording equipment didn't go unnoticed, and some people, out of shyness, expressed concern about being recorded.

"Don't worry, I just want to get some good background audio of the meeting," I said, motioning to my recorder. I casually mentioned my new podcast to anyone who would listen.

Minnesota for Pete folks gradually filled up this small coffee shop on the street level of a large office building. Apparently "Sidebar" meant that this wasn't the main Mars Coffee, but merely a satellite. That one was larger and more popular. The Sidebar had less weekend traffic, though, which made it the perfect place for our meeting.

All in all, we had about twenty Minnesota for Pete Barnstormers there, some new to me. Sarah, my bus partner from the Steak Fry, came in with her carpooling buddy, a new Sarah, *Minnesota Mama* on Twitter. This new Sarah and I had messaged each other about the Barnstormers weekend, and she had kindly offered me her extra ticket to arena seating at the Liberty and Justice Dinner that night.

When the Iowa Democrats released arena tickets to the main event, Pete supporters immediately flooded their website and tickets were sold out in about an hour. Even though I had been vigilant about getting in early, I wasn't able to score any tickets. Barnstormers for Pete assured us that there would be overflow seating in the building across the street. There were also rumors that the reason they had sold out so soon was because blocks of seats were reserved for campaigns and that those seats would be released later.

But I *had* to be inside the arena so I could record. What good would a recording in the overflow be? Sure, I could catch the Pete supporter energy, but it wouldn't be the same as the excitement of the arena while Pete was giving his speech. I knew Steve would be fine with the overflow if I could get a ticket for me in the arena. We weren't the type of married couple who had to sit together.

"Anyone have an extra ticket to the L&J?" I had posted on Twitter.

"I have a ticket you can have," *Minnesota Mama* said in a direct message. I was touched by her offer.

Now I was meeting her, my second Sarah, and making plans to get my ticket. Tickets were available at the Wells Fargo Arena box office at noon, and she'd be picking them up soon after that. We exchanged cell numbers so we could text each other about meeting up.

I could have spent the morning chatting with my Minnesota for Pete friends, but we had an agenda to accomplish, and soon, Karen called the meeting to order

"I'm going to make this quick so we can get going on what we need to do," she said.

The agenda was the same for all states. The main project was to record videos of our *Why Pete?* stories on the Storyvine app and share on social media. Also, throughout the day we were encouraged to post on Facebook and Twitter using #Petestorm as the hashtag. *Pete Storm.* That was the perfect abbreviation for Barnstormers for Pete.

"We want to make #PeteStorm trend this weekend," Karen said. I knew I was up to the task on that one.

Karen then went over the schedule for the day. The pre-rally would be at 3:00 at Cowles Commons, a green space a few blocks away. The rally would follow at 4:00 when Pete would speak. We'd then be marching en masse with Pete to the Wells Fargo Arena. I hoped the weather would cooperate, but it wasn't looking encouraging. The forecast was for a cold rain, and I was not known for my physical stamina in cold weather, despite my Minnesota roots.

The meeting then transitioned to Storyvine time, an opportunity for everyone to make their videos with technical assistance available if needed. Many paired up so they could take decent video shots, but I just did a selfie video so I could turn my attention to interviewing Karen. I had already talked to her about an interview, and now it looked like she was finally free. She was chatting with Lisa of State Fair Booth fame as I approached.

"Karen, do you have time for an interview now?" I asked, holding my recorder.

"Absolutely." she replied.

When I saw Lisa standing next to her, I thought, *Score! Now I can get Lisa too.*

"Is it OK if I include you in the interview, Lisa?"

"Sure!"

Then I pressed Record.

It was short, but sweet and included a surprise sampling of Norwegian. I was pleased.

"What's the plan now?" Steve asked when he finished his Storyvine.

"Let's go back to the Hilton, to see who's there."

"Sounds good."

"Hey—have you seen Tricia and David?" I asked.

"No, I'm sure they've been dealing with their car," he replied. Of course. They were probably lining up their rental car and dealing with insurance. Not at all what they had planned for today.

The Hilton lobby was abuzz with Pete supporters, a true Pete Storm. It seemed everywhere I turned I saw another person I knew from Twitter. I was in absolute heaven. But the commotion was about to get more intense because the bus from South Bend had just arrived. Having left South Bend for the six-and-a-half-hour drive well before dawn, the sleepy Benders, clad in comfy sweats and carrying pillows, filed into the lobby to thunderous cheers. It was one of those memorable moments, a moment I can pull up in my mind and play over and over again. I don't think they expected that kind of greeting. We'd caught them off guard. Cheering was one small way we could show our support for South Bend and its Pete supporters.

Outside it had become cold and rainy, so we stayed at base camp as long as we could chatting with people. Ever since the South Bend bus came in, the lobby restaurant was at capacity. It was fun to see AJ and Amanda again and meet some new Benders as well. But no matter where I sat, I was surrounded by kindred spirits.

"Are you doing the flash mob?" I asked the people sitting next to me at the communal table where I was eating my burger.

"We're going to try, but we haven't practiced," one woman said, motioning to her husband.

"Oh, I haven't either. I'm pitiful."

For the flash mob, we were all going to gather at the pre-rally and start doing the High Hopes dance. By now, the dance was all over social media, and if you didn't know it by now, you would soon. *High Hopes*, by Panic! At the Disco, was Pete's walk-on song. One of the Iowa organizers had made up a cheer for it, and many of us were trying to learn it. But it was Amy, *Space Nerds for Pete* on Twitter, who expanded the cheer into a choreographed dance and posted YouTube videos of herself teaching the steps. She made it easy to learn. I would be interviewing Amy for my podcast the next day, fingers crossed.

Steve and I donned our yellow Iowa for Pete T-shirts from the Steak Fry over our coats, grabbed our umbrellas, and started our trek to Cowles Commons, following others through the skyway system as far we could. All hopes of recording anything at the rally went out the window as the rain went from a drizzle to a steady rain. No way was I going to get my expensive recording equipment wet. I suppose it simplified things for me. But it wasn't the rain that canceled the flash mob. Unfortunately, the flash mob had to be nixed at the last minute because of a conflict with the musical guest scheduling. We'd still get to do it at the Pete-up in the park the next morning. It would probably be better weather.

Undaunted by the rain, hordes of people came to hear Pete speak, and the Iowa for Pete organizers cheerfully checked them in one-by-one, which was admirable. I was getting more and more cranky as the minutes passed, and I hadn't been outside as long as they had. At least I was wearing one of the disposable rain ponchos they were handing out. Savvy to Pete's campaign appearances, I chose a spot at the end of the rope line, at the side of the stage, rather than in the center behind a crowd of people. The Buttibus was parked behind the stage, and I would have a good view of Pete walking up the steps to the stage. I clung to my spot while Steve milled about the crowd.

This side vantage point gave me an excellent view of the entourage traveling with Pete as they waited beyond the stanchions. I saw Lis Smith, whom I'd met, but also Mike Schmuhl, his Campaign Manager, and Nina Smith, his Traveling Press Secretary. I tried to get up the nerve to talk to Mike and Nina as they walked by me, but the rain made it difficult for small talk.

With my eye on the backstage activity, I could clearly see Pete walk around the back of the bus and wait by the stage to be introduced. But then I lost sight of him as he hopped up on stage. I shifted position so I could at least see him from behind. This limited visibility was no problem since I'd already seen him speak in person three times before this. I didn't want to be accused of being a *Pete hog.*

When Pete finished his speech, he walked directly back to the Buttibus to get lined up for the march to the Wells Fargo Arena. From where I was standing, I caught a glimpse of the high school marching band that would be leading the march, and once I heard them play, I knew that it would only be a matter of minutes before the rally crowd would join the formation. We didn't need to think of what to do or where to go; we just followed the crowd.

For my second time in less than two months, I was marching with Pete in Iowa chanting, "I-O-W-A! Mayor Pete all the way!" This urban setting with a much larger crowd felt completely different, though. It felt like the stakes had gotten higher. And they had. Pete's popularity was continuing to grow; he was a serious contender now. With hundreds of us taking up the breadth of Third Street as we marched, even the casual onlooker could see that Pete Buttigieg was a rising star.

The rain had stopped, but it was too late. I was chilled to the bone as we walked the final block uphill towards the arena. Campaign volunteers were at the top directing us—tickets to the right, overflow viewing to the left. This is where Steve and I parted. I had found the two Sarahs while marching and gotten my ticket, but only one Sarah—Sarah Steak Fry—turned right and entered the arena with me. Unfortunately, Minnesota Mama wasn't feeling well and decided to watch in the overflow area. How disappointing for her.

I carefully removed my recorder from my tote bag and showed it to the security guard at the checkpoint.

"Is this OK?" I asked in my overly conscientious way.

"Sure," the guard replied, hurrying me through the metal detector. I don't know why I had been worried. Members of the media obviously needed recording equipment too. *I* was media.

Sarah and I took the steps up to level two and then up another flight of stairs to the third level. Next, it was a walk halfway around the perimeter to reach our section. Along the way, food and beverage stalls were staffed, ready to serve us. I was dying for something hot to drink—hot chocolate or coffee—but none of the vendors were offering it. A few had coffee listed on their wall-mounted menus.

"I'd like a coffee, please," I said, stepping up to the counter, money in hand.

"Sorry, we don't have coffee today," the woman behind the counter replied.

Today? They don't have coffee today? On the chilliest, rainiest day? Cold beer wasn't going to cut it.

Sarah and I found our seats at the very top row with a bird's-eye view of the stage below. A few rows down from us sat Tricia and David, whom I hadn't seen all day.

"Hey, Sue Ann!" Tricia called out, as I ascended the stairs.

"Tricia!" I replied. "How are you two doing? I haven't seen you all day."

At this point, I let Sarah pass me so I could dilly dally and chat with Tricia.

"We were dealing with the car and then I had to miss the rally because that was the only time I could go to the box office to get our tickets."

"It was miserable standing there in the rain," I said just in case she felt bad about missing it.

"I saw Pete's mom at the box office," Tricia added.

"You did?" I said.

"Yes. I told her about hitting the deer, and *she gave me a hug!*"

"Aww, that was nice of her!" I said with genuine feeling. Just because *I* wanted to run into Anne Montgomery didn't mean others couldn't benefit from an encounter with her too. Plus, this was the best medicine for Tricia's misfortune.

Sarah and I settled into our seats. It felt so good to finally sit down and rest in the warm arena after hours of standing and walking in the cold. It would be an hour before the program started, but the idea of sitting still in a warm dry place sounded heavenly. I got out my portable recorder and recorded a set-up piece where I talked about the preceding rally and march. The capsule microphone worked perfectly. I was able to be heard, but the arena noise was recorded as well. Not only did I get the sound of the spectators waiting in anticipation for the main event, but I also captured the hint of a dinner being served below as silverware met china plates. My listeners would definitely get the feeling of being in the arena with me.

Our seating area wasn't reserved for any particulate candidate, but we had a clear view of the Pete section in the center and down a level. With banners and gigantic letters spelling P-E-T-E and BOOT EDGE EDGE, it was hard to miss. After a half an hour of chatting with Sarah in our seats, I got a text from Steve in the overflow venue.

"We all just got tickets for the arena!" he said. "We're coming in now." I was so happy he would get to see Pete's big speech in person.

Right about the time I was relaying that information to Sarah, I noticed some Pete volunteers coming up the stairs. They were telling us to move down to the second level, center section. We happily obliged. With all of this last-minute movement, I got the feeling it was showtime. Places, everyone!

Sarah and I joined the festive crowd of yellow shirts in the center section, taking the best pair of seats we could find. I got out my Zoom H6 again and settled in to record my opening for the arena segment. Pete was first on the schedule, but it wasn't clear how many introductory speeches would come before he made his entrance. This was, after all, an Iowa Democratic Party event.

After several speeches by the local party officials, the lights dimmed, and things got serious. Then I knew I had to press Record again.

"Please welcome to the stage, Mayor Pete Buttigieg!" announced the emcee off stage.

With *High Hopes* playing, Pete walked with absolute confidence down the runway in a cloud of mist, the spotlight following him to center stage. The Iowa Democrats really knew how to put on a show.

This was our cue to go absolutely wild. The wristband lights started blinking and the cacophony of noise from the thunder bats and cowbells filled the air. But the highest decibels came from our cheering. Nearly 3000 of us were screaming. And we wouldn't stop. Poor Pete had to keep saying, "Thank you. Thank you, Iowa!" I think it was nearly two minutes before he could get us settled down. It was probably one of the most exciting moments in my life, and it was all being recorded.

Earlier in the day at the Hilton, I'd felt at home surrounded by my fellow Barnstormers community. Now I was among thousands of cheering Pete supporters in the Wells Fargo Arena, and I was struck by the fact that this went well beyond community. This was a *movement*. I recorded all of Pete's speech even though I knew I wasn't going to use it all. The speech was perfection. A rhetorical genius, Pete had a gift for relating complex ideas to everyday life, appealing to moderates and liberals alike. He expertly used the entire stage in a way that clearly showed a high level of preparedness. Extremely confident in his delivery, Pete Buttigieg looked *presidential*.

I had goosebumps. I think most of us had goosebumps, and some had tears, by the time Pete finished his speech. We were even more committed to helping him win the nomination now. He'd made us proud. But imagine what it was like for him—looking out into the sea of blinking lights and yellow *Iowa for Pete* shirts and hearing the fervent cheers of thousands of fans. I think we made him proud too.

It was anti-climactic once Pete left the stage, but we would stay to hear as many of the twelve other candidates speak as we could. I can say without a doubt that Pete Buttigieg had the strongest showing of support of any of the candidates, by far. And in this, the Barnstormers for Pete organizers succeeded in their goal of getting a high turnout for the event.

Pete's speech that night earned much media attention. The subsequent polling would show Pete Buttigieg as number one in Iowa. The Liberty and Justice Dinner had skyrocketed him. And we were part of it.

12

The Afterglow

My alarm went off at 6:00 AM Saturday morning, and I felt like I'd been run over by a truck. I'm not sure I had entirely warmed up from being out in the cold rain the day before. My entire body ached. My brain was full from the total load of social interactions I'd had, overwhelming even for this extrovert. The excitement of the day before had caught up with me, and I needed much more sleep. But what I needed more was an interview with the Barnstormers for Pete organizers. I couldn't leave Des Moines without interviewing some of the women who made the Barnstormers weekend possible. Since they still had events planned, I would need to catch them early—before their day started.

I ignored my fatigue and pressed forward, grabbing a cup of tea and quick bite to eat before catching the hotel shuttle van. I got to the Holiday Inn early, found a quiet place in the lobby, and set up. This was my big interview, and I wanted to make sure I was ready. How disappointing, then, to discover that there had been a mix-up on *which* Holiday Inn. They were at the *other* Holiday Inn.

Knowing that the window of time for the interview was slowly closing, I immediately called an Uber and made the trip across town. I tried not to look frazzled as I entered the lobby and greeted the women who started Barnstormers for Pete.

"Donna?" I asked, confirming the identity of the woman waiting in the lobby.

"Yes," she replied, shaking my hand. "Sorry about the mix-up."

"It's 8:30 now. Do you still have time for an interview?" I asked, fingers crossed.

"We have a little time before we have to head to the Pete-up in the Park." Donna replied. "Lisa and Cat had to go set up, but Abby and I can do the interview."

"You must be Abby," I said addressing the blonde woman on the sofa.

"Yes," she answered. "Thank you so much for doing this."

For this interview I'd ditched the capsule microphone and brought individual microphones—one for me on track 1, and one for them to share on track 2. With the time constraints, we just had to do the interview right there in the hotel lobby. At the time, I worried about the background noise, but in the finished product, it added verisimilitude, one of my favorite words.

I learned so much interviewing these two formidable women, again the big plus of being a podcast host. Abby started off by explaining how Barnstormers first got started over the summer with a few friends from the grassroots New York for Pete group, and then Donna added more detail. The interview then became more of a conversation between the three of us, which I loved.

In the origin story, Abby was the one who put the Liberty and Justice Dinner on the radar. As the New York group talked about attending, the plan morphed into something much larger—an initiative to get as many Pete supporters to attend as possible. And thus Barnstormers for Pete was born. Cat had already been active coordinating Pete 2020 Facebook groups, so the interface with those groups was streamlined, and Pete Twitter spread the news like wildfire. Ari handled the increasingly active Barnstormers social media and Lisa worked on operations. They had their own merchandise and a plan for subsequent events in each of the early states.

I was in awe of all that these women had accomplished. This amazing weekend wouldn't have happened without them. We were all *Barnstormers* now, and together, we would help Pete win the primary.

We were able to cover all the main points of the Barnstormers story in the limited time we had for the interview. It's amazing how a time crunch makes you more clear-headed and efficient. Since that was the one interview in the compilation I was the most concerned about, I felt like a load had been lifted off of my shoulders. I still had one interview left, but I could relax now.

It's hard to relax when you're exhausted, though. It's an all or nothing thing—up or down. I had used up all my adrenaline doing that interview and felt like a zombie as I stood outside waiting for my Uber. There was no way I could muster up the energy to go to the Pete-up in the Park. I was going to miss the High Hopes flash mob. But I had no physical reserve left. Good thing I had time to revitalize before I interviewed Amy in a few hours.

My Uber dropped me off at the AC Hotel. I got out and walked into the hotel, preoccupied with my schedule for the rest of the morning, which revolved around check-out time. The lobby was deserted, with the exception of Stephanie, my Minnesota friend, who was sitting by the window.

"You just missed them." she said. "They were *all* here, and they just left."

My depleted self wasn't prepared to receive this information.

"Who?" I asked, wanting to know exactly which members of the Buttigieg family she was referring to.

"Pete and Chasten. And Pete's mom. She came down first while I was getting some coffee. We had a lovely chat. Anne and Chasten got in a car in the front, and then later Pete came down and left for his bus tour out the back."

I just missed them. Perhaps that was the part that bothered me the most. If my Uber had picked me up at the Holiday Inn sooner . . . When you're not feeling well, things hit you harder. I remember getting in the elevator and thinking, *That's it. I'm done. Time to go home.* In retrospect, I am ashamed of this overly emotional reaction. But at the time, it seemed like everyone else had run into Anne except me—Steve, Tricia, Stephanie. Didn't the universe know that Anne and I had a conversation to finish? But then if you're going to trust the universe on these things, you have to trust that the time wasn't right. There would be another opportunity some day for the universe to intervene.

A latte and a cooked breakfast was just what I needed to rejuvenate. Steve had slept in and was ready for breakfast when I came back to our room. At least one of us was well-rested. He would be the one to drive home, then. We walked around the corner and down the street to the Scenic Route Bakery, the place Steve had tried the day before.

As we walked up to the counter to order, I heard someone calling me.

"Sue Ann! Steve!" called Tricia from the table near the cash register.

"Hey!" I responded.

Steve and I walked over to their table to greet them.

"Join us," David said.

Not only was I going to get food for the body, I was going to get food for the soul. This chance encounter was just what we needed to end the weekend. We'd started the weekend together in the middle of Iowa on I-35, but the four of us hadn't been together since. Debriefing the Liberty and Justice Dinner with Tricia and David now was the perfect bookend to the trip.

After much chatting, Steve and I said goodbye and left to check out of our hotel.

"I think I'm going to check out the Capitol Building while you're doing your interview," Steve said after we loaded up the car. I knew he would be happy doing that. He had a mental checklist of state capitol buildings, and now Iowa would be checked off.

"I'll meet you back here when I'm done." I said.

With renewed energy, I made my way to meet Amy at the Hyatt for her interview. I was on the downhill stretch now, as far as my compilation episode was concerned. Amy and her son were eating lunch in the lobby of the hotel when I entered. The plan was to do the interview there, but after they finished eating, Amy reassessed the situation.

"I'm not sure my little guy is going to be able to sit through the interview here," she said. "Is it OK if we do it in my hotel room? That way he can play his games."

"Of course." I replied. I was sure it would be quieter too.

We took the elevator up to their floor and I tried to make friends with her son using my Auntie Sue Ann charm, but like the rest of us, he was tired from the weekend and wanted to be by himself. I respected that. I would try not to take too much of his mom's time.

I'm not sure why, but I only had one microphone with me this time, which Amy and I passed back and forth. This made the interview feel more intimate, like a conversation between two friends.

I was fascinated when Amy shared the origin of the High Hopes dance. It all fit together. If a former dance instructor becomes an avid Pete supporter and sees a dance that everyone wants to learn, that person cannot sit idly by! I loved the sense of community that was developed and perpetuated through the High Hopes dance, and it wouldn't have happened without Amy.

When I asked about her Twitter handle, *Space Nerd for Pete*, her answer took an unexpected turn as she wove it into her story of why she was supporting Pete. I was spellbound as I listened to her talk about NASA, technological development, and the fact that Pete understood the importance of technology in moving the country forward.

I pushed the red stop recording button.

"That was perfect," I said.

With the addition of Amy's interview to the compilation, I knew I had a fantastic episode. Captain Karen at the Minnesota Meet-up, cheering for Pete in the Wells Fargo Arena, Abby and Donna of Barnstormers for Pete, and now the *High Hopes* dance. It was a wrap. Time to head home.

Just south of the Minnesota border on our trip home, I noticed a Facebook post from Katie of our Minnesota group.

"They need volunteers for the Charles City rally tomorrow," she wrote. "Can anyone help?"

Pete had left Des Moines on the Buttibus that morning for a tour of northern Iowa. Charles City would be the third of a four-rally day on Sunday.

Could I help? I wondered.

I checked Google maps. Minneapolis to Charles City, Iowa was a two-and-a-half-hour drive. Given that I was still on my drive home from Des Moines at that very moment, the idea of driving again the next day was far from attractive. I was looking forward to a day of rest. But how could I *not* help?

"I'll help in Charles City," I texted Katie.

"OK. Just you, or you and Steve?" she replied.

"Just me."

I knew Steve would need his Sunday at home. Others from our Minnesota group had agreed to help but were already in a carpool. I didn't want to make the drive on my own, so I set about to find a trip buddy. I didn't even consider asking my usual trip buddy, Tricia, assuming she'd already had enough driving through Iowa for a while. It would be a great opportunity for friends who hadn't officially joined Team Pete yet to see him in person, so I tried Mary and April. It turned out that less than twenty-four hours was too short notice. They both already had plans that couldn't be changed. It looked like I was going to be making the drive on my own. *I'd better get a good night's sleep.*

In all of my phone gymnastics, repeatedly taking it out and putting it away, I'd somehow pocket dialed Tricia.

"Hey, were you trying to call me?" she texted.

"Pocket dial! Sorry. Hey, I'm driving down to Charles City tomorrow to help with the rally ... "
"Do you want me to go and ride with you?"
I swear to God I did not do that intentionally.

The event was at the Elks Lodge in Charles City, a small venue in a small town. When Tricia and I arrived, the advance team met us and said they were waiting for the other volunteers to arrive, but that we could help move tables. It had been a while since I'd been in an Elks lodge or something akin to it. This was just what I was expecting—a cozy, intimate venue. We joined the advance team in the bar/restaurant to help take down tables for the overflow crowd. The larger adjacent space was set up for Pete's speech with rows of chairs. In the parking lot, workers were finishing the assembly of the gigantic American Flag backdrop for the stage area.

When the backdrop was ready to be brought inside, there was a problem. It wouldn't fit in the door. They tried the side door first, then the front door. No luck. They finally took the door off its hinges. It was a nail-biter watching them rotate the structure ever so slightly this way and that so it would fit through the doorway. It was touch-and-go for a minute, and I was beginning to wonder if Pete would have to speak in front of a plain blue curtain. Finally, they found the magic bullet and carefully eased the gigantic flag structure across the threshold.

Setup was now officially behind schedule, and I could tell the advance team was watching the time carefully as they made calls to the Buttibus entourage to confirm start time. What a contrast to the Wells Fargo Arena from two days before where no doors had to be taken off hinges. I would be experiencing the two extremes in venue size in one weekend.

Melani and Therese and a few others from our Minnesota group soon arrived to help with the event. We all had jobs for before and during the event. Some posted signs along the road outside, but still feeling the chill of the Des Moines rain, I opted for indoor sign posting. An hour before show time, a line of Iowans—and a few Minnesotans—began to form outside. A team of volunteers talked to people in line to see if they were signed up to caucus. As we opened the door to let the line in, I moved to my post in the main room.

When I entered the room, I was met with an assortment of words displayed on the far wall. As I got closer, a smile spread across my face. This was perfect. The words "Charity," "Justice," "Brotherly Love," and "Fidelity" were artistically arranged on the wall in a permanent installation. They must have been part of the Elks' pledge, but weren't they also similar to Pete's Rules of the Road? *I think they are going to like Pete.*

The room slowly filled with audience members taking chairs, and the media settled in the press area behind me. I recognized Pablo, a videographer from the Pete campaign, and waved. Ever since meeting him at the Iowa State Fair, we'd wave to each other at events. I loved knowing people inside the campaign because it made me feel like I was part of the team.

As the crowd poured in, I managed to accomplish my main task of keeping an aisle between the front and back sections of chairs clear. It was standing room only with people filling up the space on either side of the room. I assumed my bouncer position in the middle of the crowd, right by *Brotherly Love* and *Fidelity*. My eyes were trained on the parking lot door for any sign of activity, and soon I saw Lis Smith enter and walk back to the press area. This meant Pete had arrived.

Pete took the stage to a much more modest applause than what he got at the Wells Fargo Arena just two days before. Mind you, this wasn't because they didn't like Pete. No, but instead of a super-sized crowd of already-sold supporters, this small audience consisted of Iowa caucusgoers who were seriously considering all candidates. Pete knew he had to earn their caucus vote, something he often referred to in his speeches. At first, I was taken aback by the mitigated enthusiasm since all of my other Pete viewing experiences were rallies with super supporters present. But then I realized this was the real campaign—convincing undecided voters that Pete was the one to vote for.

Most people who had only seen Pete Buttigieg in debates and interviews thought of him as an extremely bright and gifted candidate, and this was true. But to sum Pete up only in terms of intellect was selling him short. To me what made Pete Buttigieg a remarkable candidate was his intuition about human nature. He understood people, people on both sides of an issue. Pete was inclusive rather than exclusive and often talked about meeting people on their journeys to progressive policies. His time as mayor had shown him the need to work together to find consensus.

Given the intimate setting, this stump speech was suitably more mellow than the many I'd heard before and allowed ample time for Pete to take questions directly from the audience. The focus seemed to be even more on community—how to help the local economy. I learned that, unlike the major metropolitan area where I lived, this community had trouble attracting workers. They had jobs and opportunity for growth, but lacked the workforce. They *welcomed* immigrants.

One question from the audience was especially poignant.

"Thanksgiving is coming up. We're so divided. How do we talk to our family members who support Trump?"

Pete gave a full answer, but it was the end of it that stuck with me.

"Just talk to them," he said. "You don't have to talk about politics—talk about anything. But keep talking."

I fought back tears as I listened to this answer from the heart. What kind of presidential candidate talks like this? He was right.

After the speech, the volunteers surreptitiously gathered in the hallway by the kitchen to wait for our turn to meet with Pete. We would each get a chance to shake his hand and pose for a selfie. I wondered if he would recognize me. He wouldn't remember me from the Iowa State Fair, which had been an encounter of less than a minute, but maybe he'd remember me from the South Bend event where he'd signed my book.

When it was time, the ten of us filed into the kitchen and formed a line around the center island, all ready to go. The timing was tight because Pete had to get to his next event, the fourth and final of the day. Still assuming secrecy, we were so quiet you could have heard a pin drop. Then all of a sudden, Pete appeared from behind the curtain and slid into the kitchen like Tom Cruise in *Risky Business*. "Let's do this!" he said.

In orderly fashion, we each waited our turn, watching those ahead of us. One by one, phones were handed to Saralena for her to take photos. Melani had brought her copy of *Shortest Way Home* for Pete to sign and her Mayor Pete *Build-a-Bear* for the photo op. That might have been a first for Pete. Tricia was in front of me, and she told him all about hitting the deer and getting a hug from his mom—Tricia got a hug from Pete too. If you have to hit a deer on the way to see Pete Buttigieg speak, you truly deserve a hug from him, no matter how belated.

As I was waiting in line, I thought of what I was going to say to Pete. Knowing that I only had a couple of minutes at the most to talk to him, I didn't want to waste time hemming and hawing. Maybe if I jogged his memory about meeting me at the South Bend Field Office opening, he'd remember me. Why was that important? To be remembered? Well, it's that personality thing again. I wake up in the morning to interact with people, to form meaningful relationships. I can't help it. In fact, it's hard to me *not* to do it. So this relationship I was forming with Pete, one or two minutes at a time, was at best, asymmetrical. Of course I realized he was an incredibly popular presidential candidate who was meeting hundreds of people a day, but that didn't stop me from wanting him to know who I was.

When it was my turn, I worried that there wouldn't be enough time to say what I wanted to say, so I rushed through it, so much so that I don't think he was able to take it all in.

"Hi Pete," I said, shaking his hand. "I'm the woman who said she could she your soul in your book. Well, I could see your soul in your speech here today too."

Pete tried to take in all of my babble, but let's face it, one to two minutes is not enough time for an in-depth discussion on the soul.

"Thank you," he said graciously, not seeming to remember me. But to his credit, how could he possibly remember everyone?

Pete and I then posed for our photo session with Saralena.

"I was in Des Moines for the Liberty and Justice dinner." I said afterwards, trying to eke out another sentence before I had to move on.

"Oh! Wasn't that fun?" he replied.

Our conversation ended there as Saralena gave me back my phone and took the next person in line. *Eventually, I'm going to finish my conversation with Pete*, I thought.

I walked back out into the hallway and was met by a staffer holding a couple of small Dairy Queen Blizzards.

"Anyone want a Blizzard?" she asked. "We have extras."

"I do!" I exclaimed, never saying no to free ice cream.

They had bought ice cream for the Buttibus, but not everyone wanted one. I got one of the *Buttibus Blizzards*. I really was part of the team now.

13

The *Good Guy Pete* Live Recording

The Barnstormers episode of *Twitter Travels for Pete* came out the Wednesday after our big weekend in Des Moines. The quick turnaround was thanks to the speedy work of my producer Michael, who had to edit the many sound files I sent him. The compilation of interviews was a proud accomplishment for me and energized me to do more and more. Since the campaign was focused on the lead up to the Iowa caucus in early February, that time frame would be mine as well. I would try to do an episode a week if possible until then. That meant traveling every weekend.

My destination the very next weekend was decided for me because there was yet another event in South Bend. How could I *not* go to South Bend? Michael, Ryan, and Lety's podcast, *Good Guy Pete*, was hosting a live audience recording event that Saturday at the field office. They would be recording two episodes: one with AJ and her sister Breana, the South Bend Organizer, and the other one with Mike Schmuhl, Pete's Campaign Manager. In addition to the locals, many people within driving distance were planning to attend, and a few were coming from farther afield, like me. I was going to make it a full weekend of fun.

Although this would have been the perfect opportunity for me to record my own interviews, I didn't want to detract from the *Good Guy Pete* recording. This meant I couldn't interview Lety or AJ, who were participating in that. But I could interview Joy for the South Bend perspective on what it was like having her own mayor running for president. We would be doing that on Sunday.

Compared to the Barnstormers episode, this next one would be simpler. Just one interview with Joy. I thought about how I could add some additional flair to the episode, so I planned on recording sound on the plane. When my flight landed in South Bend Thursday evening, I had my Zoom H6 poised to record the flight attendant's announcement.

"It's our pleasure to welcome you to South Bend with another early arrival. The local time is 9:32 PM."

For the third time in four months, I was in South Bend, Indiana again. *Let the party begin.*

"And an order of beignets, please," I said to the perky woman behind the counter at the Chicory Cafe the next morning. The New Orleans themed cafe in South Bend was just begging me to partake in the famous fried doughnut-like treats I'd had at Café du Monde in the French Quarter years earlier.

I grabbed the table marker and walked back to join Lety, Joy, and Nicole at their table. But in the time that had passed since I first greeted them, their own order of beignets had been delivered. Once mine graced the table, it was an embarrassment of puffy, sugar-dusted riches. Beignets to spare.

"How was the train ride, Nicole?" I asked as I took a sip of my latte.

"It was fun, but I probably should have slept more," she said with a laugh.

The very Nicole I'd met at the Lis Smith event in Washington had taken the train to South Bend from the Washington area rather than fly—just for the fun of it. Some of her Twitter friends would be joining her for the big *Good Guy Pete* weekend and Lety and Joy were playing hostess. I had graciously been invited to join them.

None of us had really had enough sleep, so punchy giggles invaded our conversation as we munched on beignets. As was usual, it wasn't long before someone from the campaign wandered in for their supplemental dose of caffeine.

"José!" Lety called out.

"Hey!" the man answered, approaching our table.

José, whom I recognized from campaign photos, was there with another staffer, George. Introductions were made all around, and I was again struck by how staffers were so friendly to lowly volunteers like me. After all, José was the National Constituency Director and George the Deputy National Political Director, both positions with gravitas. But I should have known by now. The Pete for America campaign was different. It really felt like we all worked as a team.

"It's so fun to meet you both!" I exclaimed. "You know I have to get a photo."

At that point, I stood up and took a quick selfie with them. I had learned that you can't hesitate when a moment like this presents itself.

"Care for a beignet?" Lety asked.

"Ooo . . . they look good," José replied, eyeing the pile of delectable treats.

"Take the whole plate," she urged.

"Are you sure?" he said.

"We have more than enough," Joy said, gesturing to the other plate of powdered sugar goodness on the table.

And with that, José and George went back to the campaign office laden with beignets.

The weekend was already off to a festive start with this chance meeting. I knew that arriving a day early was the right thing to do. There would be loads of fun right up until the recording session tomorrow night, and a lot of it involved food. After stopping by the field office on Sycamore, we ended up at PEGGS, where more people joined us for a bit of brunch. It was my third time ordering *Fred's Home Plate*.

At dinnertime we met up at the office to go to Barnaby's. I'd been dying for a slice of Barnaby's pizza ever since I saw the *Pizza with Pete* video, where Pete himself delivered the pizza to the table of contest winners. The scent of pizza filled the air as soon as we entered the bustling restaurant, and I was already thinking about what I was going to order. But my hopes were dashed as the wait for a table of eight was close to an hour.

"Let's go to Hacienda," Lety suggested.

"Is that where they serve the famous salsa and ranch combo?" I asked.

"Yes, ma'am." replied Joy.

If I wasn't going to get Barnaby's pizza that night, at least I could get salsa and ranch.

My interest in this delicacy was because Pete had been asked about it during the lightening round of an interview, "Salsa/ranch—yes or no?"

"Yes," he said without equivocation.

Twitter went into a frenzy, complete with the hashtag #salsaranch. This was worse than pineapple on pizza. Most people could not fathom a combination like salsa and ranch and deemed it something only Midwesterners indulged in. South Bend locals immediately came to Pete's defense. It wasn't a Midwestern thing so much as a *Hacienda* thing. The particular versions of salsa and ranch dressing served at Hacienda restaurant were absolute heaven when mixed together and put on a tortilla chip. If you tried this at home, so to speak, it just wasn't the same.

"I'll have a margarita," I told the server. "And chips with salsa and ranch."

I'm sure I ordered enchiladas too, but my mind was stuck on the special chip dipping combo. Would it be as good as Pete said it was? The eight of us would be sharing a few orders of chips, and when they were served, I looked across to Amanda, the other South Bender who had joined us for dinner, for guidance.

"First you dip it in the salsa, and then the ranch," she said. "And no double dipping!"

I carefully did as she suggested and put the chip in my mouth. *Yummy.* Now I could defend Pete's honor back home in Minnesota. Hacienda salsa and ranch mixed together was delicious. I certainly didn't need to wash it down with my margarita, but the margarita made it all the more fun. And you may or may not be able to detect that in the selfie I took.

The next morning I headed over to Sycamore Street with my latte to meet the gang for a tour of South Bend. Lety and Joy would be our guides and drivers. I was in Lety's car and we left the field office with Joy following behind. Lety narrated as she drove throughout the city, making stops along the way—the General, for more coffee, and Brain Lair Books, a locally owned bookstore. Then it was back across town driving by the South Bend Chocolate Company factory to the West Side neighborhood. This was the part of the tour that would prove to be the most memorable for me.

Lety had been active in this vibrant Latino community and beamed with pride as she showed us around her favorite places. The neighborhood had participated in a revitalization project called *West Side Main Streets Initiative*, part of the Smart Streets project Mayor Pete had spearheaded. After our lunch at

Taqueria Chicago, we stopped in at the West Side South Bend headquarters down the street to learn more. Since the office was closed, Lety let us in and gave us a private peek at their small community center. The walls were full of neighborhood revitalization maps and plans, some complete, some for the future. Walking along Western Avenue to the building, I had no idea the streetscape hadn't always looked this way. Before, there were no decorative streetlights and planters outside of businesses inviting you in like there were now. That was the key shift Mayor Pete had accomplished in his Smart Streets project—away from a car-centered city to one more inviting to pedestrian and bicycle traffic, something inherently beneficial for neighborhoods.

As I studied one of the plans on the wall, I came to the realization that this was the epitome of "all politics is local." These were real people working to improve their neighborhood with the help of funding facilitated by the city. Wasn't that essentially government's role? To help people help themselves? It's something Pete talked about on the trail to a lesser or greater degree. He knew it worked.

Just across Western Avenue was Lety's favorite ice cream shop—La Rosita. Of course we couldn't leave the West Side without getting ice cream, no matter how full we were from lunch. Then we piled back into the two cars to finish off our tour of South Bend. We wound our way back towards downtown, passing by the Studebaker Building and the Four Winds Field baseball stadium, places Joy had shown me in July. Lety drove by

Leeper Park where the recently restored Studebaker fountain sat in all its glory. I remembered seeing the photo of the lighting ceremony that Laura O'Sullivan had posted on Twitter and knew that it looked even more spectacular at night. Then Lety gave us a ride around one of the famous roundabouts from Pete's Smart Streets plan before ending the tour.

Getting out of the car back at the field office, I thanked Lety.

"Thank you so much for the tour, Lety," I said. "I especially loved seeing the West Side."

"I love showing people my favorite places," she replied.

As I walked back to my hotel, I thought about all I'd seen on Lety's tour. Much of it was evidence of Mayor Pete's leadership in revitalizing the city of South Bend. He would be the first to credit others for the accomplishments, but it was his vision and leadership that got it done. I knew he could do the same magic for our country as President Pete.

After a rest in my hotel room, I was ready for the main event—the live recording of the *Good Guy Pete* podcast. As one of their biggest fans, I had listened to all the episodes as soon as they were released. Tonight I would get to see Michael, Lety, and Ryan in action, which meant even more now that I had my own podcast.

Just like a month earlier, I made my way across the Colfax Avenue Bridge for an event at the South Bend Pete for America field office. This time there was a taco truck parked outside with a few hungry customers in line to order. Lety had told me there would be tacos, and I was counting on that for my dinner. But first I decided to go in and check out the seating for the show since people were filing in. *Maybe I should save a seat.*

Inside was a sign-in table staffed by volunteers. It was there where I met someone I'd been wanting to meet ever since I listened to her *Good Guy Pete* interview. In that episode, Marisel, a Notre Dame professor in Latina/Latino Literature, talked about immigration and her experience with community-based learning. One of her course requirements was for the students to volunteer at Casa de Amistad, the local Latino community center on the West Side.

I knew Marisel on Twitter as *Puerto Rico for Pete* and recognized her immediately.

"I loved your interview," I said as I introduced myself.

"Thank you," Marisel graciously replied.

"I teach ESL to adults, so it really resonated with me," I said. "The anti-immigrant sentiment in this country right now is shocking."

"It really is."

We could have talked for an hour, but with so many people coming in, I quickly made my nametag and went to stake out my seat. Rows of chairs had been set up facing a stage area with three high-top tables with chairs and Michael's sound equipment which was much larger than my portable recorder. Some audience members were seated already, but I still needed to eat, so I put my coat on a chair and went outside for a quick taco.

A few other people were standing by the truck waiting for their food, and after I placed my order, I started chatting with them. That's when I first felt a bit of fame as I was recognized for my podcast.

"I love your podcast," Jenny said. "You have a beautiful voice!"

I felt like a true podcaster now. The Barnstormers episode had only been out a few days, but apparently many had listened to it already, Jenny from Indianapolis for one. I appreciated her comment more than she probably knew, especially since I hadn't realized that people would find my voice particularly alluring. Michael had said I sounded good, but didn't he say that to all his clients? I credited my singing background, my soprano lilt, to giving me that quintessential *radio voice* I didn't know I had.

The clock was ticking and show time was almost upon us, so I gobbled down my taco and went back inside. Now stationed at the welcome table was Laura O'Sullivan. Finally, I would get to talk to her. That first time at PEGGS in October was so fleeting there was no time for a conversation.

"Hi Sue Ann," Laura said, recognizing me.

"Hello Laura!" I replied. "This is so fun! I'm excited to hear the interviews."

"I am too. We've got a really good crowd tonight."

"You don't have much longer in the mayor's office," I said, referring to the end of Mayor Pete's term at the end of December. "Any idea of what you'll be doing next?"

"I hope to be working for the campaign," she answered. "We're still working it out." *Whoa.* I felt like I'd just received insider information.

"That's great!" I exclaimed, genuinely excited at the prospect and eager to find out what that would be.

At that point, the lights would have started dimming—if they had the capacity to do so—with an accompanying announcement of *Please take your seats. The performance will be starting in five minutes.* But instead, I think it was Lety who told us they were almost ready to start. Time to get in my seat.

Before hitting the Record button, Michael warmed us up, so we'd be a good live audience. I don't know if he needed to do that since Team Pete tended to be naturally enthusiastic, but at least we knew we had permission to laugh and applaud.

The first episode was an interview with AJ and her sister Breana, the South Bend Organizer. Since they came from a family strongly rooted in South Bend, the conversation focused on the changes in South Bend from the boom time when their grandfather worked at the Studebaker factory to the decline of the city after it closed to the renewal under Mayor Pete's leadership. They talked about the changes in African American neighborhoods in South Bend through the years and recent efforts to clean up vacant properties in the mayor's *1000 Days, 1000 Houses* project. AJ talked about what it was like to come back to South Bend, making that intentional decision, and people thinking she was crazy.

It was all so fascinating to me. Two sisters talking about their own family's experience in South Bend over time. It was the perfect way for an outsider to understand the city's history because it was personal. It was even more personal for me because I knew both sisters, especially AJ.

A short intermission followed where we could stretch our legs while Michael and company set up for the next recording. I spent most of the time chatting with those seated around me. "Are you on Twitter?" I asked nearly everyone. "What's your handle?" How sad it would have been if I had squandered this opportunity to match a live person with their Twitter account, especially if we were following each other.

The audience was raucous in welcoming Mike Schmuhl, Pete's Campaign Manager. I like to think it was because by then we were really warmed up, but it was probably because we wanted to show our gratitude to him. After all, Mike wasn't on Twitter, so this was our chance to express that pent-up appreciation. There might have been some nervous energy as well, what with a proverbial celebrity in our midst. The combination of factors resulted in a noisy interview. At times, I knew I was laughing so hard I would be able to hear myself on the recording. I was right.

Afterwards, I knew I wanted to introduce myself to Mike, so I hung around, ready to jump on any opportunity. I prepared myself for a long line of people wanting to talk to him, but really there weren't that many, which surprised me. This was probably due to people's shyness rather than disinterest. But I knew this might be the only chance I would have to meet him, so I plunged forward as he was starting to leave and extended my hand.

"Hello, Mike," I said. "What a great interview!"

"Thank you!" he replied. "Thank you for coming." Mike Schmuhl shared the same traits of humility and kindness that Pete had, and I was reminded of how they had been good friends ever since high school.

"I have a podcast," I blurted out, wanting to make sure I conveyed that information to the top of the campaign. "I'm traveling around the country interviewing grassroots organizers. It's called *Twitter Travels for Pete.*"

"Oh?" he said, looking at my nametag and then my face, with a knowing smile.

I could have been imagining it, but it seemed as though he already knew about the podcast and was just matching the person to the podcast. I'll never know for sure because he was pulled away at that moment. As I made my way back to my seat to get my coat, I kept wondering, *did he just recognize me? Does he know? Does Pete know about my podcast?* Just imagining that possibility thrilled me beyond words.

A few people were still milling about, spreading the word about the after-party at the new Garage Arcade Bar, a few walkable blocks away. The partygoers filed out of the building and started our walk down Colfax

Avenue. To the casual onlooker, we must have looked like we were walking *from* a bar not *to* a bar, boisterous as we were. The Mike Schmuhl effect hadn't worn off yet, apparently.

When we got to our destination, it was obvious the Garage Arcade Bar was enjoying incredible success as the new Saturday night option in South Bend. The overflow crowd outside informed us they were full. If there had just been a few of us, we could have waited, but our group of fifteen was never going to get in. Time to regroup.

"Corby's?" Michael asked some of the South Benders.

They conferred, and soon, we were walking to Corby's, one long block away.

What I didn't know at the time was that Corby's was *the* PFA staff after-hours hangout place. I was about to walk into a bar filled with Pete for America staffers letting their hair down. Serendipity.

The place was packed with a combination of college students and young PFA staffers, which made me feel a little old even though I tried to act cool. Ordering a drink at the bar required bold tenacity, but eventually I got my gin and tonic, and that's where I recognized one of the staffers I was dying to meet. Samantha Steelman, Marathon States Organizing Director—Kyrstin's boss.

"You're Samantha, right?" I said tentatively, in case I was wrong.

"Yes."

"I'm Sue Ann from Minnesota, one of Kyrstin's organizers."

"Yes, I know about your podcast!" she replied. *Kyrstin must have told her.*

I then told her about my plans for future podcasts, which she loved from a relational organizing standpoint. Just then *High Hopes* started playing on the sound system, which immediately drew us onto the dance floor.

The *Good Guy Pete* podcast crowd joined the PFA staffers to celebrate Pete's walk-on song in unison while the college students quizzically looked on. Dancing next to some young staffers, I thought about what long hours they worked, that in a presidential primary campaign, the idea of working Monday through Friday 9 to 5 went out the window. So when they *did* have time for Corby's, they were going to have fun. They were definitely having fun. But it was short-lived because for whatever reason, they gradually left. Perhaps they were going to another bar. Or going back to work.

Some of the *Good Guy Pete* people were leaving too. Marisel and I had gravitated towards each other in middle-aged solidarity as it was clear we didn't belong in this college bar.

"There are so many students here," she said. "I think I see one of my husband's students over there."

"I feel old," I said in reply.

It would have been the perfect opportunity for a conversation about language and immigration except for the fact that we couldn't really hear each other with the loud music. Another reason I felt old.

"I think I'm going to go home, now," she said.

"Good plan. I'll probably do the same," I replied. After a slice of pizza next door, I called an Uber and went back to my hotel, exhausted from a long but magical day.

On Sunday morning, it was finally my turn to play podcast host. My interview with Joy would be the opposite of what I experienced the night before at the *Good Guy Pete* live recording. Instead of a rowdy interview with a live audience, this interview would be an intimate conversation with Joy about her Mayor Pete.

Having already checked out of my room, I'd have to do the interview in the Marriott lobby, so I went in search of a quiet spot. I found some comfy chairs in the outer reaches of the lobby and started setting up for the recording. The seemingly quiet spot—next to a meeting room that surely wouldn't be used on a Sunday—soon proved to be otherwise as some people came and started . . . *a meeting*.

Oh no. Where can I record? The hotel had the usual bustle of activity of people coming and going. There was no way I was going to find a quiet place closer to the front desk. Unless. Yes! The circle booths. The circular booths used for dining had their own built in privacy and probably the best sound possible. I secured the booth closest to the door and caught Joy as she came in the door.

"Joy!" I called out. "I've got us set up over here."

"I'm nervous," she said, as she walked up to the table. "I can't believe I'm doing this."

Like many of my guests, Joy was timid at first, never having been interviewed for a podcast before. But sitting in our intimate circular booth helped make it feel like a conversation between friends, and she soon relaxed. The mood lightened even more when the cleaning staff started vacuuming right next to our table, and I had to pause the recording. We both suppressed a giggle as we waited patiently for the vacuuming to be finished. *Now, where were we?*

The interview unfolded naturally as Joy handled my questions deftly. I loved hearing about what it was like having Pete Buttigieg as her mayor and then what it was like to have her mayor run for president. Joy's reflection was heartfelt and even elicited a few tears. I felt blessed to have been part of this very personal conversation.

"That was fantastic, Joy!" I said as I stopped the recording.

"Really?" she replied, still a bit unsure.

"I'll play it back for you, and you can see how it sounds."

We both put our earphones back in and listened to the first part of the interview together. The sound quality of the H6 Zoom recorder was amazing, something my guests usually didn't expect. It made everyone sound good.

"It will probably come out the middle of next week," I said. "I'll let you know when."

"OK. I'm excited and nervous at the same time."

"It really is a good episode, Joy," I said, wrapping the cord around my microphone. "Thank you so much for letting me interview you!"

"It was fun seeing you again!" she said as she hugged me goodbye.

I packed the portable recorder and the two microphones in my tote bag, knowing that they would soon be taken out to go through security at South Bend Airport. Security at a small airport was a breeze compared to a larger airport like Minneapolis-St. Paul. Or Washington, D.C., my next destination. Practice makes perfect, I thought.

14

Interviews

Washington, D.C.

M y plan to reconnect with my Washington, D. C. friends for an interview came to fruition as schedules miraculously meshed. Patti and Kyle, *Virginia for Pete,* would be there to represent Northern Virginia, and Raezel and Christopher, *Gingers for Pete,* would represent Maryland. I was finally going to meet my originally intended Lis Smith date, Christopher. Since it was my birthday weekend, Steve would be joining me on the trip. I decided that warranted a stay at the swank and historic Mayflower Hotel on Connecticut Avenue.

When the Uber dropped us off in front of the Mayflower Hotel on Friday afternoon, we were met by doormen clad in the traditional jackets of bygone years. Once I set foot on the glorious marble floor, the splendor of crystal chandeliers led my eyes up to the ornate ceiling and the gilded second level balcony. *Yes, this is exactly what I had in mind.*

The hotel was bustling with activity—men and women dressed in blue suits milling about wearing convention badges. We had just stumbled on the Federalist Society National Lawyers annual convention. This made us feel a little awkward, especially as we got in the elevator with some of the blue-suited convention goers. Steve looked at me and glanced down at his jacket. *I wonder if they're noticing my PETE 2020 button?* I thought for sure Steve would have taken the button off after that, but no. He purposely kept it on. That was one of the things I loved about Steve.

In the morning, we headed to the executive dining room for breakfast where we encountered mostly Federalists taking in sustenance before their morning session. After visiting the sumptuous buffet, Steve and I sat down with our plates and discussed our plans.

"You can have the whole day to yourself, Steve." I said.

"Really?" Steve replied. "Are you sure?"

"Yes. You love D.C., and you can handle walking more than I can, so go have fun."

"OK. I can meet up with you for dinner after the interview."

"Raezel wants to go to the Mandalay restaurant," I said, texting him the link. "I'll let you know what time."

Back in our hotel room, Steve grabbed his backpack and left on his walking tour. It would be a few hours before I needed to head to the Silver Spring Public Library for the interview. Since I didn't have the energy for a walking tour of my own, I did the next best thing—

found a coffee shop. What bliss to kill time drinking coffee! Eventually it was time to start my journey to Silver Spring. I left the hotel loaded down with a tote bag full of recording equipment and started walking to the Metro station at the end of the block thinking *I'm so glad I understand the D.C. Metro system!*

"Maintenance Disruption on the Red Line," read the sign at the entrance to the Farragut North station. No one else seemed to be phased by this since there was a bus that would take you to the next stop on the line. But for some reason, I was confused. What bus? Which direction? I saw a bus across the street with a Metro worker directing people on, so I got on. I soon realized that this wasn't a shuttle, but a city bus with many stops. After twenty minutes, I was sure I was on the wrong bus or had missed the critical "this is where you can connect with the Red Line" moment.

I had factored in extra time, but not enough to ride around on a bus all day. I needed to get off that bus. For all I knew, it was going in the wrong direction. Later I would learn that it was definitely the wrong bus. I pulled the cord, exited the bus, and called an Uber.

Throughout the interminable Uber ride to Silver Spring, I had no idea where I was, but of course I acted like I did. *Always act like you know what you're doing when you're traveling,* was my motto. Sometimes this requires great acting skills. At least I knew my destination, which wasn't the library, but the Starbucks nearby where I would be meeting Christopher. I was confident my Uber driver would get me there somehow. Twenty-five minutes later, my driver dropped me off at the edge of Fountain Plaza in downtown Silver Spring.

I arrived at the Starbucks before Christopher and nabbed the last two chairs at the end of the communal table, with a clear line of sight to the door. Ever since Christopher had missed out on the Lis Smith event as my guest, I felt an unmet agenda item in my mind. I was supposed to have met Christopher that day. Now I needed to set that right.

There was a constant stream of customers going in and out the door, but it was easy to spot *Gingers for Pete* when he walked in. He was the epitome of a ginger with that full red beard.

"Christopher!" I exclaimed after I caught his attention.

"Hello, Sue Ann," he replied as he joined me at the table. "It's nice to finally meet you!"

"It's been a long time coming," I said. "Should we get in line?"

"I'm impressed you made the trip all the way out here," he said as we waited to order our drinks.

"This is fun for me," I replied.

Hot drinks in hand, Christopher and I went back to the crowded communal table and settled in to get acquainted. Unlike me, he had had many years of experience working on political campaigns, and that made his support of Pete even more meaningful, in my view. I liked Pete because he used his amazing intellect to advocate for others, but I wasn't experienced enough to know how rare a breed he was. In all of Christopher's 30 years in politics, he knew that Pete was special.

During our conversation, I had been keeping an eye on the time. I didn't want to be late for the big interview.

"I think we should head to the library now," I announced at a natural break in the conversation.

"I'm glad Raezel reserved a space at the library," Christopher replied as we gathered our things to leave. "It should be a good place to record."

We stepped outside into the street and tried to get our bearings.

"Do you know how to get to the library from here?" I asked.

"I think so," Christopher replied, alternately checking the street signs and his phone.

The library was only two or three blocks away, but Christopher and I managed to get turned around in our directions and took the least efficient path. My luck with directions that day must have rubbed off on him too. We arrived at the door to the library just as the others did. There was Raezel, our fearless leader, along with Patti and Kyle.

"Hey!" I said as we approached. "I'm so glad you all could come."

"It's a miracle that we were able to find a day all five of us could get together," said Patti with a laugh.

Patti and Christopher were closer to my age, give or take, and Kyle and Raezel were in their late twenties. Together, we were a fun mix. We all headed up the stairs to the main entrance of the library where Raezel checked in with the librarian for our room. Raezel knew the place well and led us to a beautiful room with a large conference table. *Perfect!* I thought. Plenty of room for the recorder and all the microphones. Just as we were taking off our coats and getting settled, two teenagers walked in the room.

"Can we help you?" asked Raezel.

"We have this room now," said one of them.

"Really? We scheduled it." replied Raezel.

"We did too. We're working on project for school."

Raezel went to check on this and found that the library had double scheduled in error. Now, were we going to make the high schoolers leave? Were we going to compromise their academic success? No. Pete would never do that. We would be the ones to move.

We gathered up our coats and bags and traipsed through the library to a small room near the entrance. This will be OK, I thought. Except there was a distinct lack of furniture—just one small table, coffee table height rather than desk height, and four chairs. Raezel went in search of another chair while the rest of us quickly moved the small table and chairs to the center of the room. We had lost valuable time in the room change. Now we were backed up against library closing time, something I was painfully aware of as podcast host. This was the only opportunity to do this interview.

The table was just big enough for the recorder and the four microphone cords. Sitting around the small table, I felt like we were gownups visiting a kindergarten classroom. Thank God we didn't have to sit in tiny chairs too.

Raezel and Christopher were from the Maryland Pete group while Patti and Kyle represented Virginia. I structured the interview with segments between the two state groups, with some room for give and take. I was blown away by all of the things they had done and were doing in their respective groups to support Pete. They were very well organized from early on. Christopher, with his vast experience, was a key organizer in Maryland and Kyle wasn't *Virginia for Pete* in Twitter name only. I found his leadership remarkable. Both Raezel and Patti were heavily involved every step of the way. I loved hearing all their stories, especially what they liked about Pete, things not previously mentioned in my other interviews. Patti, a veteran, spoke about the importance of Pete's military service. Raezel, with a political science degree, talked about how Pete fit her description of the ideal candidate.

I was feeling confident that we'd finish the interview in time, but I knew Raezel had her eye on the giant clock on the wall as she answered her last question. Just then, an announcement over the loudspeaker system startled us.

"The library will be closing in fifteen minutes."

I knew we'd have to edit that out. Raezel started her sentence again and tried to wrap it up.

"The library will be closing in ten minutes." Wow. We really needed to finish.

Then a security guard popped his head in the door, "The library is closing in five minutes."

"Thank you," I said. Each interruption would have to be edited out, but I knew Michael could handle that. I thanked all four of them for participating, and we closed out the episode together with a rousing "Go Pete!" cheer.

"The library is now closed."

Whew! We made it.

The security guard had now returned and was waiting for us to vacate the room. I hastily packed up my recording equipment while the others moved the furniture back. We grabbed our coats and dashed down the stairs. In my experience, libraries are very strict about closing *on time*. The five of us stood talking for a while inside the door on the street level, but it wasn't long before we were chased out of the building entirely.

Raezel, Patti, and I would be continuing on to dinner at Mandalay, but unfortunately neither Christopher nor Kyle could join us. So, it was hugs goodbye on Wayne Avenue and then we went our separate ways.

It was only a few blocks walk to the Mandalay Restaurant, and since Steve was on schedule for meeting us, we arrived at just about the same time. I loved introducing Steve to Raezel and Patti because it was a way of connecting my two worlds—Twitter and real life.

"You took the Metro from the hotel, didn't you?" I asked. "Did you have problems?"

"No, it was easy."

Later on we would have a complicated discussion about shuttle buses, but suffice it to say, I had gotten on the southbound shuttle when I needed to have crossed the street to get the northbound shuttle.

"How did the recording go?" Steve asked.

"It went really well," I answered. "It's a fantastic interview."

"It was so much fun!" added Patti.

The restaurant was as busy as you would expect for a Saturday night. Raezel checked in with the host on our reservation, and we were shown to our table.

"How was your day?" Patti asked Steve, as we settled in at our table.

"It was great. I walked around a lot and then went to the Holocaust Museum," he replied.

"What did you think of it?" asked Raezel.

"It was impressive," he replied. "I'd like to go back again someday. There were so many exhibits." Steve went on to elaborate on his day as we waited to order.

I had never been to a Burmese restaurant before, so Raezel recommended her favorite dishes and we all ordered something different. When the food came, we tasted each other's selections. The complexity of the spices used in the sauces made for a mouthwatering, memorable meal.

As we ate, I was happy to let Steve take charge of the conversation since I had already done my fair share of talking for the day. As a master conversationalist, Steve had no trouble getting to know Patti and Raezel. He often asked the kinds of questions I neglected to ask people, which meant I ended up learning more when he was in the mix. It was such an interesting discussion all around that I didn't want it to end, but it was inevitable.

After we'd paid the bill at the table, Patti gathered up her purse and coat. "I'm sorry to be a party pooper, but I've got to get home to my husband," she said. To be fair, it was getting late.

"We should go too. We still have to take the Metro back to the hotel," I said. "Raezel, can you show us where the station is?"

"Sure!"

We said goodbye to Patti and started walking towards the station. But at some point along the way, Raezel thought of a different plan.

"Why don't I just drive you to your hotel," she said.

"Really?" I asked. "That would be fantastic." I wasn't going to argue.

"Are you sure?" Steve asked out of politeness.

"It's no problem at all," she replied. "I'd love to do it."

Raezel had proven to be the complete host—from making arrangements with the library to reservations at Mandalay and now chauffeur service back to our hotel. I was grateful she had taken care of all of those details.

Our walking path now diverted to the parking garage where her car was parked, which wasn't too far. What a relief it was to sit in the front seat of Raezel's car with my tote bag at my feet, knowing that she would be taking us directly to our hotel. With the day's excitement over, I let Steve handle the talking, while I sat quietly relishing the fact that I had managed to record an interview with four people that day. This D.C. episode was going to be impressive, and it just made me want to do more.

✈

Miami Beach

When lining up episode ideas in my mind, I penciled in a trip to New Orleans to interview Myndee. But it turned out that Myndee was working in Miami Beach for a few weeks, so I'd have to meet her in Florida. I thought about it for a split second. *Why not?* In fact, how could I *not* go to sunny Miami Beach in late November, especially when there was snow on the ground in Minnesota? Indeed.

I'd already done the great Minnesota wardrobe switch in my closet, so packing was tricky. *Where are my summer clothes? Where are my sandals?* I had forgotten what I even wore in the summer. In the end, I was proud of my wardrobe plan for the trip. I chose something that transitioned well from winter to summer in just a few hours. I left Minneapolis wearing a sweater over a black linen sundress, leggings, and boots. Then at Miami airport, I took off everything except the sundress in the ladies room and put on the sandals that were in my tote bag. Score!

This really did feel like an escape, especially since I was just staying one night. My Uber driver was surprised when I told him I would be going back to

Minneapolis the next day. Most people who come to Miami Beach stay longer. For obvious reasons.

The Royal Palm Hotel wasn't on the beach, but it was only a few blocks away, and most importantly, I could see the beach from my upper floor hotel room. Once in my room, I opened the sliding glass door and stepped out onto the balcony to breathe the sea air. I needed to change out of my black travel outfit into something more Miami Beach. Myndee and I would be meeting for dinner and then would come back to my room to do the interview.

Myndee, *Mayor Pete Fangirl* on Twitter, had first caught my eye on Twitter when she posted about plans to meet Pete at a fundraiser in New Orleans. As a writer, she had a natural flair for getting to the essence of her experience in her posts, and for long form, she posted pieces on her blog. At one point, she asked for people to submit their *Why Pete?* stories, and I submitted mine. Anytime you interact with someone on Twitter beyond normal posting and direct messaging, your relationship broadens. Myndee and I were starting to bond as fellow writers.

As I followed Myndee during the summer, I saw that she was struggling with mental health issues, something she felt comfortable sharing with Team Pete. Things got so low for her that she contemplated ending her life. Instead, she drove herself to the emergency room. Myndee wrote about her experience and posted it on the online publishing platform, Medium. It was difficult for her to write, even harder to share, but she felt it was important for others who might feel the same way. Pete had released his mental health plan over the summer and had talked about "deaths of despair." Myndee's story of her close escape from a death of despair was important for people to hear, and fortunately, she was willing to talk about it.

As I waited for Myndee on the veranda of the Royal Palm Hotel, I felt the miracle of a summer evening in November. No coat, no sweater. *No socks.* I wasn't even a little chilly. This must be the temperature of heaven.

Soon a car pulled up and out jumped Myndee.

"Sorry for keeping you waiting, Sue Ann!" she said, dashing towards me. "It took forever to get an Uber."

"Well, it's Friday night!" I replied, good-naturedly.

"I was thinking we'd just walk down Ocean Drive and pick a restaurant," Myndee suggested.

Good plan. There was no shortage of choices there. We walked a few blocks, and then as soon as we turned onto Ocean Drive, I felt like we had walked into one giant party. So many people were out and about enjoying their vacation. Every restaurant and bar was bustling and festive.

"Cuban food!" I said when we came to the Havana 1957 restaurant. "Is it OK if we eat here?" I loved Cuban food, and to me, this was very Miami.

"Sure!" replied Myndee.

We took a table for two on the sidewalk and ordered cocktails. My mojito had the largest "sprig" of mint I'd ever seen, more like a *stalk* of mint. How fitting for my summer in November experience. Myndee and I made a toast, taking a selfie to mark our first meeting in real life. Over dinner we got to know each other better. I heard more about her husband and three children and her digital design profession. With the ice officially broken, a conversational podcast interview would come naturally.

Back at my hotel, I set up the recorder and two microphones on the table. Myndee and I sat across from each other, and we each grabbed a mic. We did a sound check and then I pushed Record. I've said before that the beauty of being a podcast host is that you never know exactly what content you will get, but it's always an amazing experience. This interview was no exception, but it was much more. During the interview, Myndee invited me into her private world. As our conversation was unfolding, I knew it was special. I knew that she was trusting me with her story, a story that had some unexpected turns. I took her trust with great honor and humility. It reminded me of when a student would unexpectedly tell me a very personal story. They needed to tell me. Myndee needed to tell me her story, and I would be its caretaker through my podcast.

The next morning, Myndee and I planned to meet at Starbucks for coffee before I had to get back to the airport. Starbucks with a beach view is the best kind of Starbucks, I always say. I was already seated at a table outside when Myndee arrived.

"Hey!" she said.

"Good morning!" I replied, tilting my face to the sun. "It's a gorgeous day."

Myndee sat down and said, "Would you mind if we do another recording?"

"What?" I wasn't expecting this. Last night's recording was perfect as far as I was concerned.

"I wasn't comfortable with how I told my story," she said.

"Really? I thought it was great!"

"I know, but I wasn't happy with the way I told part of the story, the order I said things."

I always wanted my podcast guests to feel comfortable with their interviews, so of course we were going to record it again. I had to wrap my mind around it first, though. I wanted to make sure I covered all the same content, asked the same questions, as the night before. I wasn't worried about Myndee's contribution. I was worried about mine. Last night's was a great interview.

"I think we have just enough time to do it again," I said. "Thank God for late check-out!"

We did the interview again. No two interviews can possibly be the same, and these weren't the same. One wasn't inherently better than the other, except for the fact that Myndee was happier with the second one. And that made it the better interview.

✈

Omaha

I arrived in Omaha the night before the big interview and had time to kill. Maybe my old Minnesota buddy Wes was available.

"Husker women's volleyball is playing in the tournament," Wes messaged. "I'm meeting some friends at a sports bar to watch it. You're welcome to join us."

"Thank you! That would be great." I responded, relieved that I wouldn't have to spend the evening alone.

I was going to a sports bar. To me, this was comical since I didn't follow sports. At all. What does one wear to a sports bar? I thought about it for a minute and then decided not to change. Instead, I went down to the hotel lobby early to wait for Wes to pick me up. Not sure of what car he would be driving, I examined each vehicle that approached. Eventually, a car stopped, and the passenger window lowered. There was Wes waving at me.

"Hey, Sue Ann!" he called out.

"Hi Wes! Thank you so much for letting me join you tonight," I said as I got in.

With two extroverts in the car, the conversation was non-stop from there on. Wes hadn't forgotten his Minnesota for Pete friends and wanted to know what everyone was up to. I updated him on what the group was doing to promote Pete, and although it was the perfect opportunity for me to ask him what Nebraska was doing, that would have to wait until tomorrow when Jana and Jodi joined us for the interview. Instead, I asked him how his new teaching job was going.

Soon we were pulling up at DJ's Dugout Sports Bar in Aksarben Village, west of downtown. I commented on the unusual name for the village and Wes informed me that *Aksarben* was *Nebraska* spelled backwards. *Ah ha!* Aksarben Village was billed as a premier shopping and entertainment community, and it sure was hopping on this Friday night.

When we walked into DJ's Dugout, my jaw dropped. So many screens! A mosaic of large and small screens covering every wall and the center bar area as well. You had your choice of which game to watch, but tonight, Wes and his volleyball teammates would be watching the University of Nebraska Huskers women's volleyball.

We found Wes's friends at a communal table and joined them.

"This is my friend Sue Ann," Wes said, introducing me to the group of five.

"Hello, everyone!" I said, knowing that I was an imposter. I was not here to watch volleyball or any other sport. I decided that I'd just fess up. "I don't know anything about volleyball, so you'll have to tell me what's happening."

"Sure thing," one of them said. "Have a seat!" I ordered a margarita and settled in for casual banter with Wes's friends. When you have no vested interest in who wins and who loses, a sports bar can have a neutral, but energizing vibe. It was a fun night out with Wes. But since the Huskers lost, Wes and his friends didn't have as much fun.

"I'll pick you up tomorrow morning to go to Jodi's house," Wes said as he dropped me off back at my hotel.

"Thank you. That makes things so much easier." I replied. "I'm so excited!"

"It will be fun," he said.

Wes effortlessly navigated through suburban Omaha to get to Jodi's house that morning, having been there before. I wouldn't be meeting Jodi for the first time that day. We had met in the summer when I flew to Omaha for the day just so I could meet her for lunch and give her a PEGGS for Pete T-shirt from South Bend. Jodi had been unable to make the trip herself, so I wanted to bring South Bend to her.

Now I was showing up at her front door with Wes.

"Jodi!" I exclaimed when she opened the door for us. "It's great to see you again."

"Come in!"

Jodi's house was spotless and her middle school-aged kids nowhere to be seen.

"Thank you for letting us come here to do the interview, Jodi," I said.

"Is Jana here yet?" Wes asked.

"No. She texted that she'd be here soon." Jana was coming from Lincoln, about an hour's drive away.

Jana and I had met at the Steak Fry in Des Moines and had become buddies on Twitter talking about our similar personality type, her artwork, and the fact that her daughter was going to college at my alma mater in St. Paul, practically my backyard.

Jodi showed us into the great room to the large dining room table where we would record. She moved her laptop and homework for her library science class out of the way, and I set up the recorder and four microphones.

Ding dong!

Jodi went to the door, and I could hear the hubbub of Jana's arrival in the background.

"Hello everyone!" Jana announced, making her entrance. *Another extrovert!*

"How was your drive?" I asked.

"It was all right. There was a little construction I had to get around. Sorry I'm late."

"We're just getting set up."

I was patting myself on the back for the fact that I had met all three of them before the interview, forgetting that the three of them knew each other better than they knew me. This became obvious as they started chattering away like long-lost friends. I was the fourth wheel. Wait. That's a good thing, right? Especially if you want a good episode. The fact that I didn't know what they'd been up to in their political organizing for Pete made for authentic questions and attentive listening on my part.

In the course of the interview, I discovered just how involved Wes had been and how he had been the catalyst to their meeting each other. I was delighted to learn that Jodi ran the *Nebraska for Pete* Twitter account and had been chatting with the other two state accounts I'd met—*Virginia for Pete* Kyle and *Minnesota for Pete* Melani. Jana had often been making the drive to Omaha for Pete events and even beyond to Council Bluffs, Iowa.

How embarrassing it was to only now be learning that Council Bluffs, Iowa was just across the river from Omaha, Nebraska. A ten-minute drive. Since Nebraska was a late primary state, this meant that much of the focus of their organizing energy would be in Council Bluffs canvassing for the Iowa caucus. Wes was already taking on a volunteer leadership role there.

In both Nebraska and Iowa, rural issues were important to voters, and I loved hearing about conversations they'd had with farmers on Pete's rural plan. It was interesting to learn about farmers' concerns about climate change. Flooded farm fields were devastating to their livelihoods, and those once-in-a-century floods were happening too often.

The episode essentially ran itself with the four of us in natural conversation. Was I getting better at this, or was it the Wes/Jodi/Jana effect? In any case, I was starting to get the hang of this podcast thing and having the time of my life. It was a blast spending the morning with my Nebraska for Pete friends.

After the interview, Wes drove me to the airport to catch my flight back to Minneapolis.

"You know what, Wes?" I said en route to the airport.

"What?"

"I think I'm going to do something crazy."

"Really?" he replied with interest.

"I'm going to go see Pete in Coralville, Iowa tomorrow," I said.

"Cool!"

"That's not the crazy part. The crazy part is I'm going to stay at MSP airport when I land and catch a flight to Cedar Rapids later this afternoon."

"That *is* crazy." Wes said. "I hope it all works out!"

With many Iowa rallies scheduled in preparation for the Iowa caucus, I wanted to take advantage of any I could attend. Seeing Pete in person was energizing and added spark to my relational organizing. Plus, I knew all of this excitement wasn't going to last forever. That made it all the more meaningful. I had this plan to go to Coralville in the back of my mind when I left for Omaha on Friday and even told Steve it might be happening. Now that I had made it on the Omaha to Minneapolis flight, Plan B was now becoming Plan A.

I had four hours to kill at MSP, so of course I bought a carry-on bag at Tumi. Now I know why they have shops like that. If you have a long layover and you're annoyed with your bag, why not rectify the situation right then and there? This new bag would be much better for hauling around my recording equipment, and I could start using it right away.

My plan was only going to work if I actually got on the flight to Cedar Rapids. Those smaller market planes only had 50-100 seats. I didn't want to book a hotel until

I was sure I got on the flight, but I was ready to do so once I knew. The rally was going to be at the Coralville Marriott Hotel Conference Center, so I would stay there at the Marriott. Safely on the plane in my assigned seat, I reserved a room.

Once I arrived in Cedar Rapids and called for an Uber to take me to Coralville, I set about contacting campaign organizers to sign up to volunteer for the event. Kathryn, my Iowa Twitter friend, facilitated this, and soon I was on the volunteer list.

There were hordes of volunteers at the pre-rally training session the next morning, making me feel unneeded. Still, it was interesting to see how the campaign machinery worked in Iowa. Like clockwork. I was assigned to directing pedestrian and car traffic outside, and then once the doors opened, I was tasked with checking people's event stickers as they entered the event space. I'm not sure how many attended, but let's just say Pete was gaining in popularity.

As I listened to Pete do yet another great stump speech, my mind was distracted by the worry that I might not make it to Cedar Rapids airport in time for my flight back to Minneapolis. It was the last flight of the day, and I didn't want to get stranded. I had to teach the next day. I knew Pete would be meeting with the volunteers after his speech, and I wanted to stay for that, but it was going to be close. I had to determine the latest I could stay before bowing out, Pete or no Pete.

Since there were so many volunteers for Pete to meet, we gathered outside and got in four groups of twenty so he could do smaller group photos rather than one huge group. As we were waiting for him to come out, a woman standing behind me in my group shrieked. Pete had come out from behind and startled her. We all giggled as good-natured Pete sneaked into our group for the first photo. He thanked us all as he moved from group to group. Then he disappeared into a black SUV and left.

I looked at my watch. I had barely enough time to catch my flight. I called an Uber and raced to the hotel front desk where my luggage was being kept. On the way, I ran into Nina Smith, Pete's Traveling Press Secretary. I had been too shy to talk to her at the Iowa State Fair; no way was I going to be too shy now.

"Nina!" I said getting her attention.

"Yes," she said as she stopped.

"I'm Sue Ann Rawlins from Twitter."

"I think I recognize you!"

"I wanted you to know that I'm traveling around interviewing Pete supporters for a podcast."

"Really?" she replied

"I was just in Omaha doing an interview yesterday."

"That's amazing. Thanks for telling me!"

Neither of us had time to talk more than that because Nina was also headed to the airport. She had just called her Lyft. Too bad we couldn't have coordinated that trip.

I got to the airport in time for my flight, and as I was stretching my legs, I noticed Nina sitting at another gate waiting for her flight. *Should I talk to her again?* I wondered. I decided not to bother her. Maybe that would have been too much. Sometimes you have to know when your Pete weekend is over.

15

Elise and Nicola

It was now the second week in December, and I'd already done six podcasts since the first one came out on Halloween. That's one a week—breakneck speed. But time was critical. The Iowa caucus was coming up soon. I was committed to knocking out as many episodes as possible before then. This was much to the consternation of my husband Steve, who was starting to get annoyed by the disruption my traveling was causing the household.

"Do you have to travel *every* weekend?" he had asked. "Can't you interview someone local?"

"No," I replied. "The show's called *Twitter* Travels *for Pete,* so I have to *travel.*" I thought it was obvious.

The conversation got me thinking, though. Maybe during the upcoming Christmas holiday when the flights were too full for me to get on, I could interview someone local. Light bulb moment. I could interview someone local who had traveled for Pete. It would still be traveling.

I immediately thought of college student Elise. Elise and I had met at Katie and Kelly's house back in

May for that Fox Town Hall watch party. She hadn't been active with the Minnesota group much since then because she'd been in Iowa over the summer working as an intern for the Pete campaign and then in London for a study abroad semester, where she was involved in the Americans Abroad for Pete group.

Elise would be coming back home in a few days. Wouldn't it be fun to interview her about both Iowa and London? It would make for an interesting episode, a break from what I'd been doing up to this point. I messaged Elise on Facebook with my proposition. It was a plan. I would interview her as soon as she got home. The day after she made her transatlantic journey, as a matter of fact.

That Sunday morning, I drove to Elise's parents' house a mere twenty minutes away—definitely a local interview. I'd met her mother a couple of times at Pete events, but hadn't met her father yet. I had heard, however, that he was a volunteer in my school's evening program. Small world. We had many common acquaintances.

The other member of Elise's family present was Zat, the cat.

"I hope you don't mind my cat," Elise said. "He's missed me."

Zat would become part of the interview. He paced back and forth on the dining room table repeatedly brushing against Elise in that feline way. "Zat, get away!" she scolded as she took up the microphone to start the recording. Yet, Zat stayed put. It was my first interview with a cat. If only he would have meowed on cue!

Poor Elise had caught a cold in London. She said she'd had it for weeks, probably the result of her college student lifestyle. Considering that she was also severely jetlagged, her lucidity was impressive as she described her experiences on both sides of the Atlantic.

To start, I asked her the "Why Pete?" question I usually asked my guests. As a fellow member of the LGBTQ community, Elise's initial impression of Mayor Pete was that of admiration for his historic candidacy. It didn't take long, though, for that admiration to become all-encompassing. Maybe this guy could win. Elise decided she would do everything she could to help make that happen.

I loved hearing about her time as a summer intern in Grinnell, Iowa, where she attended college during the year. When I last saw Elise in the early summer, she talked about heading down to Iowa even though she didn't have an internship lined up yet. I remember thinking, *Good for you!* During the interview, I joked about her being a squatter while she was waiting for the internship to come through. Elise had fun stories of setting up the early days of organizing for the Iowa caucus. Can you imagine the one coffee shop in town that nearly all the candidates were using as their office? I wish I could have seen that.

The London part of her story was fascinating. Elise had done so many interesting things in the past four months as she got involved with the Americans abroad for Pete campaign. Canvassing takes on a different meaning when you're trying to reach expats and involves some creativity. At least American college students studying abroad were easy to find, and that was the group targeted for a big event with Chasten in London. Elise worked hard to promote the event at various colleges, which resulted in a sizeable turnout.

At the Chasten event, Elise met another Buttigieg— Nicola Buttigieg, Pete's second cousin. Nicola, an Australian now living in London, had been active on Twitter as she worked on her Pete Mosaic project. The Pete Mosaic was a digital image of Pete's face made up of thousands of photos from campaign events across the country. I knew about the Pete Mosaic; I had even submitted photos for it. But until this interview, I had no idea it was Nicola who was doing it.

After meeting Elise, Nicola invited her to participate in an event at the school where she taught. It was a panel discussion on American politics with journalists. Elise would present the American view. The magnitude of this request intimidated her, but in the end, Nicola would tell me, Elise came through with flying colors. What a phenomenal opportunity for a young college student.

Before leaving the UK, Elise had time for a side trip to Malta. Malta was the birthplace of Pete's father— Nicola's father too—and thus, the origin of the *Buttigieg* name. From Elise's description of the beautiful island nation, I knew Malta would be added to the list of places I wanted to visit.

We wound down our conversation with what was next for Elise.

"This is the most historic election of my lifetime," she said. "So, I'm taking the semester off to work on the campaign in any way I can." Elise had unwavering commitment.

We concluded the interview with the usual "Go Pete!" cheer.

"Whew!" Elise said, out of breath. "I hope I made sense."

"You were fantastic!" I assured her. "I can't wait to get this episode out. People are going to love it!"

My idea for a local *Twitter Travels for Pete* episode was a success.

A few weeks later, I was ushering in the New Year on a flight to London. I didn't have my recording equipment with me this time, so I guess it was a leisure trip. It was still a Twitter trip, though, because I was traveling on my own to meet up with some friends I'd met on my other Twitter account, my non-political account. I'd met up with my English Twitter friends Sarah, Delia, and Sharon the year before when we enjoyed an elegant afternoon tea together. Hoping to make it an annual event, I suggested a return trip this year. I was flying to London to go out to tea. That was the only thing I had planned.

I would be in London with some downtime. *Surely there must be someone on Team Pete I could meet while I'm there,* I thought. By the time I thought about this, it was short notice for making plans, and the fact that it was still the Christmas holiday made it difficult to connect with people. *Should I try to contact Nicola?* I hadn't interacted with her on Twitter much. Would she want to take the time to meet me? At least I knew she'd listened to Elise's episode because she'd shared it on Facebook. It was worth the try. I shouldn't have worried because Buttigieges are nice people, and of course, Nicola was willing to meet me on Friday.

In London that Friday, I met Sarah and Delia at Selfridges for afternoon tea. Unfortunately, Sharon wasn't able to join us, so it was just three for tea. We were all dressed up for the occasion and took multiple photos of ourselves at the elegantly appointed and heavily laden tea table. So many sandwiches, scones, and cakes! But no worries. The first rule of afternoon tea is that there are no calories. Especially if you fly all the way to London for it.

After tea, I wandered down Oxford Street until it was time to meet Nicola, and then the chain of texts and messages began.

"I will be able to meet you in the next half hour. H Club is 24 Endell St Covent Garden," Nicola wrote. "I'll meet you in Reception."

I wasn't quite sure what "h" Club was, but I was going to find out, once I found that address. I wonder how many people realize their dependence on Google maps. As a Baby Boomer, I pride myself in being able to read a paper map. But I had millenialized myself to the point of relying strictly on my phone. That works just fine when you can connect to a cellular network when you're out and about traveling. But in the UK, my phone only worked with Wi-Fi. I didn't realize I could have downloaded the navigation maps. Oh well.

As I tried to find 24 Endell Street, I popped in and out of shops that had Wi-Fi to check on my location. I thought I had a good sense of direction, but London streets aren't on a grid like New York and Chicago. I would exit a shop with a concrete idea of where I was headed only to get turned around again. To add insult to injury, when I asked a shopkeeper for help, he gave me the wrong directions. I was so close, but he told me to walk in the opposite direction. Had the building still been St. Paul's Hospital, the reason it was called "h" (for "hospital") Club, it would have been easier to find.

I finally made it to my destination, forty-five minutes late. Poor Nicola had been patiently waiting for me all this time. The entrance to the building was unassuming. I'd walked right past it the first time. Perhaps this was intentional—it was a private social club. Walking into h Club was a little like walking through a magical wardrobe. One minute in bustling Covent Garden, the next minute in a dimly lit oasis of quiet.

Once in the lobby, I approached the reception desk.

"Who are you meeting?" the concierge said with decorum.

"Nicola Buttigieg," I answered.

"And what is your name?"

"Sue Ann Rawlins."

He looked at his book to confirm that I was allowed admittance.

"Please sign here," he said, rotating the register so I could sign.

That's when I started to get the idea of how classy h Club was.

"Ms. Buttigieg is waiting for you on the fourth floor," he said, gesturing towards the lift.

The lift opened to a wood paneled hallway, which with the dim light, felt especially warm. I could hear the faint sound of quiet conversation as I walked towards the private cocktail lounge. This was *fancy*. Good thing I had dressed up for tea; otherwise, I might have looked like a tacky American tourist.

I was nervous about meeting Nicola. *Pete's cousin*. The DNA alone made her famous in my mind. What would she be like? I was glad to have sixty-one years of experience under my belt as I embarked upon yet another social challenge.

I'd never been to a private cocktail lounge. The small space made it feel more like a room in a private home. The decor was contemporary with sofas and comfy chairs carefully placed in small groupings against large windows looking out onto the city. The night sky twinkled with a thousand lights.

The lounge wasn't particularly busy this evening, so it was easy to pick out Nicola, who stood up to greet me as I entered. Nicola, with wavy long blonde hair, was smartly dressed in her teacher attire, a gray A-line skirt and blouse, which to me, was a very English look.

"Hello, Sue Ann!" Nicola said in her beautifully resonate voice.

Immediately, I was under her spell. I needn't have worried about meeting Nicola.

"I'm so sorry to have kept you waiting!" I said apologetically.

We hugged, and then I sat in the comfy chair next to her on the sofa.

"I've started already," Nicola said, gesturing to her drink.

Soon the waiter approached to take my cocktail order.

"Gin and tonic, please," I said.

We settled in for a long conversation that naturally started with Elise, our common acquaintance. Nicola told me more about the panel discussion for her school that Elise had been part of and sung her praises. Elise had impressed Nicola as being extremely competent in her answers that day, especially for a college student.

We soon shifted to talking about Pete, and I wanted to know all about the family history. She was his second cousin—their fathers were first cousins who grew up together in Malta. Her father ended up in Australia, Pete's father, in the United States. Both studied English literature, and both were named "Joseph." Nicola and Pete had never met, but since she was about six months older than he was, she joked that he was her "baby" cousin.

Nicola's impressive resume included work in the arts as a singer, writer, composer, director, actor, and voice artist. This is how she became a member of the h Club. H Club was a private members' club for people working in the arts. Not just anyone, mind you. You needed three referees (references) to be considered for admission.

Professionally, Nicola had shifted to a more dependable line of business—computer science. She was teaching computer science at a high school while working on her master's degree in computer science. The Pete Mosaic was a project for one of her classes.

As a British subject, Nicola was conscientious about following American campaign finance rules, so she limited her involvement in Pete's campaign, not knowing exactly where the line would be drawn. Involvement of foreigners in expat campaigning seemed unclear, and it was better to be safe than sorry.

"You know I can't order any Pete merchandise." Nicola said, eyeing the Pete 2020 pin on my coat.

"You can't?" I replied.

"No. It's considered a donation, and I'm a foreigner."

"You can have mine," I said, taking the pin off my coat.

"Are you sure?" she said, taking it from me.

"Yes. It's from the South Bend field office." Breana had given it to me when I was in South Bend for the *Good Guy Pete* podcast recording. It was my favorite pin, but I knew Nicola should have it. This was the perfect "selfie" moment as evidence of meeting Nicola Buttigieg in London.

We ordered food and continued talking. I shared that my husband was also in computer science and worked as a software developer. Knowing his approximate age, Nicola was immediately interested in what he could tell her about the early years of Fortran programming. I knew Steve would love to talk to Nicola. But I also chuckled to myself that he was going to be asked about the old days of programming, something he referred to as his "old geezer" days.

During a rare break in the conversation, I sat back in my chair and looked out the window. I had a perfect view of the London Eye, all lit up. The juxtaposition of London nightlife against the interior calm of the h Club lounge was something I would probably never experience again. Tourists never got to experience this. It was getting late, but I didn't want to leave. Couldn't I just stay there talking to Nicola forever?

Finally, we paid our bill and got ready to leave. As I stood up, my knees creaked from the stiffness of sitting too long. After a visit to the ladies' room, we rode the lift down to the street level. The concierge offered a polite "Good night" as we went out the door.

"I'll show you where the Covent Garden tube station is," Nicola said. "I'm going there too." What a relief it was not to worry about finding my way through the labyrinth of London streets again.

We talked as we walked, and soon, we were at Covent Garden station, teeming with Friday night revelers. We would be getting on different trains, so this was the moment of farewell.

"It was lovely to meet you, Sue Ann," Nicola said.

"Thank you for meeting me today," I replied.

"I do want to talk to your husband," Nicola reminded me.

"He'd love to answer your questions," I said as we went our separate ways.

I smiled at the thought of Nicola and Steve becoming IT buddies. That meant I could stay in touch with her.

Nicola was one of the most accomplished and interesting people I'd ever met, but instead of talking about herself the entire evening, she had genuinely shown interest in me too. This is where I saw some similarity to Pete, at least from what I'd read about him. They were both intellectually gifted people who fearlessly jumped at the chance of a new challenge. With curious minds, they both seemed to love talking to people and listening to what they had to say. It was all learning. I took this to be a Buttigieg family trait, and I truly hoped the two cousins would someday meet.

16

Door Knocking in Iowa

January was kicked off in high gear as the campaign made its push to the Iowa caucus finish line. Pete was busy crisscrossing the state, making four to five appearances a day, trying to meet as many Iowans as he could before February third. Team Pete volunteers from all over the country were text and phone banking into Iowa, something the Minnesota for Pete group took on as our top responsibility. As Minnesotans, we were especially valuable in conversations with caucusgoers as neighbors to the north who had chosen Pete over our own senator, Amy Klobuchar. Plus, we could easily drive south to knock on doors, so we had two big weekends planned for an all-out Minnesota invasion of northeastern Iowa.

Before that, however, I would hone my canvassing skills in the diagonally opposite region of the state— Council Bluffs, Iowa. Why? Because Wes asked for help, and how could I say no to Wes? Plus, now I knew that I could fly to Omaha and easily drive across the river to Council Bluffs. And maybe I'd be able to catch an interview with some of the organizers. My next episode had to be about the Iowa caucus. That's what everyone was focused on.

By this stage of the campaign, Wes had become heavily involved in the Council Bluffs field office, spending all of his free time working on canvassing. He was the best of the super volunteers, more like staff. Wes kindly picked me up at my hotel that morning and we crossed the river to report for duty. As soon as we entered the office, Wes checked in with the two PFA organizers, Shalini and Antonia, and together they reviewed the plan for the day. They scrutinized the county map posted on the wall for status. Who was still uncommitted? I had no idea this sort of fine-tuning was going on, but it made sense. They had been canvassing every weekend trying to reach everyone out in the rural areas. But today I would be canvassing in Council Bluffs proper.

I had entered the office self-consciously dragging my luggage behind me, snow from the sidewalk stuck to the wheels. I would be heading back to the airport later that afternoon. Luckily, I would be able to store it in Antonia's office while I was out canvassing.

Jana, having made the trip from Lincoln, was seated at the welcome table, which was indeed a welcome sight.

"Hey Sue Ann!" she said.

"Jana! It's great to see you again!"

"My daughter is here," she said gesturing over to the other side of the room. "She's going to do the training this morning."

"That's fantastic!" I replied.

I introduced myself to Jana's daughter, and knowing she went to my alma mater, I said, "You're on J-Term break now, right?"

"Uh-huh."

"What a perfect opportunity to work on the campaign!" I said.

"Yes, it is," she replied. "I love it."

While waiting for the training to begin, I walked around the office, surveying the tasks I'd done the night before to help with the prep—the snack baskets I'd assembled and the "commit to caucus" cards I'd added to the display wall. It wasn't much, but it was something. Shalini & Antonia had been crazy busy prepping for the weekend's canvassing event, so no interview was possible last night. And now Lizzy, their regional organizer, had arrived to help with the canvassing weekend, and I could tell there would be no interview today, either. Everyone was much too distracted and busy with the task at hand: knock on as many doors as possible. I was beginning to learn that there is no free time in an Iowa campaign office in January. That was fine with me. I just wished I hadn't lugged my recording equipment around for nothing.

After the training, it was time to pair up and take a route. With no car myself, I was dependent on getting paired with a driver, but most volunteers arrived in pairs. Wes took pity on me and agreed to be my partner. I was going to go out canvassing with a pro.

We suited up for the cold and left the office, clipboards in hand. I used to think that Omaha was warmer than Minneapolis just because it was farther south, but I now knew about the wind, the cold wind that swept across the prairie into Iowa too. It had snowed the night before, but today was clear and cold with a subzero wind chill.

With Wes, I was always ten steps behind, literally and figuratively. It became painfully obvious that he could get many more doors knocked than I could. He knew the neighborhood well since he'd already knocked it the weekend before, so he had a strategy for where to park and which side of the street we'd each take in which direction to circle back to the car. I noticed that he'd kindly skewed it so that he had more houses than I did.

It was bone-chilling cold as I walked from house to house, and luckily, that meant those who were home, invited me in. I had a few good conversations with undecided caucusgoers in which I could say that I'd met Pete and he was the real deal. But then it was back out into the cold.

On the next segment of our route, I wimped out. I was miserably cold. Not wanting to leave anything undone, Wes offered to tackle the remaining houses while I waited in the car. And I let him. It would be faster this way.

We got back to the office with our paperwork and I was surprised to learn that Wes would be taking one of the rural routes next. I was completely done for the day, and he was just getting started. I had undying respect for that man.

As I was gathering my luggage and about to call my Uber, I got talking to another volunteer. We eventually figured out that we knew each other on Twitter. *Lady Liberatoire* was there with her mother, and since they were headed back to Omaha, she was happy to offer me a ride to the airport. The gods were truly smiling upon me. I put my bag in Erin's trunk and dropped into the front seat of her car, depleted of physical energy. I still had social energy, though, and enjoyed the brief time we had to chat on the way to the airport.

Sitting in the gate area waiting for my flight back to Minneapolis, I posted the selfie I'd taken with Erin on Twitter and mindlessly scrolled through my timeline.

I'd come to the realization that I really wasn't good at door knocking. I was probably the least efficient, least effective canvasser. But because I still wanted to help, and I still wanted to be part of the "Caucus for Pete" experience, I would continue to sign up for shifts. I wouldn't be good at it, but I was still going to do it. And somehow, I still felt that I belonged.

The next weekend would be the big canvassing event in Mason City for the Minnesota for Pete group. Katie and Irish Katie were busy coordinating carpools with messages and group texts. In the meantime, though, everyone was talking about Pete's town hall schedule that week, and who was going to drive down to see him.

Waterloo? Dubuque? Des Moines? Mason City? Pete was going to be in Mason City on Wednesday, January 15. Could I pull that off? Drive down after school and back again?

A weekday event in a small town, two hours south of Minneapolis would limit the crowds. It would probably be my last chance to see Pete in a small venue. If he did well in the Iowa caucus, he'd be attracting thousands and thousands of people at events even if I could travel to them. And it wasn't clear he was going to make it to Minnesota at all before Super Tuesday. THIS was my last chance to talk to Pete. I wanted to tell him about my podcast, especially Myndee's episode. I wanted him to know that he had helped prevent a death of despair.

Who else would want to drive two hours down and back in winter weather? I needed a travel companion. I immediately thought of my friend April. When I'd asked her if she wanted to help out in Charles City in November, she seemed genuinely disappointed that she had prior plans. Maybe she'd be game for Mason City. Lucky for me, she was!

I'd met April on Twitter through my non-political account, my English tea account, and realized that we lived in the same city. Now April was following me on my political account too, and I'd won her over to supporting Pete in the primary. Mind you, that wasn't especially difficult since Pete sold himself. April was dying to meet Pete in person.

Everything was set, but would the weather cooperate? A two-hour drive on a freeway sounds like a no-brainer, but two hours on Interstate 35 with snow blowing across the road from one flat farm field to another sounded treacherous. Even if it didn't snow, we'd have to worry about visibility. The chance of snow was low, but how could we really know what the weather was going to be like in Iowa? One thing I knew for sure: it was going to be bitterly cold with below-zero temps.

Fully aware of the travel risk, April was ready to join me on one of my Pete adventures. But we'd take her four-wheel-drive Ford Flex SUV rather than my Honda Accord. The next question was, how early did we need to arrive to be first in line? We planned to arrive in Mason City two hours before and then scope it out.

Driving down I-35, there was only a brief stretch with blowing snow limiting visibility, which luckily passed before we had to discuss turning back. As an expert Minnesota driver, April handled it all well. I was so glad I wasn't the one at the wheel, especially driving back in the dark.

Once in Mason City, we found our way to the North Iowa Events Center, a multipurpose regional fairgrounds, which looked as though it was hibernating for the winter. The events center building was unassuming with no evidence that a political superstar was about to appear. We were definitely early. Enough time to go to Starbucks just down the road for some sustenance. I certainly had a Starbucks guardian angel because so often, there was one "just down the road."

I ate my sandwich with one eye on my watch. When would other people arrive? When would it be too late to be first in line? Looking out the window, I could see cars turning down the road heading to the events center. I was getting antsy.

"We'd better get back there," I told April. There's nothing worse than not being the head of the line when you arrived early enough to do so.

When we got to the parking lot, we could see a few other cars parked with their engines running, but no one in line. There was no one anywhere near the door to the building. It was like everyone was trying to judge the perfect moment to get in line.

"We'd better get in line before all these other people," I said to April.

"I agree," she replied.

April shut off the engine. We exited the warmth of the car and dashed up to the door of the building. Just as we did so, the other parked car people did the same and were close behind.

"Do you think they're going to make us wait outside?" one person asked, shivering.

"I hope not!" I said. "The wind chill must be -20° now."

Soon, a volunteer appeared at the door and let us into the entryway. From our place at the head of the line, I could see volunteers setting up the main event space, something I was becoming accustomed to. The stage with a huge American flag on the wall behind, the stool with the microphone placed on it, and a bottle of water were in the desired set-up position. All was ready for Pete. Rows of chairs were set up in front of the stage, with a small set of risers behind the audience for the media.

"Look," I said to April. "There are chairs. We don't have to stand."

"Score!" she replied.

It wasn't long before a volunteer moved the stanchions and let us in. April and I walked directly to the front row, center stage, and took our seats. We watched the room fill up behind us, and I wondered how many people were from Minnesota and how many were true Iowans. I know the people next to us in line had driven south like we had. There were about 300 in the audience, by far the smallest venue yet. And the fact that we were all sheltering inside from subzero temperatures on this winter night made it feel all the cozier.

I kept my eye on the back edge of the stage for any activity that would portend Pete's arrival, and it wasn't long before the introductory speakers gathered. Two of the regional organizers took the stage with a primer on the Iowa caucus, highlighting new rules for this year. What I didn't know at the time was they were stretching their speeches until Pete was ready to take the stage. I told them afterwards that they should do that caucus primer at every town hall. I know I learned a lot.

As soon as I heard the opening bars to *High Hopes*, by Panic! At the Disco, I knew it was time. Usually, for these small-town events, Pete wore his signature white shirt, open collar with no tie, and blue dress pants. But tonight, he wore his full suit. Anyone looking at photos from that event wouldn't know the reason why. But anyone in attendance that night did. He needed that suit jacket for warmth on this frigid January night.

Pete hopped up on stage, greeted the crowd, and started in on his stump speech, something I would never tire of. I occasionally looked to April to see how she was reacting to seeing Pete in person for the first time. She was spellbound. *Ah, I remember the first time I saw Pete speak . . .*

Mayor Pete's rhetorical gift was that he could synthesize complex issues into manageable talking points. He made sense in a way that other politicians didn't, making it seem like no one had ever said it quite like that before. His delivery was genuine and his demeanor one of calm kindness. I really didn't understand how anyone could *not* like Pete Buttigieg.

For the Q&A segment, Pete took questions directly from the audience. One of the questions was from a man wearing a Trump button. Pete steeled himself for a potential onslaught of criticism, but the man had an honest question in reference to something in Pete's stump speech: "How do you define the middle class?"

In Pete's answer he referred to an assumption people had about the middle class, that if you're middle class, you have enough money to take an occasional vacation and maybe give to your place of worship. But he went on to say that so many people who are considered middle class are hurting right now. As Pete spoke, the man listened in rapt attention. Pete's answer was compassionate and showed a real understanding of the challenges faced by rural communities. At the end, I could tell by the man's face that Pete had earned his respect.

With the Q&A finished, Pete thanked the audience for coming and started greeting those of us along the rope line. Saralena followed behind as usual, taking photos for people. Soon he would be coming to April, and then to me. I mentally reviewed what I was going to say to him. I would only have a minute or two to talk to him, so I would have to come straight to the point. I knew he wouldn't recognize me from our previous brief encounters.

The awkward thing about talking to Pete in a rope line was that the physical proximity was much closer than you would normally have when meeting in another setting due to the crush of the crowd. And because you only had a short time to talk, it was an intense interaction.

Pete got to me, and I was ready for the handshake, after which I launched into what I wanted to say.

"Pete, I wanted you to know that I'm doing a podcast called, *Twitter Travels for Pete* where I travel around and interview supporters about their grassroots efforts on the ground." He laughed at the name *Twitter Travels for Pete*. That seemed to tickle his funny bone. But as I continued, his facial expression shifted from interest to concern as I told him about Myndee.

"Thanks for talking to people," he said earnestly, knowing he had to move on. Saralena then took the official selfie photo and moved him along the line.

I did it. I had accomplished my goal of telling Pete about how he had indirectly helped Myndee, how Team Pete had helped her feel like she belonged. It was something I had desperately wanted him to know ever since I'd interviewed Myndee for that episode. I felt like the circle had been completed.

While Pete was still talking to people, I noticed Nina Smith, his Traveling Press Secretary, standing nearby.

"Hey, Nina!" I called to her.

"Hi Sue Ann," she said with a smile.

"I told Pete about my podcast—in particular a special episode with a supporter struggling with her mental health," I said. "Do you know how I could get the link to him?"

"You can send it to me," she said. "DM me on Twitter."

Now the circle really was complete. I wasn't sure if he'd have time to listen, but at least he knew where to find it.

With the excitement over, April and I turned to each other.

"What did you think?" I asked.

"He was *impressive*," April said. "I didn't know what to say to him. I told him he gives me hope and that he's the voice of reason. He thanked me and said that yes, that's what we need right now."

"Aww, that's great!" I said. "I'm so glad you got to meet him!"

"This was amazing," she said. "I got some great photos of you with Pete."

"Really? Thank you!" I said. "I took a couple of you with him too."

We showed each other the photos we'd taken and texted them to each other. Now April had evidence of meeting Pete in person, definitely making the trip worthwhile.

What a relief to know that April had enjoyed the evening. Not that I really worried about the power of Pete, but a part of me felt like I had imposed on April by inviting her to drive down to Iowa two hours and back on a bitterly cold, January day. For someone to want to do that, it had to be worth it. This had definitely been worth it for both of us.

As the weekend for canvassing in Mason City approached, we were all watching the weather maps. Blizzard conditions with dangerous wind chills were predicted. But we were hearty Minnesotans! Surely that wouldn't stop us. By Friday, decisions had to be made. Even if we could make it down there, were we going to risk frostbite? The answer was no. Unfortunately with the clock counting down to Caucus Day, and every weekend critical for door knocking, Minnesota for Pete would not be canvassing in Mason City. We'd have to take a snow check for the next weekend.

As a door knocker, that was OK for me, but as a podcast host, it just meant one more week without an episode. Getting an Iowa caucus episode was eluding me. It had been a month since my last episode had come out, the one with Elise. I knew I had to keep up the momentum of my show. I needed to put out an episode somehow. *Maybe I could have Steve interview me and we could call it "Snowbound in Minneapolis."*

My experience had been that people were generally curious about spouses of people they knew. I was banking on the assumption that my listeners would tune in just to see what Sue Ann's husband was like and what he thought of her traveling around so much. It was worth a try. It would be a turn the tables episode where I was the guest. When I proposed the idea to Steve, I knew that with his gift of oratory, he'd do well. I also knew he'd have fun with it.

So, date night at the Rawlins household entailed the two of us seated at our dining room table with my Handy 6 Zoom recorder and two microphones. I have to say that being the guest was a completely different experience than being the host. There was slightly more pressure to come up with a good answer. Asking the questions was easy.

"Thank you for doing this, Steve," I said when we ended the recording. "I really appreciate it."

"It was fun," he replied. "I think it's going to be a good episode."

I still needed a photo for the episode, though. For verisimilitude, I decided to go outside in our driveway and take a selfie with the snow falling against the wintery background for the *Snowbound in Minneapolis* episode. It was obviously a posed photo with me in my down coat and Russian hat talking into a microphone in the snow, but it did the trick. It was definitely eye-catching.

The next weekend, Minnesota for Pete was out in force canvassing in Mason City, as promised. Irish Katie had resumed coordinating volunteers and had been in close communication with the Mason City folks. Steve and I were signed up for Sunday and made sure to leave early enough to get there on time for training.

Checklist for the trip: down jacket with Pete buttons, snow boots, mittens, Pete hat. Lisa had ordered navy blue Pete hats for us, and Steve was wearing his, but I had upgraded to a hand-knit Pete hat. A few months earlier I approached my daughter's friend who was a master knitter.

"Would you be willing to knit a Pete hat for me?" I texted Maddie. "I'll pay you."

"Sure!" she replied. "Do you have a pattern?"

Why, yes, I did. Someone had posted it on Facebook, and the intricate snowflake pattern had gotten many oohs and aahs. And thus, I commissioned my very own Pete hat. When we arrived in Mason City that morning, I was wearing the coolest Pete hat in the bunch.

The bulk of our group had volunteered on Saturday, so there were fewer of us on Sunday. After receiving our instructions and synching up the MiniVAN app with our route, Steve and I were ready to take on our territory. It reminded me again of *The Music Man*, this time the opening number with the salesmen on the train.

We had to know the territory. And our territory was Charles City. I don't know why I was surprised that we would be venturing beyond Mason City to do our door knocking. How else would they reach Floyd County? After Steve and I wrapped our minds around the fact that we had another hour to drive before we'd begin canvassing, we got in the car and set the GPS. Steve drove, and I navigated. I'd driven to Charles City before, but that was from Minneapolis, not from Mason City.

City folk like us didn't have a true grasp of the vastness of rural Iowa. We weren't used to seemingly endless roads in a monotonous winter landscape. Everything was starting to look the same, and despite Google maps, we got confused by the highway markings and turned off on a secondary road rather than wait for the highway turnoff. I thought we were lost.

When the snow blew across the road, it was difficult to see the side of the road. Where did the road end and the ditch begin? It reminded me of something Pete had written about in *Shortest Way Home*. When canvassing for Obama in 2008, he and his canvassing partner drove into a ditch in the dark of night and had to ask a nearby farmer for help pulling the car out. Now I knew how easily that could happen. In fact, I'd find out later that one of the Minnesota volunteers really did drive into the ditch.

Luckily, we arrived in Charles City without incident. Before starting the route, we stopped at Kwik Star to take care of necessities. I grabbed some sandwiches too, knowing there would be no time for a proper lunch. I hungrily wolfed down half of my sandwich as we drove into the neighborhood we'd be canvassing.

We decided to park the car in the middle of our territory, so we drove down North Jackson Street, looking for a parking spot.

"Let's park here next to the library." I said. "We can hang out there if one of us finishes first." Steve loved libraries, and I knew I'd be slower. But Steve wasn't thinking of books, he was on task checking the MiniVAN app, planning his strategy. Soon he took off at a brisk pace.

The library was the *old* library, the one on the historic register, a turn-of-the-century *Carnegie* library. But it was open, so I went inside before starting my route. When I saw the vintage librarian's desk, I thought back to playing Marian the Librarian in *The Music Man*. I imagined myself in costume, standing behind the desk, stamping books, waiting for Harold Hill to come in and sing to me.

My reverie was cut short by the realization that I was not alone. In fact, I was interrupting a meeting of some sort.

"You're welcome to join us," the librarian said. "We're discussing—." I had stumbled on a book discussion group, and as usual, I hadn't read the book.

"Thank you, but I just stopped in to see the library," I said, sheepishly. I turned around and headed back to the door where I saw the hours posted. The library would be closed in an hour. So much for choosing it as a meeting place.

As I started my route, I was grateful it wasn't as cold as Council Bluffs. It was actually quite comfortable for January, so the few people who were home didn't feel the need to invite me in. We kept our conversation to the doorway. Some people were still undecided, but I wondered if that was truly the case at one house. They just couldn't bear to tell the nice lady in the pretty Pete hat that they had decided on a candidate other than Pete. At one house, I was told that someone from the Bernie campaign had just been there. One household was split between Pete and Bernie.

With each door, I marked my results on the MiniVAN app and was surprised to see that I was actually making progress on my list. I was almost done.

"Where are you now?" I texted Steve. He was working his way back in my direction, so I met him on Main Street.

"How's it going?" I asked once we'd reconnected. "I'm done with my section up there."

"I have a few down this stretch," he answered. "There's a guy canvassing for Bernie and he's been knocking the same doors."

"Is that him?" I said, nodding towards a young man laden down with a clipboard and flyers.

"Yep."

"Bernie, huh?" I said. "I had some Bernie voters."

In all my Iowa door knocking so far, it seemed like it was a Bernie/Pete/Amy race with a bit of Warren and Biden thrown in. With a little over a week to go until the caucus, whoever had the best ground game had a good chance of winning Iowa. Whatever the Minnesota group was doing in Mason City and Charles City—and Wes and Jana were doing in the Council Bluffs area—was happening all over the state. Fired-up organizers and volunteers were hard at work making sure every Iowan knew who Mayor Pete Buttigieg was. And Pete? He was traveling around making as many personal appearances as possible.

On our drive back to Minneapolis, I thought about the overwhelming task of canvassing all over Iowa and of the relational organizing it would take to reach everyone. I knew I wasn't doing as much to help as others were. Many Minnesota for Pete volunteers had been canvassing both Saturday and Sunday and were planning to do the same the next weekend. I marveled at their energy. Unfortunately, I lacked that kind of physical stamina.

But I could still contribute. *The Iowa Caucus* episode of my podcast was set to be released on Tuesday. Thank God I was able to get that interview with Barbara in time.

17

The Iowa Caucus

I found myself in the gate area for a flight to Cedar Rapids, Iowa for the second time. Hopefully, this time I'd make it. The last time I tried this trip, I didn't get on the flight and had to call Steve, who had just dropped me off at the airport an hour and a half earlier, to pick me up again. Everything had been arranged for an interview with Kathryn in Iowa City—she'd even recruited two more people to participate. But I was going to be a no-show. How embarrassing. I was disheartened as I got back in the car.

"I'm sorry you didn't get on the flight," Steve had said, feeling bad for me.

"Oh, well," I replied. "This gives me a chance to catch up on my Christmas shopping." As an optimist, I always tried to roll with the punches.

That was December, and now it was Friday, January 24th and I was going to try to squeeze in a trip to Iowa City via Cedar Rapids and still get back in time to go door knocking in Mason City on Sunday. Since Kathryn wasn't available, she had recommended Barbara Clark as someone I should interview. Barbara was on Twitter, but I didn't know her well yet. Our interview at a coffee shop that morning would be the first time getting to know each other.

There was plenty of room on the 9:15 AM flight that morning, but a different problem arose. There was no plane. The departure time listed on the sign behind the agent's desk was changed to *Delayed* with no time listed. That wasn't good. How much of a delay? I overheard other passengers speculating. I overheard the gate agents talking. Something about snow and ice in Cedar Rapids. Or was it a mechanical issue with a plane? All of the above. Estimated departure was now 11:00. OK, I can still make it in time. The estimated departure was then updated to 1:15 PM. The flight was so late it was now overlapping with the second flight to Cedar Rapids, and I worried about passengers from that flight opting for my flight, taking my seat. I had that sinking, déjà vu feeling.

I sat tight because I didn't have any other option. I kept up hope that it would all work out. In the meantime, Barbara said she would wait for me. I apologetically kept her updated on my estimated departure time. Good things come to those who wait. At last, I made it onboard a flight to Cedar Rapids, Iowa. Once on the ground, I waited twenty-five minutes for my Uber to arrive to take me to Iowa City, a thirty-minute drive. I finally arrived at Java House, four hours late.

Java House was bustling with college students on this late Friday afternoon, so it wasn't hard to find

Barbara, a woman close to my age, seated at a high-top table by the espresso bar. She had a full head of wavy blonde hair and the easygoing countenance of someone you'd want to get to know.

"I finally made it!" I said, introducing myself. "I'm sorry to keep you waiting so long!"

"That's OK," Barbara said. "It gave me a chance to catch up on Twitter and Facebook."

A girl after my own heart. That's exactly what I would have been doing too.

"I checked the back room, but that's actually noisier," Barbara said. "Do you think it will be OK to record here?"

I looked around and assessed the sound level. The only thing that worried me was the espresso machine nearby, but frankly, we didn't have many options.

"Sure!" I replied. "Let's do it. The background noise will add some fun energy to the episode."

So, on our high-top table for two, I set up my portable recorder with two microphones and looked around to see if anyone noticed. I'm pretty sure we were the only ones recording a podcast episode at the Java House that day. Sitting as close to the wall as possible, Barbara and I took up our mics and leaned in towards each other conspiratorially as we recorded. It must have looked like a top-secret operation was in progress. But this intimacy made it easier for me to build a connection with Barbara as I interviewed her. We hit it off immediately and had fun with the interview. The coffeehouse ambience was magical.

Once again, I was fortunate to have a guest who just ran with the interview. All pressure was off me for content, and I just moved it along with quips and follow-up questions. Barbara painted a fascinating picture of what it was like to live in Iowa during the presidential primary season with easy access to all the candidates. She took the process seriously and made sure to meet as many candidates as she could during the lead up to the caucus. For some candidates, the lead up started a year and a half before. She latched onto Pete fairly early in the game after hearing him speak a couple of times.

Then we got to the nuts and bolts of the caucus, a primer of sorts, for those of us new to the process. What would it be like on Monday, February 3? As a precinct chair, Barbara was able to give insider information on how the precinct caucuses would be run. She wasn't the Pete precinct captain; she was in charge of the entire event for her precinct. I was in awe as she explained what she was responsible for and all the work that still needed to be done before February 3rd.

We finished the interview with the quintessential *Go Pete!* cheer. What a feeling of accomplishment—I finally had my *Iowa Caucus* episode! And it was *good*. I let Barbara listen to some of it so she could hear how it would sound. She seemed pleased.

As I packed up my recording equipment, Barbara and I talked about what to do next.

"I'm going to see if Kathryn can meet us for dinner," Barbara said as she texted.

"That would be great!" I replied.

"Do you want to see the campaign office?" Barbara asked. "It's near here."

"I'd love to!"

"Kathryn will meet us there," Barbara said, reading the text Kathryn had just sent her.

We left the Java House and walked the few short blocks to the Pete for America Iowa City field office, another selfie venue. It was my second Iowa campaign office so far in January, adding to Council Bluffs. Mason City would make it three. I met the Iowa City organizers who were busy with various tasks getting ready for the weekend of canvassing and witnessed Barbara in her element, as she sat at the front desk to check on something.

Kathryn, a perky older woman with a pixie haircut, soon arrived and joined us in the office.

"Hi, Kathryn!" I said. "Thank you for connecting me with Barbara. She was perfect for the interview!"

"I knew she would be," Kathryn replied, winking at Barbara.

"Where should we go for dinner?" Barbara asked.

I let Barbara and Kathryn brainstorm restaurant ideas since I had no idea what was what and where was where, but I did chime in with the fact that I was in the mood for a good burger.

Barbara and I got into Kathryn's car, and we headed to Big Grove Brewery in Eastside Iowa City. As one would expect for a Friday night, the vast brew pub was already bursting at the seams with cacophonous revelers when we arrived. We'd have to wait a long time for a table. The three of us looked at each other with similar expressions.

"Let's try somewhere else," Kathryn said.

We got back in the car and ended up at a much more suitable place, the polar opposite to the chaotic brewery—Short's Burgers Eastside. This neighborhood burger bar was quiet and cozy and had a booth just for us. Kathryn and Barbara sat opposite me, and I could tell that they had gotten to know each other over the past few months of volunteering. Both were retired from the world of academia—one a professor and one on the administrative side.

I wish I had a recording of our dinner conversation. I learned even more about what was happening on the ground for Pete in Iowa City and beyond from these two super volunteers. There was something about Pete Buttigieg that inspired people to give up all of their free time, and then some, to help him win the primary. The dedication was something I was seeing across the country in my interviews. Pete was special; he was a true servant leader with a balance between head and heart. And we needed someone like him right now.

On my flight back home early the next morning, I listened to the Barbara interview. The background noise wasn't too bad. At least I'd said something about the coffee shop at the beginning of the interview. *Surely, my listeners will be forgiving,* I thought. The episode wouldn't have many edits, so hopefully, Michael would be able to get it out early in the week so that people would have time to listen to it before the caucus the next Monday. The timing was tight.

I was scheduled to canvass in Mason City again the next weekend, the last chance before the caucus. But I was also being pulled in another direction—Des Moines. The Barnstormers were organizing a big canvassing event for the weekend and the Monday of caucus. Everyone was talking about being in Des Moines to help on Caucus Day, but unfortunately, I didn't have any personal days left to take time off. Technically, I could join the Barnstormers for the weekend canvassing in Des Moines, but I didn't want to let my Minnesota group down in Mason City. I was torn. Maybe, just maybe, I could do both.

At the last minute, I decided to drive down to Des Moines from Mason City on Saturday after I was done door knocking. There was a Barnstormers party, and I didn't want to miss it. There was also, coincidentally, a Pete rally there on Sunday, his last before the caucus. I would drive down to see my Barnstormer friends, stay the night, go to the rally the next day, and drive back home. Was I crazy? I kept wondering this throughout the entire 120-mile drive south. You see, I was doing this on my own.

The winter driving conditions would be good, something I made sure to check before leaving. I was more worried about getting sleepy while driving, which was starting to become a problem in my advanced years.

There would be no one to take the wheel if needed. I would just have to pull over.

I kept my mind occupied by repeatedly checking my trip progress on Google maps navigation. Although I wouldn't need directions for the 100-plus miles of I-35, I needed to know how to get on and off the freeway, so navigation was set. I kept glancing at the "time remaining" info and bargaining with myself to wait at least fifteen minutes before checking again. It worked to keep me alert and make me feel like I was indeed getting closer to Des Moines despite the unchanging landscape. I wondered if I increased my speed, would the time remaining decrease? My bored mind actually thought about the physics and mathematics involved in the calculation. My experiment showed that actual speed rather than the speed limit was being factored into the miles remaining to calculate estimated arrival time. *Fascinating.*

Once I saw signs for Ames, Iowa, I knew there would be enough roadside variety to keep me awake, so I quit playing my navigation game. At Ankeny, I knew I was on the outer fringes of the Des Moines area. When the freeway made a sharp curve towards the west, I knew I had to start paying attention or I'd be headed to Omaha rather than West Des Moines.

The Barnstormers base camp was at the Hampton Inn just across the freeway from where I was staying at the West Des Moines Marriott. I checked the time. If I headed straight to the Hampton Inn, I'd be able to catch someone at the Barnstormers welcome table. I needed to know where everyone was meeting for dinner.

I parked my car and stepped out into a surprisingly temperate climate. Had I really driven that far south? Or had the weather changed? Both. I took off my coat and threw it in the back seat. Two hours on the road had stiffened my joints, so I did a mini stretch before walking into the hotel.

What a relief to find the Barnstormer table just inside the door of the Hampton Inn. I didn't even have to look for it.

"Hello!" the greeter seated at the table said, cheerfully.

"Are you Julie?" I asked. I recognized her as *Buttons for Pete* on Twitter and the face of Barnstormers.

"Yes, I am!" she replied.

"I'm Sue Ann from Twitter," I said. "I'm staying at the Marriott across the way."

"Nice to meet you. I think I recognize you."

"Where is everyone going for dinner tonight?" I asked.

"Exile Brewery," Julie said, giving me a slip of paper with the address and time.

"Fun!" I put the paper in my pocket and looked around the lobby to see if there was anyone I knew. The crowd was sparse enough to indicate that people were regrouping, resting up for the brewery.

"Help yourself to any buttons or stickers," Julie offered, motioning to the display on the table.

What caught my eye, however, was a flyer about the next event in New Hampshire.

"What's the McIntyre-Shaheen Dinner?" I asked.

"That's like the Liberty and Justice Dinner, but for New Hampshire. All the candidates will be speaking."

"I think I might go to that," I said, checking the date in my mind.

"Great!" Julie replied. "Do you want to buy a ticket? I have a few tickets to sell."

"Yes!" I replied getting out my wallet. "That way I won't have to worry about getting one."

How fortuitous. If I hadn't driven down to Des Moines, I wouldn't have been able to score a ticket to the McIntyre-Shaheen Dinner in advance.

"See you at the Brewery," I said, getting ready to leave.

"For sure." Julie replied as she started packing up the table. The Welcome table was now closed. I'd gotten there just in time.

I got back in my car and drove over to the Marriott and checked in. After a short rest, it was time to head over to Exile Brewery. Instead of my usual Ubering on these trips, I was the one driving. I not only had to worry about directions, but I had to worry about parking, too. My GPS easily got me to 1514 Walnut Street in Des Moines proper. Had I been a local, I would have known the tricks to finding a parking space, but instead, I actually had to read the No Parking signs.

Walnut Street. That sounded familiar. Could it be that Pete's Rally for the Liberty and Justice dinner had taken place just ten blocks down, on Cowles Commons? Here I was three months later in a much different landscape, seasonally and politically. It was winter now, and Pete was poised to win the Iowa caucus, fingers crossed.

As I walked the two blocks to the brewery, I realized that I was nervous about walking into a crowd of people who had already been together canvassing, a little like a party crasher. Unlike my other trips, I wasn't meeting any one person in particular. I wouldn't have a buddy. Still, I knew I would recognize people from Twitter. And I certainly wasn't shy.

The lobby of Exile Brewery was absolutely packed with Barnstormers, the din of their exuberant chatter filling the small space. I fit right in with my Pete buttons as I stood in the crowd waiting for seating for our group of forty. I introduced myself to a few people and confirmed some Twitter identities. Everyone was having such fun just being together, I found myself wishing I could have participated in the entire Barnstormers weekend.

More and more people were coming in the door to join us, and among them was a familiar face. What a relief to see Paula from California.

"Paula!" I cried.

"Hi!" she replied.

"How is door knocking going?" I asked, knowing that she had taken time off work to canvass in Iowa.

"I'm exhausted," she replied. "I'm not going to stay long. We've got an early start tomorrow for canvassing."

"That's too bad you're not staying." I said regretting the loss of a buddy. "I understand." Her face soon disappeared in the crowd as the flow shifted.

Eventually, Julie moved mountains, and our group was shown to the private room upstairs. I joined a friendly table of eight where I felt more like an observer as I listened to the simultaneous conversations, adding my two cents whenever possible. Where was Sue Ann, the social butterfly?

Perhaps the reason for my diminished social nature that night was because I was exhausted. Two hours of driving to Mason City, door knocking, and then a two-hour drive to Des Moines had tuckered me out. And unfortunately, the microbrew I was drinking made me sleepy rather than gregarious. I still felt like I belonged, though, because with Team Pete, *belonging* was the most treasured rule of the road. I loved being part of the group, sharing a meal together.

Before leaving, I made sure to ask around to see who was going to Pete's rally the next day. A few were forgoing the rally so they could get more canvassing in. More were squeezing their door knocking in before and after the rally. I had great admiration for their commitment and felt a sense of shame that I wasn't doing the same.

"How early do you think we need to get there?" I asked someone.

"I have no idea. Maybe two hours before?"

"That's what I was thinking," I said. "Maybe I'll see you there!"

I left the brewery as the party started winding down and walked to my car, happy to see that I didn't have a parking ticket. I drove back to my hotel, eager for a good night's sleep.

Sunday morning, after a substantial breakfast meant to hold me for a while, I checked out of my hotel and made my way to Lincoln High School, fifteen minutes away. It was two hours before the event, and the parking lot was still fairly empty, so I felt good about my prospects as I walked through the school to get to the line. How could I know that a busload of high school students from out of state would get there before me? *No fair!* But then I calmed down and thought about it. Of course they should see Pete speak in person. Of course they should be in the front. I'd already seen him many times.

High school students sure know how to wait in line. They simply get settled on the floor in small conversation groups. It's no big deal. Sitting on the floor is a big deal if you have two artificial knees, though, so I preferred to stand. More and more people were joining the line behind me and within an hour, I could see a line forming outside. It seemed to go on for blocks. I had no idea how long the line inside the school was and where the outside line would join up. But one thing was certain: Mayor Pete was attracting a huge crowd at his final rally on the eve of the Iowa caucus.

The mood in line was festive, and I chatted with those around me, bonding over various political views. Reporters were strolling the hallway with cameras, interviewing people on what they thought about Pete. The reporters had to try a few people before finding an actual Iowan to interview, however. So many people had come from out of state for the rally, like me. Guilty as charged.

Just before the appointed hour, the volunteers opened the doors to the gym and let the line in. I quickly gathered up my coat and followed the students ahead of me, wondering if I would still be along the rope line. As we entered the gym, I noticed the students were bunching up to the center of the stage, rather than extending along the rope line. I knew how important it was to be on the rope line if you wanted to talk to Pete, even if it was on the far edge, so I was happy to get one of the last places on the right side, stage left for Pete.

Feet firmly planted in place, I looked across to the Pete cheering section behind the stage. I couldn't believe it. Directly across from me, along another rope line, were three very familiar faces: Laura O'Sullivan, my friend AJ, and Arielle Brandy, the Indiana State Organizer. The South Bend contingent was positively beaming. They noticed me too and waved. I snapped a pic and immediately shared it on Twitter. It was too perfect. More and more people were filing into the cheering section, many of them Iowa organizers and volunteers. I saw Paula amongst them and waved. I knew how much all of this meant to her. And to me.

From where I was standing, I had a great view of where Pete would be coming in. Wouldn't it be great if I got a close-up video of him entering to *High Hopes*? After a succession of introductory speeches, it was finally time. I had my phone ready. *But, what?* Don't tell me he was entering from stage right instead! Dang. By the time I noticed this, the jaunty guy had already jumped up on stage. I was at the exit, not the entrance. I felt ridiculous.

My strategy for being on the edge of the rope line wasn't the best for my line of sight. Standing behind the stage and off to the side offered a somewhat obstructed view, one mostly of Pete from behind. I wouldn't have minded this since I'd already seen many of Pete's speeches from the front, but the spotlight meant for Pete was aimed directly at me. The intensely glowing orb was sure to trigger a migraine if I kept looking in that direction. I tried to position myself behind a tall man in the crowd so his head would block the bright light. This worked, but then all I could see was the back of the man's head. At least I could still hear Pete. As I looked around the gymnasium, I could see a sea of people filling the room and then more in the balconies above. I gasped. *There are thousands of people here.*

At the end of his speech, Pete started greeting the audience along the rope line, joined by Chasten. I watched as Pete made his way down the line with Saralena taking selfies, as usual. What I thought would be a straightforward path down to my end turned into a zigzag as there was the rope line with the volunteers on the opposite side for him to greet as well. He darted back and forth between the lines as he was pulled to meet various people. I worried he would miss me. No, now he was back on my side, only one person away. I got ready to give him my good luck hug. Just then, Saralena saw me, and recognizing me from a prior rally, pulled Pete to the other rope line to give someone else a chance. I could have taken this personally, but to be fair, she was only doing her job of making sure Pete met as many people as possible. He'd already met me, and maybe I should give others a chance.

But that didn't mean I couldn't shake Chasten's hand. He was following Pete but sticking to my line. When he got to me I was quick to take a selfie, which I later regretted because I had been a little abrupt in getting his attention. Still, he was consistently cordial and friendly with each person he met, even the bossy lady at the end of the line. I imagined how tired he must have been and wished I had just let him be. After all, I already had one selfie with him from when he was in Minneapolis.

When Pete finished greeting supporters, he made his way to the exit. Now I could get my video. Pete turned around and humbly waved to the cheering crowd before disappearing behind the curtain. And I got it all. I got that final wave before the Iowa caucus.

It was over. I sighed as I gathered up my coat and followed the rest of the crowd through the hallways of the school out the back entrance to the parking lot. Walking to my car, I noticed some people gathered around a side entrance of the school with black SUVs parked outside, so I went over to investigate. It was obviously something akin to the stage door. The SUVs were waiting to take Pete to his hotel, just like a rock star.

The media stood in waiting, with reporters poised for one last question and photographers ready for one more photo.

At last, Pete and Chasten emerged from the building to the sound of applause and the snapping of cameras, making a beeline for the car. They waved at us and quickly got in the car. Then they were off. *Good luck tomorrow, Pete,* I thought as I watched the black SUV drive away.

The mood was definitely anticlimactic at this point, and there was nothing more to do but drive home, something I wasn't looking forward to. But since I wanted to drive as many miles as possible before it got dark, I knew I had to get on the road. No time for dillydallying.

I followed my GPS to get back onto northbound I-35, at which point it was clear sailing back to Minneapolis. Having missed lunch, I stopped at the Panera in Ankeny for sustenance before taking on the bulk of the journey. I was still in an emotional cocoon from the rally, finding it hard to detach, so I appreciated running into some other rally-goers as we stood in line to order. The retired couple was from Minnesota as well, on their way back home like me. I surveyed the seating area and wondered if anyone else had been at the rally.

I sat down and ate my autumn squash soup and half of my sandwich, saving the other half for the drive.

After making a pit stop in the ladies' room, I was ready to hit the road, but with trepidation. I had three and a half hours of driving ahead of me. What if I got sleepy? So before leaving Panera, I bought something sugary and chocolatey to take with me, just in case.

Back on the interstate, I knew the next 100 miles would feel very remote as I drove through rural Iowa. It was getting dark, and still winter, so I had my headlights on and the heat going. I felt a great sense of vulnerability on my own. In fact, I was downright scared. What if my car broke down? How long would it take to get help? Would I get hypothermia? What if I sleepily drifted off the road?

It was pitch black now, and I felt like I was driving through a tunnel. The glow of the headlights formed an arc that enclosed me in the darkness. I could only see as far as the lights shone in front of me. There was little other traffic—just me on the road. At this point, I remembered that my night vision wasn't all it should be. I strained to see the lane ahead of me. It was impossible for me to relax my mind because I had to give full attention to those white stripes. This was going to be a long drive home.

Music. Music saved me. I played every CD I had in my car, singing to every song to stay awake and focused on my lane. Taylor Swift was an especially kind companion as I played *Lover, 1989,* and *Reputation.* Adele's *21* and *25* switched things up, and then Queen energized me with the soundtrack to *Bohemian Rhapsody.* When I took out one of the CDs to start another, I noticed how warm the disc was. No, it was actually *hot.* Was this a problem? Was it OK to keep playing CDs while the heat was blasting?

At some point, I took a break from playing CDs to let the player cool down. With no music, I had time to think. As I reflected on the progress of my journey, I thought, *I'm going to make it. I'm really going to make it.* My fear shifted to pride as I felt a sense of accomplishment for making this trip on my own. I now relished this time alone, this time singing in the car. No companion would have put up with that much singing. And the darkness? Now, it was magical.

Once I passed the exit for Mason City, I had a frame of reference. From this point on, it would be as if I had just gone home after canvassing yesterday. But instead, I had taken a chance and gone the other direction to Des Moines. *It was worth it,* I thought. In twenty miles, I was at the Minnesota border, and although I still had over an hour and a half to go, at least I knew where I was. The succession of exits seemed to speed along now—Albert Lea, Owatonna, Faribault, Northfield. Soon I was in exurbia, then suburbia. Finally, I reached Minneapolis. *Home.*

On Monday morning, I went to school and taught my adult ESL class despite the distractions of the looming Iowa caucus. I thought of Paula and the Barnstormers spending the day canvassing, the precinct captains getting organized. And I thought of Barbara and her responsibilities as the chair for her precinct. I was vicariously nervous for her, for everyone. For Pete. I was almost too nervous to watch the results come in that evening. What time would we know?

As I was cooking dinner, I was mindful of the time. Caucusgoers were now assembling. I imagined all the Pete supporters gathering in their precincts across Iowa. I imagined all the Iowa organizers for the campaign keeping tabs on every precinct. After washing the dishes, I turned out the light in the kitchen and took my favorite spot on the futon in front of the TV to watch the results come in.

I don't recall ever being as nervous waiting for returns as I was this night. The stakes were high, and I was deeply invested in Pete's candidacy. Pete *had* to do well in the Iowa caucus to have a chance at winning the primary. If he didn't, it would signal insurmountable challenges to his viability.

The numbers were slow to come in. Something about some mix-ups with the new cell phone app they were using. There was great confusion as many precincts weren't able to submit their results on the app, thus overwhelming the phone-in center. I thought immediately of Barbara, wondering if she was having to deal with chaos.

"Do we know who won yet?" Steve asked, popping his head in the room.

"No. There's a problem with the app," I replied.

"Are you going to stay up?"

"Of course, I am. Is that a real question?"

"I'm going to bed," he said pragmatically.

As the night wore on, the delay in the results was so great that the candidates were starting to make their thank you speeches. Bernie's was fairly early in the evening. As he thanked his supporters, he said he was optimistic about the outcome. I could tell that Pete was waiting as long as he could to speak, just in case those numbers became clearer. Eventually Pete came out with his speech. It was a victory speech.

The venue was packed with supporters. I could see Laura, Arielle, and AJ again among the crowd standing in the first row of the risers behind the stage. This time, they were waving small American flags as *High Hopes* played, and Pete walked on stage. He looked so happy and proud. The crowd chanted and cheered wildly, almost not letting him start his speech. I immediately got a lump in my throat and had tears in my eyes.

"Thank you, Iowa!"

Cheers

"What a night! Because tonight, an improbable hope became an undeniable reality," Pete said.

Boot Edge Edge! Boot Edge Edge!

"So, we don't know *all* the results, but we know—by the time it's all said and done—Iowa, you have shocked the nation."

Cheers

"Because, by all indications, we are going on to New Hampshire VICTORIOUS."

Pete was doing an all-out victory speech even though the race hadn't been called. That's because based on the campaign's internal numbers, they knew Pete had won. And with the level of organization Pete for America had in Iowa and back at headquarters, I knew they were right. They didn't leave anything to chance.

Pete couldn't wait for the final results—he had to hop on a plane for New Hampshire. He had people to meet, places to go.

New Hampshire? What a coincidence. That's where I was going next.

18

New Hampshire

The best way to get to Manchester, New Hampshire is not to fly from Minneapolis to Boston and then take a very expensive Uber. As I was sitting in the back seat trying to enjoy the pastoral scenery between Massachusetts and New Hampshire, I couldn't help wondering how much this was going to cost. The first Uber driver I was matched with changed his mind once he calculated his round-trip driving time of one hour there and one hour back. When the second driver arrived, I made sure to confirm the plan. He was game.

I'd chosen to fly directly to Boston Logan rather than through Detroit to Manchester because trying to find a seat on *two* flights was riskier than making it on one. I had to get there on Friday so I could canvass the next morning before the McIntyre-Shaheen Dinner. Otherwise, why go? I searched the internet for transportation options between Boston Logan and Manchester, and I swear to God—I found a shuttle bus. But at Logan Airport ground transportation, no one knew what I was talking about. So, I called an Uber.

A hotel room in Manchester for the weekend of February 7–9 was a hot ticket. With the presidential primary debate on Friday night and the McIntyre-Shaheen Dinner on Saturday night, nearly every political reporter covering the Democratic primary was in town. As a result, I stayed at the Fairfield Inn just outside of town, near the Manchester airport. I would need to Uber into town for everything, and that meant I had to decide whether to take my recording equipment with me and carry it around all day.

Even though I'd probably be able to get some good interviews at the canvassing training the next morning, I planned not to take my recording equipment with me in the morning. I knew I wouldn't be able to handle carrying that heavy bag with my clipboard, house to house. No, I'd leave it at my hotel for my interview with Julie later that afternoon. I was eager to talk to her about how she started Buttons for Pete and had contacted her a few days before to line it up.

In the lead-up to the debate at Saint Anselm College that night, all the campaigns were "doing visibility" along the road to the entrance to the college. The Pete campaign planned for a strong showing, asking volunteers to come hold up signs. Sure, I could do that. Then I could head over to the Barnstormers debate watch party at Stark Brewing Company.

The weather was complicating things. It was raining. But since it was early February, it was a *cold* rain. I'd dressed for snow, not rain. I decided that I'd wait in the hotel until peak visibility time to join them along St. Anselm Drive. While waiting to leave, I scrolled through Twitter and saw photos of Pete organizers and volunteers already in place holding signs and chanting. *In the rain.* They were tougher than I was.

In the next hour, the temperature plummeted, and the rain turned to snow. Now I had the right outwear, even snow boots. I ordered my Uber, typing in "St. Anselm College" as my destination. It was 5:00 PM and already getting dark as my car pulled up. Once on St. Anselm Drive, we could see staffers and volunteers for the various campaigns lining up along both sides of the road for several blocks. I spotted the Pete group close to the St. Anselm College sign.

"Where do you want me to drop you off?" the driver asked, seeing that the entrance to the college was blocked off to unauthorized vehicles.

"Just pull over here at the entrance," I said, ready to jump out quickly. "Thank you!"

There was no sidewalk, so I walked on the trodden snow along the road towards the Pete group with my head down, fighting the cold damp wind. Oh, that's right. I'm in New England now.

"Hi! I'm here to hold signs," I said to someone I identified as being in a position of leadership.

"That's great!" he said with a smile. "Pick a sign."

At first, I tried two smaller signs, but I wasn't strong enough to hold them up against the wind. The conditions were brutal. One large sign worked much better for me. I took my place along the road amongst the other Pete volunteers and joined them in their chants to the cars driving past.

Boot Edge Edge! Boot Edge Edge!
Gooooo PETE!
Hey Hey! Hey Hey! Mayor Pete all the way!

After only fifteen minutes of holding my sign, my mittened hands were freezing, and my feet were doing the proverbial stomping to keep warm. My cheeks stung every time I faced the wind. I wondered what the wind chill was. Being from Minnesota, I should have been able to handle this, but we have *dry* cold, not *damp* cold. I looked around at all the Pete people there. Some of them had been out for hours. *How can they handle this?* I couldn't.

Maybe there was a coffee shop nearby where I could warm up. It wasn't likely, though, because this wooded residential setting wasn't anywhere near a commercial area. If I ordered an Uber, how would they be able to find me? *Surely, I can walk somewhere.* Not knowing my plan, but knowing I couldn't stand the cold anymore, I'm ashamed to say, I bailed on the visibility event. I hoped Pete would forgive me.

I gave my sign to a staffer and walked back to the entrance to the college where a continuous stream of cars filled with reporters and dignitaries were being admitted through the checkpoint.

"Is there a coffee shop nearby?" I sheepishly asked one of the traffic officers.

"They're all down the road," he said, gesturing several blocks eastward. "But I'm sure they're closed now."

"Thank you," I replied. "Sorry to bother you."

There has to be somewhere to go to get warm, I thought as I moved away from the traffic. *Maybe if I walk down this street, I'll eventually get somewhere.* It was better than standing still.

Perpendicular to St. Anselm Drive was College Road. I'd seen cars turn down this road. It must lead somewhere. I carefully crossed the street and started walking down College Road, down the hill. As I looked back at the college disappearing behind me, a strange sense of relief washed over me. I was free from standing still in the freezing cold and on my way to a place of warmth. But I was alone. Alone in the dark, in a seemingly remote area.

On my left was what must have been a wooded area—I couldn't see well enough to confirm—and to my right were dimly lit residential streets with suburban houses. As I walked, I looked down the road to see the streetlights planted at intervals too far apart for my liking on this dark night. I would have to walk fast. Luckily, this also kept me warm.

In the distance, I could see a major intersection, so I knew I would eventually reach civilization. I wondered how long it would take me to get there. Like my drive back from Des Moines, at some point, I knew I'd be OK. Once I knew this, I could relax. My walk had become a peaceful evening stroll. I looked up at the sky to see a few stars and a gibbous moon. I stopped to take in the quiet and appreciate it all.

My path became better illuminated as I approached Mast Road where there was a stoplight. I surveyed the area for a place to warm up. *Pizza.* It was like an oasis in the desert—Golden Acres Pizza Market. I couldn't ask for anything better, and it was right there. I didn't even have to cross the street.

"I'll have a slice of pepperoni pizza and a coke," I said decisively to the woman at the counter.

She knew I wasn't from around there, for whatever reason. Maybe it was my Minnesota accent, maybe my Minnesota down coat. I wondered if she could tell that I'd walked from St. Anselm's college, a half a mile away, and that I'd nearly frozen to death. It's all hyperbole now because in truth, it was only a fifteen-minute walk. Distances seem greater when you don't know where you're going.

I took my pizza and found a table. That first bite into the hot, cheesy slice was heaven. I stared down at the red and white checkered tablecloth as I wolfed the rest of it down, reaching an almost hypnotic state. As I gulped down my Coke, I immediately felt the magical effects of the caffeine and sugar. I felt rejuvenated enough to take on the next phase of my evening—the Barnstormers debate watch party.

The press should have been interviewing Uber and Lyft drivers that weekend in Manchester to get the pulse of the people during the primary. For me, it's very difficult to stay silent in an Uber if the driver is friendly.

"So, what brings you to Manchester?" he asked.

"The primary. I'm volunteering for the Pete Buttigieg campaign."

On my various Pete travels, I had talked to many Uber drivers—some had heard of Pete, some hadn't. In either case, I was doing relational organizing, and a little bit went a long way with an Uber driver, literally and figuratively.

"Stark Brewing Company," he announced as he pulled up to my destination.

"Hang in there this weekend," I said playfully, knowing that he'd be swamped with ride requests.

I walked into Stark Brewing and immediately caught a view of the brewing room behind glass, complete with huge tanks and paraphernalia I didn't understand. *Hmm . . . I wonder how all of that works . . . Now, where are the Barnstormers?*

The Barnstormers were hanging out at the bar.

"Hi Julie!" I said as I approached.

"Someone got our room," she said with disappointment. "We're waiting to see if they can get us in the smaller room."

There had been a mix-up in the reservation, and now the brewery was trying to rectify the situation. In the meantime, I ordered a beer and joined the others around the bar area. There weren't many familiar faces, but in conversations, I discovered some were Twitter friends.

Finally, we were shown into the small room on the other side of the brewing room. There was a large TV at the end of the room, already tuned to the pre-debate coverage, so we had all we needed. I ordered some food since one slice of pizza wasn't enough for dinner. But my stomach was already doing flip-flops worrying about how Pete would do in the debate. Not that I worried about his competence, it was more that I worried about what the other contenders were going to do to him now that he was the presumptive winner of the Iowa caucus. They weren't going to be easy on him.

I loved watching the debate surrounded by Pete supporters just a few miles away from the actual event taking place. Pete did well, but at the end, when there wasn't enough time for him to respond, Amy Klobuchar hit below the belt. She quoted only the first part of something he'd said during the week, but not the rest of the quote. The first part painted a negative scenario that the second part resolved. It was an unfair misrepresentation for Amy to state the first part only. I couldn't believe my senator would stoop that low. Everyone watching with me shared my disgust. Since it was near the end of the debate, Pete didn't have an opportunity to fully defend the accusation. It might have been water under the bridge, but Amy had come across as a strong debater. For the first time in the primary, she was a contender and would get a lot of press before the primary election here the following Tuesday. As a similarly moderate candidate, she would take away votes from Pete. And through dishonest means, in my opinion. Politics is not for the faint of heart.

The next morning, I arrived at the Manchester field office on Elm Street wearing my hand-knit Pete hat ready to knock on some doors. The small office was packed with volunteers and staffers at various stages of the training process. Volunteers from all over the country were entering in a steady stream and checking in at the front table where they'd be grouped for the next orientation session. As I waited, echoes of instructions from the various stations peppered the air among the hubbub of casual chatter. The energy within those four walls at that moment was electrifying. *We were going to win this thing.*

I eventually got to the last step in the training process where I was to establish my canvassing partner and get my list. I didn't have a partner. Nor did I have a car. I needed to find someone who had a car but no partner. My prospects were limited since most people arrived already paired up. Finally, a young man from Maine took me under his wing, just like Wes had in Council Bluffs. We picked up our lists and headed out the door to his car.

My new friend had driven from Maine that morning, a two-and-a-half-hour drive away. Why was I surprised to meet someone from Maine in New Hampshire? It was just like Minnesotans going to Iowa. Our canvassing territory was in a suburban area just outside of Manchester. As we drove, we shared our Minnesota/Maine backgrounds and our Pete campaign experiences. I loved hearing his *Why Pete?* story.

Once in the neighborhood, we each took one side of the street and off we went with our clipboards. The weather was partly sunny and in the mid-twenties, definitely manageable. As usual, most people weren't at home, but also as usual, I had some excellent conversations. It was mostly split between Pete, Bernie, and Amy, with a little bit of Warren and even less Biden. Pete had definitely impressed the primary voters, but because he was new on the scene, he was considered risky. If Pete came with a guarantee of beating Trump, it would be Pete all the way for the moderate voter in my estimation. Everyone I talked to liked Pete.

We finished our route in a couple of hours and drove back to the office where my Mainer would get another list to work on, and I, of course, would not. That's all the stamina I had. The office was still buzzing with activity when I turned in my list. Dodging the crowd of volunteers, I exited the building and planned my next step. Directly across Elm Street from the campaign office was the SNHU (Southern New Hampshire University) Arena, the venue for the McIntyre-Shaheen Dinner later that evening. I was so close, but way too early. Signs for the various candidates were already placed in abundance along the block in front of the arena, building the excitement.

I'd missed my morning latte, so I headed down Elm Street in search of a coffee shop. I knew I'd eventually find something. I just didn't know how far I'd have to walk. Most people would have simply Googled "Coffee near me," but I wanted to see where my feet took me.

How fun to explore, looking at the various storefronts until I found the perfect place: *The Bookery*, a bookstore cafe. When I first walked in the door, a display table with political memoirs greeted me, Pete's book front and center. I smiled at that prominent position.

The bookstore had an energy different from what I presumed was their usual Saturday. It was festive. I got my latte and a snack and found a comfy chair near an outlet to charge my phone. I eventually started chatting with the couple sitting on the sofa next to me.

"Where are you from?" I asked.

"Boston," the woman answered.

They had made the trip just to see if they could catch some of the candidates. It was a tradition for them. I imagined that there were probably many Bay Staters in town that weekend. As we talked, I learned who they were rooting for. She was for Pete; he was for Biden, the safe choice. They wouldn't get to cast those votes until Super Tuesday, though.

I let the Boston couple have their space and checked my phone for messages. Julie and I were trying to coordinate a time to meet for our interview back at my hotel. As with other canvassing weekends, I knew it would be tricky to fit in when there was real work to be done. And with Barnstormers in town, Julie was being pulled in many directions. In the end, we just couldn't make it work.

As I sat there, I reflected on the future of *Twitter Travels for Pete*. The pace of episodes had definitely slowed down, whether I liked it or not. The campaign was in hyper-drive now leading up to Super Tuesday. After the New Hampshire primary on Tuesday, Pete volunteers would be focused on text and phone banking for the Nevada caucus with some traveling for in person canvassing. Then it would be on to South Carolina. I could tell it wasn't the time for podcast interviews.

Since Julie couldn't meet me for an interview, there was no need to go back to my hotel. It would have been nice to get my recording equipment for the event, but I decided to save my energy and stay downtown. I had already recorded the Liberty and Justice Dinner; I didn't need to record the McIntyre- Shaheen Dinner too. But now I had time to kill. Since I didn't have one of those high-priced dinner tickets, an early dinner was just the thing to pass the time. I found a good burger at the *Thirsty Moose Taphouse,* right on Elm Street.

As I was enjoying my Rocky burger (cheddar, bacon, and BBQ sauce), I looked out the window and noticed more and more sidewalk traffic. It was still a couple of hours before the event would start, but the energy was already building. It was almost time for Pete volunteers to line up at the office to get their T-shirts and event tickets, so after I paid my bill, I headed back down Elm Street for the five-block walk.

The closer I got to the office, the more people joined me on the sidewalk, like an intricately choreographed dance number. At one point, I noticed a familiar face, and she noticed me too. It was Tracy, a Bay Stater, from Twitter. Knowing I was making the trip, she had reached out to see if I needed help with any of my arrangements, which I appreciated.

"Sue Ann!" Tracy called out.

"Tracy!" I replied with a hug. "At last, we meet."

"Were you canvassing today?" she asked.

"I just did a morning route," I said. "How about you?"

"All day. It's been crazy," she said. "I'm off to get my ticket now. Maybe I'll see you later."

Her group was walking much faster than I was, so I let them go ahead.

Eventually, I made it to the campaign office and joined the line outside to get a T-shirt. The Liberty and Justice Dinner in Des Moines had taught me the importance of having us all wear the same T-shirt. There was nothing like a sea of yellow in the stands to show the phenomenal support for Pete. And just like Iowa, the New Hampshire shirts were that same bright yellow.

"I already have a ticket," I said, once I got to the front of the line. "I just need a shirt."

"Awesome," the staffer said, handing me an extra-large so I could just throw it on over my sweater.

I walked to the intersection and waited to cross the street with the other Pete people. Everyone seemed to be in a hurry to get inside the arena, so when the light changed, the herd carried me all the way to the front door. I wouldn't have been able to walk that fast on my own. I chuckled to myself thinking about how I never went to sporting events or rock concerts, but in under four months, I'd been in two sports arenas. All because of Pete.

As we entered the arena and walked to our seating area, I looked around to see if I knew anyone, but surprisingly, there was no one I could buddy up with. I ran into Julie briefly, but she was on a mission at the moment and wasn't able to chat. I would continue to be on my own—not with Minnesota for Pete, not with Steve, just me. But I wasn't alone. I was with hundreds of Pete supporters wearing yellow shirts. *I still belonged.* And I knew I could strike up a conversation with any one of them.

I took a seat on the outer edge of the Pete section, on the aisle for easy bathroom and snack breaks. Across the aisle from me to the left, journalists were setting up in the area reserved for the media. When I glanced to my right, I could see a field of yellow shirts stretching out far and wide. I had no idea how many Pete people were there, but it was a lot of yellow. The SNHU Arena was a step down in size from the arena in Des Moines, but still large enough to get an impressive crowd.

The young man sitting next to me wasn't wearing a yellow shirt. He was undecided. He was undecided, yet he chose to sit with the yellow shirts. To me, that said something. He had come from New York for the event as it was the perfect opportunity to see all the candidates at once. After a few attempts to convince him that Pete was the one, I sensed that he preferred making up his own mind, so I left him alone. I did warn him, though, that it would soon become very noisy. Pete was the first candidate scheduled to speak.

Across the arena from the Pete section was the Bernie section, and already they were getting rowdy. Surely, they'd quiet down once the speaking program started, but unfortunately, I was wrong. After several speeches by New Hampshire party leaders, Pete was introduced. On cue, we all stood up and cheered at the top of our lungs.

Not long into Pete's speech, the Bernie section started heckling. It wasn't just a few bad apples; it seemed to be the whole basket. And it seemed to be a coordinated effort. I was in shock. *Really?* My eyes shot daggers across the arena with a message saying, *you think this is OK? Knock it off!* We started chanting to drown them out. I watched to see if Pete was getting thrown off by the taunts, but the accomplished speaker just increased his volume and talked over it. But I could tell he wasn't expecting this to happen *during* his speech. Oddly enough, the heckling wasn't noticeable on the broadcast version of the speech, so we must have done a good job chanting over it.

The Bernie section heckled a few other candidates, but only lightly. Nothing compared to what they did while Pete was speaking. That just meant that Pete was a threat. A huge threat. It seemed like this was a Pete/Bernie race now.

At the end of the event, I joined the throng of people exiting the arena. Once outside, I could see that it would be too chaotic for an Uber to pick me up there, so

I started walking down Elm Street to get away from the crowd. The police were out directing traffic as the sidewalks filled with people headed to their parked cars. Many side streets were blocked off in an effort to guide the traffic out of town. But that just added to the congestion, with cars moving at a snail's pace. At the time I didn't put two and two together that it was going to take a long time to get an Uber.

I stopped outside a restaurant a few blocks down from the arena and called my Uber. At least it would be clear where I would be waiting. The app said that it would be a twenty-minute wait. That was to be expected. I would just wait. Except it was dark, and the cold New England damp was setting in. It wasn't going to be a fun wait. But what worried me more was my phone was running out of battery. I had taken so many photos and videos during the event that I'd used up most of my battery life. I was kicking myself now for not paying closer attention to that.

I suddenly felt very vulnerable. I was able to call an Uber, but what if my battery died in the meantime? The indicator now showed red, the danger zone. How could I check on the status of my Uber? How could I see the driver's info? What if the Uber never came? How could I get back to my hotel? I was alone. Again, I was kicking myself. After twenty minutes, the app switched drivers on me. It was obviously chaos out there on the streets. I had a new driver now that I was waiting on. I tried to memorize the info before my battery died. And my battery did die. I prayed that the car would find me soon because I had no way to confirm or correct. If it weren't so cold, I would have been sweating bullets. Instead, I was shivering pellets.

Many cars passed me as they slowly made their way down Elm Street. My hopes were dashed as approaching headlights became passing taillights. At traffic breaks, I looked down at the oncoming cars waiting for the light to turn green and hoped one of them was my Uber. So many cars, and none of them were for me. Then, unexpectedly, a car made a turn from the side street and pulled up to the curb.

"Are you Sue Ann?" the driver asked.

"Yes!" I said as I hopped in.

"Sorry for the wait, but the traffic is crazy. There are so many blocked-off streets," he said.

"It's a busy night," I replied. But what I wanted to say was, *Thank God you got here because my phone died, and I can't call anyone else and I hope to God you know where my hotel is because the address is on my phone.*

"You're going to the Fairfield Inn at 860 S Porter St, right?"

"Yes."

Whew. He knew where to take me. Now I could finally relax. An hour after leaving the SNHU Arena, I was finally on my way back to my hotel. I was ready to go home.

On Tuesday night, I sat in front of my TV and watched the results of the New Hampshire primary come in. It was neck-and-neck between Pete and Bernie, just like the Iowa caucus had been. In the end Bernie had a clear win with Pete coming in a close second. Amy Klobuchar had, in fact, received a boost from the debate; she came in third. We will never know how many of those votes would have gone to Pete. Nor will we ever know if a clear win in Iowa would have catapulted him to a win in New Hampshire. But it was clear there had been some sort of effect on both counts. Whether Pete should have won or could have won New Hampshire was a moot point now. The reality of the race was that Pete had to do well in Nevada and South Carolina. But I wouldn't be able to help in those states. I'd be staying in Minnesota to prepare for Super Tuesday.

19

Minnesota Super Tuesday Prep

Back in Minneapolis, I was reconnecting with my Minnesota for Pete group. In addition to text banking for Nevada, we were all steam ahead for Super Tuesday. We now had two Pete for America staffers assigned to our state, Kevin and Nate. They probably didn't know what hit them when they jumped into the robust team of grassroots organizers here. Gina, Lisa, Katie, Irish Katie, Karen, and so many others had kept the wheels oiled in preparation for this moment. And what better time for another Minnesota episode? I had started *Twitter Travels for Pete* back in October with the "Home Base" episode. How fitting to circle back now on what Minnesota for Pete was doing to prepare for the big day on March 3rd.

The big rally to kick off early voting was coming up on Saturday, February 22, so I sat down with Gina earlier that week to talk about plans. We met at a Starbucks near her office during her lunch hour and found a spot to record, complete with barista background noise. I'd loosened up about recording conditions in the past few months, and that made me feel like a real pro. Gina was an easy interview because I didn't have to worry about anything. She would tell me everything we needed to talk about. Frankly, I'd been traveling so much I'd lost track of it all. It was so much fun to see Gina again and catch up.

Gina was ready with all the stats on what Minnesota for Pete had been doing—grassroots by the numbers, so to speak. I don't know how she had them all off the top of her head, but let it be known that I was a witness to the fact that she wasn't using notes. So much was going on to spread the word about Pete all over Minnesota. Yard signs from Iowa had been picked up and were now being distributed throughout the state. It would be the first time Minnesotans would be putting up campaign signs in the snow, which amused me. Yard signs ahead of an election were always a sign of fall in my mind, but now that Minnesota had shifted to a presidential primary election in lieu of the usual caucus, signs would be out in the snow. Gina and I finished the interview with talk about plans for the rally on Saturday. I would be able to catch some more interviews there and make this a compilation episode.

That Saturday morning, I donned my favorite Pete shirt—the gray and navy baseball tee—and headed out the door with my recording equipment. After the short drive downtown, I needed twice as much time to park and walk to the office building where the rally was being held. I had forgotten about the Farmer's Market effect. Not wanting to miss the start of the program, I walked so quickly I was out of breath as I made it to the door of the building. What a happy sight to see Elise there as the greeter.

"Hi Elise!" I said, panting. "Has it started yet?"

"No, I think they're still waiting on people." she replied.

"Great."

"I think they have doughnuts," Elise teased. "Get me one if there are any left."

"Yum. I'll try," I said as I started up the grand staircase to the main gathering area in the atrium.

I could see why this building had been chosen for the venue. With views overlooking the river, the spacious atrium was gorgeous. The warmth of the woodwork combined with contemporary furnishings made for a welcoming ambience, and the addition of Pete signs, banners, and balloons made it festive, especially with the ebullient energy of the volunteers assembling.

I bypassed the line at the sign-in table with plans to go back later and started chatting with people.

"Hi Tricia!" I cried as soon as I saw her standing off to the side with David.

"Hi Sue Ann," she replied as we hugged. It had been a while since we'd seen each other.

"Did you come early to help set up?"

"Yes, we did."

At that point, I noticed the boxes of doughnuts set off to the side, apparently for the set-up crew, not for general consumption. But there were a lot of doughnuts left over. Just sitting there. And they shouldn't go to waste, right?

"Is it OK if I have a doughnut?" I asked.

"Go ahead," she replied, gesturing to the box.

I took an apple fritter and continued my conversation with Tricia, catching up on all we'd been doing for the campaign. I forgot all about getting a doughnut for Elise. I hoped to God she would be able to score one later because the program was about to begin.

Nate and Kevin kicked it off followed by several other speakers endorsing Pete. We were fired-up and feeling bolstered by Pete's showing in the first two states—a win and second place. Winning Super Tuesday was in sight. Everyone was so excited about canvassing and phone banking. It seemed that it was just a matter of making contact with as many people as possible before March 3. And now that early voting had started, we needed to get as many people to vote early. There's nothing like an "I voted early" sticker to bring awareness.

After picking up info sheets on early voting, the crowd dispersed to join either the policy conversations upstairs or the canvassing training session downstairs, with some going directly to vote. My plan was to wait until the training was over—I already knew how to use the MiniVAN app—and then catch some interviews with people before they headed out. And then maybe I'd go vote if it wasn't too late. In the meantime, there was no casual chit-chat to be had. The event was over, and the cleanup had already begun.

Kevin and Nate had started moving furniture back in place and were taking down signs. I offered my help since it was the least I could do after taking a doughnut earlier. But in my cleaning up, I encountered those doughnut boxes again. There were still a few extras in each box. Too bad Elise had already left. Of course I took another one—a chocolate-frosted doughnut this time—but what to do with the rest? I put them all in one box and carried the box around, cigarette girl style, looking for takers. No such luck. Everyone had apparently maxed out on doughnuts already. So, instead of throwing the doughnuts away, I gave them to the building security guard. I made his day.

I gathered up my coat and tote bag and walked down the open staircase to the entrance level below. At the bottom of the steps was a swank, glassed-in conference room where the canvassing training was taking place. I peeked in the window to assess the status of instruction. A fairly large group of volunteers was squished together around the large conference table with Irish Katie at the head conducting the training. It was definitely still in progress, so I'd have to wait a little longer to catch people leaving.

Not wanting to miss the moment when it came, I took out my recorder and plugged in one of the mics. I wanted to be ready to record as soon as the door to the meeting room opened. But I was nervous. Even though I was already a seasoned podcast host, I wasn't used to impromptu interviews. Everything up until now had been scheduled. People were expecting to be interviewed and were prepared. Now I was going to pounce on unsuspecting volunteers, and that made me self-conscious.

The door opened and volunteers began filing out. I noticed Stephanie and Jeff huddled together with Mary, another volunteer. They were looking at the MiniVAN app on their phones planning their attack. I approached them with my recorder and microphone, very much looking like a reporter on the street.

"Are you guys going out canvassing now?" I asked.

"Just for a couple of hours," said Stephanie.

"Can I do a quick interview for my podcast before you go?" I asked the three of them.

"Sure," said Jeff.

I got down to business and started the interview right there, standing in the foyer of the office building. Using one microphone, I passed it around as I asked them questions. First, we talked about plans for canvassing, and then I got to the *Why Pete?* question, my favorite question. Mixed in with the more common answers was something unique to each individual.

Mary, who'd been involved in politics for years, said that Pete was probably the most authentic, compassionate, empathetic politician she'd ever known. "He is a wonderful human being," she said.

"He is the opposite of so much of what is ugly in our world and society right now," added Stephanie, a second-grade teacher. "He truly just gives me hope."

"He's inspiring people to get involved who haven't been involved before," said Jeff, who was seasoned in

Minnesota politics. "The best leaders are the best listeners, and he's by far the best listener."

This was the most succinct interview I'd done thus far, coming in just under five minutes, and just what I wanted. I captured the energy of the moment just before they headed out door knocking.

I looked around for other people to interview. Most people were on the move, but I noticed two men sitting on the bench by the waterfall feature, talking about their door knocking plans.

I hadn't met Philip or JD before today, nor had they met each other. And now they were going out canvassing together. Minnesota for Pete was continually bringing people together like this. When I asked if I could interview them, they both welcomed the opportunity to talk about our favorite candidate.

From a small conservative town in Minnesota, JD felt that Pete appealed to people back home like none of the other candidates did with his message of inclusivity. Philip talked about how Pete was the right person at the right time now when the country needed healing. He talked about the importance of welcoming what Pete referred to as "future former Republicans" to vote for him. As a member of the LGBTQ community, JD felt it was inspiring to see people who had condemned his sexual orientation during the Bush era now were supporting Pete, a viable candidate. We all agreed that Pete had the same calming effect as the waterfall feature next to us, which could be heard in the recording.

I caught one more interview before I left. It was with Emily, a young woman who had been at many of the Caffe Bene meet-ups over the summer. As a mother of two young children, Emily saw how Pete could truly make a difference in her children's future. It was a fantastic interview. But you won't hear it. Not even I heard it because I had done the unthinkable: I failed to press Record. I had been pushing different buttons on my recorder to listen back to the other interviews and to move to the next file, and in my hasty start of the interview, I pressed the wrong button. But of course I didn't know this until later. I was mortified. I'd committed the first sin of podcasting. I contacted Emily right away. We tried to set up another time to record, but our schedules didn't jibe. I had to release the episode without her contribution.

With my interviews finished, I packed up my recording equipment and walked back to my car. I looked at my watch and saw that I still had time to vote, so I headed north on I-35W to the early voting center on East Hennepin Avenue. This was the first Saturday of early voting. I wondered if it would be crowded, if I'd have to stand in line.

As I walked from my parking space to the building entrance, I could see several people standing outside as if they were waiting for someone to arrive or for someone to leave. They were checking their phones and casually chatting. A few had cameras. Were they reporters covering early voting? They didn't seem to want to interview me because I walked right past them undetected.

There was essentially no line, and after the initial step at the front desk, I took a seat at a table to complete my voter information. I glanced out the window and immediately knew why the press had gathered outside. There was Amy Klobuchar in her iconic harvest-gold coat doing a media interview. She had just voted early. Unbeknownst to me, we'd crossed paths near the check-in desk. I couldn't believe the timing. My vote for Pete Buttigieg was going into the same ballot box as Amy Klobuchar's vote for herself.

As soon as I got back to my car, I tweeted about my early voting experience, complete with an Amy sighting. In my scrolling, I noticed tweets on the Nevada caucus. I swear to God, I knew it was Nevada caucus day when I woke up in the morning, but I'd been so focused on doing my interviews that it completely slipped my mind. And now early numbers were coming in. Nothing was conclusive at this point because early voting had to be incorporated into the in-person voting numbers. I didn't understand how they could do early caucus voting and how that would work in the ranking of candidates.

There was confusion over how to count these early votes—should they go in with the in-person votes and thus affect viability, or go in after viability was determined? From what I heard in news reports, it sounded like the method chosen by the party wasn't being consistently followed, and that might have favored one candidate over another. It was a little like the Iowa caucus all over again.

In the end, Bernie Sanders pulled ahead with a clear win. Biden, who up until now was off the radar, came in second. Pete was third. Unfortunately, we'll never know for sure if the confusion on caucus procedure lost votes for Pete, but the difference probably wouldn't have been enough to overtake Bernie. What did the results tell us? Joe Biden was now a contender, especially going into South Carolina, where he had a toehold. It also told us that Bernie was on track to win the nomination with his consistent performance. I was starting to worry.

The pundits were saying the reason Bernie was doing so well was because the progressive wing of the party had chosen their candidate and was rallying around him. The moderates had not. Their vote was being split between Pete Buttigieg, Joe Biden, and Amy Klobuchar. Even my math-challenged brain knew how that was going to play out, especially with the Michael Bloomberg wild card in the mix.

I started to mentally prepare myself for the possibility that Pete might have to drop out of the race after Super Tuesday. He wasn't the type of person to hang on longer than his candidacy was viable. I knew I had to be realistic, but that didn't mean I had to like it. At least I had ten days to prepare myself. Until then, there was still a chance he could win the nomination, which made everyone work even harder on phone banking and canvassing.

The Saturday before Super Tuesday, I was out door-knocking with Minnesota for Pete friends just as the South Carolina primary was underway. How strange it was to be talking to folks under a set of assumptions that might change by the end of the day. We could all feel it.

That evening the results trickled in as usual, and it was unclear how Pete was doing. But in the end, Joe Biden had a resounding win. Bernie took a modest second. Tom Steyer, who had invested a lot of campaign dollars in the state, took third. Pete came in fourth. Biden had proven he could win the African American vote, something the pundits questioned Pete could do.

How was this going to play out now? Bernie and Biden were in it for the long haul. But what about Pete? The nomination wasn't going to be a quick win. Maybe it would go all the way to the convention. Maybe even a brokered convention. I was starting to get a sinking feeling.

20

Doing the Right Thing

On March 1, the day after the South Carolina primary, Pete suspended his campaign. I was shocked. *Blindsided*, more like it. It wasn't supposed to happen yet. I was preparing myself for after Super Tuesday, if it had to happen. Not before. This was absolutely devastating. When I heard the news after getting home from canvassing that day, I fell into a stupor I couldn't shake. I knew I couldn't handle meeting my Minnesota friends at a bar to watch Pete's speech later that evening. Instead, I watched the speech at home, by myself, with an awful feeling in the pit of my stomach.

Pete had returned to South Bend to address a crowd of supporters at the Century Center, a place I'd walked through a few times. A familiar place with some familiar faces in the crowd as well. I could only imagine the heartbreak my South Bend friends were experiencing at that moment.

Chasten introduced Pete with a heartrending and tearful speech that also brought me to tears. Then Pete took the stage for his most difficult speech of the campaign, the one ending it. Yet, he handled it beautifully. Amidst his deep disappointment that things hadn't turned out differently, the focus of his speech was to thank everyone for supporting his candidacy, for all of the hard work. And then he thanked South Bend for welcoming him home. He and Chasten were home now.

I didn't sleep well that night. In fact, I don't think I slept at all. The next day at school, my brain was in a fog, and my emotions were still raw. Many of my teaching colleagues approached me with their condolences since they knew how active I'd been on the campaign.

"Sue Ann!" they said. "I heard that Pete dropped out."

"Yeah," I replied dejectedly. "I didn't sleep last night."

"I'm so sorry. I really liked him."

Yes, everyone liked Pete. And they were as shocked as I was that he'd suspended his campaign before Super Tuesday. But then it all started to make sense. *Pete was doing the right thing.* He had made the difficult decision to step aside now when many others in his place would have let it play out. Why? *Integrity.* The very quality that made us fall in love with Pete also meant he wasn't going to stay in a race he didn't have a chance to win. And if he stayed in the race any longer, it might have jeopardized a Democratic win in November.

With the moderate vote being split between candidates, Bernie Sanders had most of the progressive vote and was well on the path to winning the nomination. But it was widely thought that Bernie's

Democratic Socialist policy positions would cost him the election. Trump would win. By getting out of the race before Super Tuesday, Pete signaled the consolidation of the moderate vote around Biden while there was still time for Biden to win the nomination. And Biden could win in November.

Some said Pete fell on his sword, took one for the team. I believe that was true. How else do you explain dropping out only days after attracting 10,000 people at his rally in Arlington, Virginia? I'm sure he would have loved to see those Super Tuesday numbers come in. But Pete had a way of seeing the long view, ironically another thing that drew us to him. The long view was a Democrat in the White House.

The Democratic presidential primary landscape then quickly shifted as Pete formally endorsed Biden that night at an event in Dallas. It was bittersweet seeing him onstage with Joe. They shared many of the same ideals and had the same level of integrity. With the age difference, they looked like father and son. Joe even commented that Pete reminded him of his late son, Beau. If Pete had to throw his support to another candidate, Joe was the one. Pete and Joe did a short video saying they were working together now. Team Pete would transfer our support to Biden. *Because that's what Pete wanted.*

The next day was Super Tuesday already, and I didn't know what to do with myself. I had been planning on doing visibility for Pete—holding up signs over the freeway—but no need for that now. Those signs would still be in my trunk months later. I didn't need to go vote because I'd already voted early. *For Pete.* Nothing to do but go about my day as usual until the results came in.

Before Pete dropped out of the race, Minnesota for Pete had booked space for Super Tuesday at the 508 Restaurant downtown to watch the election results. Kevin suggested that we keep the reservation and still get together. I wouldn't have been able to handle that two days earlier, but now I was ready. In fact, I was eager to see the numbers come in for Biden, knowing so many of them would be because of Pete. Following Pete's lead, Amy Klobuchar had dropped of the race and endorsed Joe as well, so Biden was slated to do well in the state.

"Tricia!" I cried as we greeted each other with a hug.

"This is hard," she replied. "But I knew he was going to drop."

"You did?"

"Yeah, I could just feel it, especially after South Carolina."

I don't know if detecting it earlier made it easier for Tricia or not. It lessened the shock, but I'm assuming it didn't lessen the disappointment, the sadness. Seeing Tricia, my Iowa travel buddy, at the 508 that night helped bring my Pete campaign involvement full circle. The same for seeing Gina and Lisa, who were both there as well. I'd gotten to know them working on the campaign and shared many special memories. I was in awe of their immense contribution of time and effort for Minnesota for Pete. This was the night to celebrate accomplishments rather than to focus on defeat, especially since we would be instrumental in sealing up a win for Biden.

The mood was festive as we watched the Super Tuesday results pour in from around the country. Biden was doing well. Biden won Minnesota with Bernie coming in a strong second. If Pete and Amy hadn't dropped out, Bernie would have won Minnesota. All in all, Biden won ten states on Super Tuesday; Bernie won four. Biden now had an overwhelming lead in total delegate count. Boom! The Pete Effect.

The next day, an email went out from the Pete campaign to all donors and volunteers , thanking us for our support and inviting us to join an audio call with Pete that evening. I was eager to hear from him in person but knew it would be bittersweet.

Mike Schmuhl, his Campaign Manager, started out the call and then quickly handed it over to Pete. It was heartbreaking to hear Pete's voice just three days after he'd suspended his campaign. I could only imagine the emotions he was feeling. But he gave none of that away as he earnestly thanked us for all of our hard work on the campaign.

Pete also talked about how this was just the beginning. That it was always much more than putting him in the White House. It was about *Winning the Era,* his signature slogan. He didn't know exactly what form that would take, but he said he would still need our help.

The community we had built should stay together. After Pete left the call, the staffers ended it with "Talk to you soon!"

So, it wasn't over? We would still get to work with Pete? I wondered what form this would take. A political action committee (PAC) or non-profit organization, perhaps. We were all dying to know what it was going to be and when we would find out.

Those weeks of not knowing were excruciating. Team Pete Twitter was in a state of mourning. I was starting to process my own emotions and come to acceptance only to witness the emotional pain of my friends. South Benders were especially hit hard. In fact, many tweeted, "Don't ask us how we feel. WE ARE DEVASTATED." Similar messages were tweeted by Pete for America staffers, some of whom I'd met. "Don't ask us how we're doing . . . " They had worked so hard and achieved so much, and suddenly, it was over. They were going to miss each other. The rank-and-file were distraught as well. So many of us had devoted our free time to working on Pete's campaign for the past several months. We felt un-moored without our ship's captain. *What do we do now?*

In my observation, I noticed that supporters handled their grief in one of three ways. One group headed for the lifeboats saying it was too painful to stay, some of them to return later after their wounds healed. But a second group remained and took the helm in Pete's place, re-forming Pete groups and starting new organizations. The Barnstormers for Pete group became *Barnstormers for America*; Kristi started *Building Bridges*, an organization promoting grassroots organizing, with many joining her. A larger third group stayed on the deck of the ship for the community we'd developed and to support Pete in his future endeavors. That was my group, and we started using #TeamPeteForever as our hashtag.

Three weeks after that call with Pete, I got an email announcing Pete's PAC, *Win the Era*. At last. But something else had been brewing during those three weeks—a novel virus. On March 11, the World Health Organization declared a global pandemic for COVID-19. The only frame of reference I had for a pandemic was the H1N1 pandemic in 2009, which had little impact on my life, so I took the term *pandemic* with a grain of salt. But something was different about this one. Things were changing fast. For the March 10 primary elections, neither Bernie, nor Biden—who had won five out of the six states—held rallies. That was jaw-dropping. So, no more rallies were going to be held?

Studio audiences were being cut from various shows, including *Jimmy Kimmel Live* that Thursday night when Pete guest hosted. The studio audience had been cut just the night before, but since a group of Pete supporters had driven all the way from San Diego, they were allowed to be seated in the audience, but spaced out. Pete excelled in his role as guest host, but the camera shots of the audience members scattered six feet apart was sobering and an indication of what was about to become the new normal.

The walls were closing in. Companies were exploring "working from home" options and schools were headed towards distance learning. Steve moved to his home office that next Monday. My last day of in-person teaching was Tuesday. Restaurants had shifted to takeout only; movie theaters were shut down. Governor Walz declared a "Stay Home Minnesota" order for all except essential services on March 27. *What was happening?*

It was then that I realized Pete had dodged a bullet. If he were still in the race, how could he have won over voters with no rallies? When people met Pete in person they were sold, but many who hadn't met him were reluctant to take a chance on someone new. And even if he'd won the nomination, it would have been difficult to sell himself to voters all over the country as a relative newcomer on video only. No glad-handing, no conversations, no meet-and-greets. This wasn't his time. I felt sure of it.

Back on the ship, I said that I was in the third group, the one there for community. But I was also in the second group, the one that was rebranding. You see, I couldn't bear to see the end of my podcast. I loved it too much. In mid-March, I had a new idea and texted Michael about it.

"Hi Michael—Heads-up. I'd like to talk to you on Monday or Tuesday about doing a new podcast with remote guests, something about the Rules of the Road," I texted.

"Sounds good!" he replied. I loved how Michael was always up for a new adventure.

And so, *Twitter Travels — Rules of the Road* was born.

21

The Rules of the Road

At first, I had no idea what I was going to do with the Rules of the Road podcast. I just knew the rules were important to cover. But *how* to cover them was still in the developmental stage. My local Twitter friend April helped me sort it out at lunch one Saturday before we went to a matinee, the last one before shutdown.

"I've got news," I said while we were waiting for our food. "I'm going to do a new podcast series on the Rules of the Road."

"That sounds like a good idea," April replied.

"Except I don't really know how to structure it. There are ten rules. Do I do ten episodes?"

"You could take two at a time . . ." she suggested.

I had honestly not thought of this possibility. Sometimes you just have to talk about your project and let others think of things you should have thought about yourself but couldn't have because of all the clutter in your mind. Taking the Rules of the Road two at a time would create a five-episode series, much more manageable than ten. And since some of the rules were more challenging to discuss than others, I didn't have to worry about filling time in a stand-alone episode. With two rules each time, odds were there would be plenty to talk about. But who would I interview?

This was my opportunity to interview Team Pete Twitter friends I had wanted to interview in the first round during the campaign. I started putting feelers out there for potential guests. *Respect and Belonging* would be the first episode and I wanted to interview Paula for that one. Paula and I had developed a friendship as we commiserated with each other on the suspension of Pete's campaign, helping each other grieve. When I was down, she lifted me up; when she was suffering, I tried to comfort her. From our conversations, I knew she would be able to discuss *Respect* and *Belonging* with great depth, exactly what I was looking for.

Now I needed to find some structure for the discussion. Why not start with the descriptions used by the campaign? Yes! We could parse out the definition for each rule and talk about the various aspects mentioned. It was the easiest way to do it and allowed for uniformity among the episodes. This easy way out was actually the best way to do it because the definitions covered angles I'd never thought of. In fact, I hadn't really examined the descriptions before.

Respect, Belonging, Truth, Teamwork, Boldness, Responsibility, Substance, Discipline, Excellence, and Joy. I knew what those words meant. But I didn't understand the fuller meaning until I examined them with my guests. And that was the beauty of doing this podcast series. Although my guests and I couldn't always answer the question "What did Pete mean by this?" we had our own interpretation to contribute.

Rebranding my original *Twitter Travels for Pete* podcast to a post-campaign Rules of the Road series of episodes was something I carefully considered. I didn't want it to look like I was still campaigning for Pete, like I hadn't accepted reality. Yet, I wanted to honor Pete's legacy. Yes, that's how I'd position it—the Rules of the Road as Pete's legacy and how they apply to everything we do in life, personally and professionally. I switched out the album photo of me with Pete at the Iowa State Fair for one of me wearing my Rules of the Road T-shirt. I recorded a new intro and outro with new music. I renamed the podcast *Twitter Travels,* removing "for Pete." I would try *not* to talk about Pete and the campaign. That was easier said than done, however, since my guests couldn't help themselves. I soon relaxed my own rule and let the episodes take on a life of their own, and in hindsight, I could have kept the "Pete" in the name.

Remote online recording would be new to me. Michael recommended Zencastr to record the two tracks, but I'd supplement by recording my own track on my recorder, as well. "We want the best sound for you because you're the host," Michael said. I would need to use plug-in headphones for Zencastr, but I would be speaking into my handheld microphone connected to my H6 recorder. I would invite my guest with a link via email, and they would connect wearing headphones. We would be able to talk to each other just like a phone call until I was ready to push Record. At this time, Zencastr was audio recording only, so we didn't have to worry about video comfort level. It would just be a conversation between friends who lived miles apart. And Paula lived 2000 miles away from me in California.

It seemed as though all of the Rules of the Road were interrelated and interdependent, so for each episode, I challenged my guests to find a way that the two rules were related. In the *Respect and Belonging* episode, Paula and I found that the first two rules were inextricably intertwined. If you didn't respect someone, they would never feel like they belonged.

Lauren, *Grandmas for Pete*, joined me for the *Truth and Teamwork* episode, and we found that those two rules tied together because truth is essential for good teamwork.

My guest for the *Boldness and Responsibility* episode was Cleo, a Team Pete Twitter friend from North Carolina I hadn't met in person. We determined that the two rules were directly connected in that we have a responsibility to be bold.

Kristi from the Northern Virginia group joined me for the *Substance and Discipline* episode. Since the campaign's description of discipline centered on the stewardship of resources, we tied the two rules together by saying you owe it to donors to be disciplined about substance.

Verity, from the New York group, was my guest for the last two rules, *Excellence and Joy*. In her newsletter for Team Pete alumni, Verity had been exhibiting excellence and joy herself. When asked how the two rules were related, she said that joy provides our mind with necessary fuel for excellence.

All five episodes came out in quick succession— nearly one a week, over a six-week period. We were in the height of the coronavirus lockdown, so it was easy to schedule my guests. No one had anywhere to go. But that also meant it was a life saver for me, and I hope for my guests as well.

April 2020 was scary. We knew how deadly the virus was because we were seeing news reports of how hard New York City was being hit. There was a shortage of supplies, no masks to be had. All non-essential businesses were closed. We didn't know how long the social isolation would last. Doing my podcast interviews and working with Michael helped distract me and stay connected to people. It gave me energy. And because people were staying home, they had time to listen to podcasts as well. I hoped the Rules of the Road episodes uplifted them.

I loved exploring Pete's Rules of the Road in depth with my guests. Since we all had been deeply involved in the campaign, the discussions offered a way to process our time working for Pete, a much-needed debriefing of sorts. But I still wasn't ready to move on. I wanted to continue to do podcasts. I'd already covered the Rules of the Road themselves, why not interview some staffers and ask about how the Rules affected their work?

Nina Smith, Pete's Traveling Press Secretary, was kind enough to accept my invitation for an interview. Now that I had a high-profile guest coming on, I felt I was in a whole new ballgame. And that made me nervous. But as I went on to interview Samantha Steelman, the Marathon States Organizing Director, and Garret Brubaker, Video Post Production Manager and Editor, I could see that they all welcomed the opportunity to talk about the campaign.

Nina was the first to refer to the team beyond professional relationships. They were a family. And the grassroots organizers were part of the community along with them. I asked them all what their favorite Rule of the Road was. For Nina it was *Joy*—you needed joy to get through the tough days. Samantha said that Discipline and Responsibility were her favorites. Since *Joy* was a given, Garret said *Substance* was his favorite Rule of the Road.

Then I contacted Laura O'Sullivan to see if she'd be willing to talk about her experience as Pete's Chief of Staff in the mayor's office in South Bend as well as her stint working on the campaign. I was elated she was game. I thought back to my limited interactions with Laura over the past year, which had progressed from my initial handwritten note of goodwill to a quick handshake at PEGGS to a brief conversation at the *Good Guy Pete* podcast live recording. Now, we'd finally have a longer conversation. Laura was a delightful guest, full of stories of South Bend. I knew my listeners would love this episode. Not surprisingly, *Joy* was her favorite Rule of the Road.

As the summer progressed, quarantining lessened as people could gather outside with social distancing, which was a relief. We were getting used to the new normal. I was off teaching for the summer and still had a few more podcast interviews in mind before closing down shop. I thought about one of the things that brought us *Joy*—the Pete Mosaic. I still didn't know all the details on how Nicola accomplished the huge project of compiling hundreds of grassroots photographs to form a mosaic of Pete's face. If I was curious, other people on Team Pete must be curious as well, I thought. Plus, Nicola and I had hit it off so well when we met up in London I was dying to talk to her again. So, in early August, we both logged on to Zencastr for an interview.

I didn't have to worry about filling time with Nicola as my guest. In fact, I had to worry about going over time. It was a fascinating discussion, made even more engaging by her British accent. I had to stay on my toes with such an articulate guest as Nicola. She had those Buttigieg rhetorical skills and intellect to match. But she was also fun and indeed brought joy to the episode. After I stopped recording, we continued talking for over an hour afterwards. I knew another trip to London was in the cards, but with the pandemic, it would have to wait.

In my post-recording conversation with Nicola, I learned that Julie, *Buttons for Pete*, would soon be offering Pete Mosaic merchandise. Julie was another person who brought *Joy* to Team Pete, and since I missed interviewing her in New Hampshire, now was my chance. We could talk about all of the things she'd done for Barnstormers and her Buttons for Pete story. The Pete Mosaic merchandise would be launched just before Thanksgiving, so the episode was timed to come out after that.

My interview with Julie reminded me how much I loved being a podcast host. Talking to interesting people about their backstories always brought up the unexpected. I never would have known that Julie's button making experience dated back to Bernie's 2016 primary run when she supported his candidacy. She easily shifted to supporting Pete in the 2020 primary and started up the button making machine again for him as a fundraiser. After Pete suspended his campaign, Julie was one of the rebranders as she transitioned from Pete 2020 merchandise to Win the Era offerings. All proceeds were donated to Win the Era. Now the Pete Mosaic was added to her repertoire.

How fitting that Julie was the last guest for my series on the Rules of the Road. Our conversation was a celebration of what we all shared working on the campaign together, a tribute to Team Pete. Through Barnstormers and her buttons operation, Julie had interfaced with many Pete supporters from all over the country, providing many photos for the Pete Mosaic. We'd all devoted so much our time to the Pete 2020 campaign and had accomplished so much.

The sudden end to Pete's candidacy hit us all hard, and because of the pandemic restrictions, we weren't able to gather together in person for closure. I like to think that the Rules of the Road episodes provided a path towards acceptance as we celebrated Pete's legacy and the campaign itself. Had I intended that from the start, I'm not sure it would have worked out that way. The momentum built as each guest brought their own thoughts and experience into the wider discussion. We needed to celebrate the campaign in order to heal.

There was one episode in my Rules of the Road podcast that never saw the light of day. I'd finally been able to schedule an interview with Anthony Mercurio, who had been Pete's National Investment Director and was now on board with Win the Era. The episode was all about fundraising, and it was full of important information for newbies like me. This was the one and only time that I had technical difficulties with Zencastr. After recording, Anthony's sound file failed to finalize. That dreaded blue circle continued spinning without end. Usually this part of the process took only a matter of seconds. Anthony had to get to another meeting, so he didn't stay on to see that the file was never processed. I didn't have his soundtrack. Just mine. I was devastated. And embarrassed to have this happen with such a high-profile guest. How could I ask him for a re-do? At least the error wasn't mine. But it wasn't his either.

That was October 12. With less than a month before election day, Anthony would be swamped with Win the

Era business. There was no way he'd have time to do another interview. I just had to accept the fact and think that maybe, somehow, this was meant to be. I understood Anthony's commitment to Win the Era. After all, I was part of the team.

22

Win the Era

With the pandemic still raging, everyone was staying home. There were no vacations, no parties. So, it may surprise you that my calendar from May to October was packed full of events. Being a Boomer, this was a *paper* calendar with something nearly every day of the week listed in both Eastern Time and Central Time. I often got confused about the time zones. Not because I didn't understand them, but because I would sometimes do the conversion in my head and think of that as the time, only to convert it again and show up early. So, I wrote both times for each event, forming an array of ETs and CTs across the page. Win the Era PAC was in full swing now with fundraising events for endorsed down ballot candidates.

Thank God Chasten had kept us entertained with his Instagram account while we were at loose ends back in March and April. He brightened those quarantine days with shots of home life with Pete and the dogs and then upgraded to doing Instagram Live video interviews which he called *Chasten's Chats*. I felt like I was checking in with Chasten on a regular basis, maintaining some sort of connection and sense of community. Joining in for the live chats brought a smile to my face and made my day. Later on, those chats would turn into teasers for his memoir, *I Have Something to Tell You*.

When Win the Era launched, I somehow joined the Circle, a group of serious fundraisers from the campaign. I didn't know how I would be able to compete with the other members of the Circle in fundraising, but I was willing to try. Luckily, Paula was also in the Circle and provided a lifeline to me. We were both on the host committee for the big Win the Era PAC fundraiser on May 28 and had our own dedicated fundraising links to track our goals. Paula and I often compared notes, commiserating on our lackluster numbers. But we both raised money, and I was proud of myself for my efforts as a neophyte fundraiser. And now I was getting regular emails from Anthony.

My laptop was balanced on a large shoebox placed on an antique writing desk, turned to an angle for optimal window light. This was how I logged on to my online Google Meet ESL class every day from my bedroom. I'd learned early on the importance of camera height and lighting. If your students are going to see you up close and personal for two hours straight, it'd better be good. Or as good as you can make it. On the wall behind me was a large map of the London Underground from one of our trips in the '90s. After my recent trip to London, I knew the map was far from up-to-date, which amused me.

From my perch on the second floor overlooking the street where Amazon, FedEx, and UPS trucks roamed, I spent my mornings teaching ESL and my late afternoons and evenings attending fundraisers for down ballot candidates endorsed by Pete's Win the Era PAC. Win the Era was both an action fund that advocated policy issues and a political action committee that endorsed 2020 candidates up and down the ballot across the country, twenty-two in the first round and twenty-one in the second, with an Indiana group of candidates in between. These candidates met several criteria for selection, such as representing underserved populations, but most importantly, they shared Pete's values and followed the Rules of the Road. I often found myself thinking, *Wow. He really reminds me of Pete. She's so much like Pete!*

My Act Blue account was my constant companion as I RSVPed to as many events as possible. What else did I have to spend money on anyway? With the pandemic, I had nowhere to go to spend money. Plus, we had an era to win. In most of the Zoom fundraisers, Pete introduced the candidate, and then the candidate took the virtual podium. Sometimes there were two or three candidates, but there was always time for questions at the end, either pre-submitted questions or directly from the chat.

Some events were small with everyone's cameras and microphones on, whereas other times we had cameras on, but the microphones muted. Some larger events had us all off camera with the chat open, but sometimes even the chat was turned off if there were too many people. I tried to ascertain which permutation of media would be available for each event so I'd be prepared. Would I be able to type something in the chat? Would I be seen?

Paula was my Zoom buddy. Nearly every day we direct messaged about upcoming events.

"Are you going to the Lucy McBath event tonight?" I asked.

"Yes, but I'll be running late. I don't know if I'm going to put my camera on. I look a wreck."

"You always look great," I said. "Plus, you've got that great background that Pete likes." Paula's Zoom background was a photo of a PETE 2020 campaign sign in a field of bluebells, and once when she asked a question, he commented on it. I just had the London Metro map behind me. But I liked to think that Pete noticed it.

Invariably, Paula would manage to gussy herself up in time for the event, and we'd see each other on camera. Although we were there to meet the candidates, it was fun to see my Team Pete friends there and to type in the chat. "Hello from Minneapolis!" I always wrote as my greeting.

I could tell Pete was looking at faces and reading the chat whenever he could, especially towards the beginning of the event. One time, I noticed him scrolling through our video feeds with an amused smirk on his face. He later said, "I see a lot of familiar faces here today. Other frequent flyers." Oh, no. Did he think we were stalkers? Was it a good thing? Now I was self-conscious. In future events he'd say the same thing. I decided to interpret it as a good thing. He *liked* seeing us.

I found myself looking forward to all the Pete events. Was it because I had nothing else to do? Or was it because I was obsessed with Pete? The two were interrelated. Because of the pandemic restrictions, I had nothing else to distract me from my obsession, and it was threatening to take over. There is a point where an interest becomes an obsession, and I was on that path. I remember trying to temper it. *It's just because of the pandemic,* I told myself. *You have nothing else to keep your mind busy.* But then one day, standing in front of the bathroom mirror, I had an epiphany. *What if it's not about Pete? What if it's about everyone else? The Community.*

Yes, we were a real community. Team Pete wasn't there just for Pete. We were there for each other. Occasionally, Pete would end the Zoom sessions telling us to "continue lifting one another up." We were doing just that. It was our *Joy.* You could see that joy on display as people sent each other cards and small gifts through the mail, hosted book discussion groups, and had zoom parties just to see each other. You could see it in the way we all rallied around someone having a particularly tough time. Real friendships were developing.

I was still mostly on Twitter at that time, but I'm sure the same thing was happening in the Facebook and local Pete groups. What united us were the shared values of Pete's presidential primary campaign, the Rules of the Road. I know that Jodi, *Kansas for Pete,* shared her joy on Twitter, Facebook and beyond as she mailed out Win the Era swag to grassroots donors. Wristbands, stickers, pens. A little something fun to get in the mail for any donation amount. Jodi had been a topnotch grassroots fundraiser during the campaign and didn't miss a beat as she transitioned to fundraising for Win the Era PAC and the action fund. I never even tried to compete with her.

Jodi also started the *Heartland Movement* newsletter, which contained updates on various Democrats up and down the ballot in addition to news about what Pete was doing. Jodi wasn't the only one civically engaged. Pete had awakened in us a sense of responsibility for enacting change. So many of us had been new to politics and had thought it was for others to get involved, not us. What that meant, though, was other people were going to decide what happened, not us. If we truly believed in our values, we needed to take action.

From phone banking and post card writing to formal training through organizations such as Arena Summit, Team Pete was activated to help Democrats win across the board. Many local Pete groups had stayed together and were now working on their state and local elections. Pete had awakened a whole new grassroots movement. Biden's team must have noticed the army that Pete had built, especially after that hugely successful grassroots fundraiser he had with Pete that took in over one million dollars.

But how to harness that wild energy for a more traditional campaign? At first, as we mixed with the Biden team online, we were like the unruly cousins coming to visit until we found our place at the table. Biden's campaign knew about Pete's Rules of the Road and wanted to create their own similar "Campaign Code," with Pete's blessing, I'm sure. After surveying which Rules of the Road were our favorites, the Biden campaign added *Joy* and *Respect* to their list. Many of the others on the list were manifestations of Pete's other rules, evidence of their shared values. Joe and Pete were a lot alike.

Another way to harness Pete's grassroots army was to engage us in their digital efforts online along with some of the other primary candidate's supporters. Thus, the Biden Digital Coalition was born. Laura De Veau from Team Pete was one of the Digital Coalition leads, making good use of her Arena Summit training in the Organizing Director track. Laura helped coordinate five teams, something for every skill level and interest: Data, Content, Policy, Rapid Response, and Hype. Once again, we felt *belonging*.

Team Pete showed up for Biden offline as well as the Barnstormers organized a huge effort in their "Signs Across America" campaign leading up to the Democratic National Convention in August when Biden would formally accept the nomination and name Kamala Harris as his choice for Vice President. The convention would be virtual this time around, thus lacking in the usual excitement of thousands of delegates and spectators arriving in town for a big wingding. We needed an exciting buildup, and Barnstormers for America thought of a fun way to get everyone involved.

They created five routes where photos of Biden/Harris signs in cities across the country would be posted relay-style, on the path to the Democratic Convention in Milwaukee. Seven days of happy faces across the country "United for Biden." Karen led our Minnesota effort, making sure that the whole state was covered. As you can imagine, thousands of grassroots supporters participated, and the culminating video collage brought tears to my eyes. Joe made sure to thank the Barnstormers in a video message.

The closer to the election the more frenzied the volunteer efforts. The race was much too close for comfort. The stakes were high. How would we feel if Biden lost, and we hadn't done all that we could? So many people were working tirelessly. Kristi and Wes and Building Bridges rallied their forces to write postcards and phone bank. Vanessa in Florida seemed to be working around the clock, engaging new volunteers in the process. After text banking nearly every day, Paula had taken on a more formal volunteer position with the Biden campaign answering emails. Everyone was doing so much. I couldn't hold a candle to any of them.

In October, Pete's book *Trust* came out, and he split his time between book promos and stumping for Biden. But the closer it got to the election, he was working every day for Biden in Zoom calls, on news shows, and some in person events with proper social distancing and mask wearing. His cool rhetorical skills made him a huge asset everywhere he went, especially on Fox News.

Election Days for the past twenty years have been busy ones for my husband, Steve. As Chief Judge, he has to get to the polling place at 6:00 AM to get things set up for 7:00 AM opening and then work until the polls close at 8:00 PM when they cross all of their t's and dot all of their i's. Then he and the co-judge drive the ballots to the collection site. Usually, he doesn't get home until 10:00 PM. It's exhausting but rewarding.

This Election Day was no different. Even though Steve woke up before his 5:00 AM alarm and disabled it, I was well aware of his stirring. I always slept lightly the night before because I worried he'd oversleep. Now there was no way I was going to be able to fall back asleep. It was finally ELECTION DAY, the day we'd been waiting for.

I had already cast my vote for Biden/Harris back on September 18, the first day of early voting in Minnesota, so I wouldn't be going to my polling place like usual. I wouldn't be able to wink at my husband as I voted. Today, I'd still make an appearance, but it would be only to bring him some coffee and a doughnut. There were no ESL classes that day, so I had the freedom to saunter over to my local doughnut shop mid-morning. I bought several doughnuts and fritters because you never know how many you're going to eat.

Steve was just going on break when I arrived with his apple fritter and coffee.

"How's it going?" I asked.

"Surprisingly well," he replied. "We haven't had any problems with the mask requirement."

"Has it been busy?"

"There's been a steady stream," he said. "Looks like we'll have a good turnout."

I was crossing my fingers for a Biden win in Minnesota. Early voting numbers had been well above average, and a good turnout usually meant a Democratic win.

With my mission complete, I was starting to feel the effects of a short-night's sleep. My brain was in a fog. I needed more coffee. When I got home, I fired up the espresso maker for four shots out of habit. I'd only drink my usual double. I sat down at the kitchen table with my double latte and the box of doughnuts and started eating. The more coffee I drank, the more I needed. I couldn't believe how tired I felt. I walked over to the espresso machine and poured the remaining shots in my cup with some more milk. It was Election Day 2020, and I was drinking a quadruple latte.

I mindlessly stared at my phone, about to check Twitter, when a call came through. It was an unknown number, but I answered it anyway.

"Hi Sue Ann," the voice said. "This is Anthony."

"Hi Anthony!" I replied. *Was this about rescheduling the podcast interview?* I thought.

"I have someone very special who wants to talk to you," he said. "Hang on while I patch the call through."

Oh. My. God. I knew at that moment that it was Pete. Pete was calling me.

"Hello, Sue Ann," he said. "This is Pete Buttigieg."

"Pete!" I cried, walking into the living room to sit down. "You're calling me on *Election Day?*"

"We're feeling pretty good about it," he said.

My heart was racing. This sudden opportunity to talk to Pete on the phone was both exciting and terrifying.

"I'm calling to thank you for your support for Win the Era," he continued. "I saw you on all the Zoom calls. You were like the MVP of the Zoom calls!"

I laughed at that sports reference, but I felt embarrassed that he'd noticed me. So, I *was* a stalker, but he appreciated it? I'm sure I was blushing.

"You're welcome," I said. "Pete, we support you because we believe in your message. It's so important."

"Thank you for your support," he replied.

What do I say next? I knew I couldn't waste time hemming and hawing. I had to make the most of this opportunity but be respectful of his time. Luckily, I had something in mind. It was something I was going to put in an email to Anthony, but now I could tell Pete directly.

"You know, endorsing all those candidates helped with their fundraising, but it also helped us during that dark time. It was so nice to get to know all those new faces," I said.

"That was fun for me too," he said.

"I'll really enjoy watching the election returns tonight because I'll be looking for how they all did."

"For sure. Enjoy the next 48 hours," he said.

"Thank you for calling, Pete."

And that was it. I put my phone down and stared into space. *Did that just happen?*

We didn't have the results on election night. Nor did we have them the next day. Or the next. All the many mail-in ballots took time to count, and since they were falling in large proportion to Biden, each day Biden's lead grew. Finally, on Saturday, November 7, 2020, Joe Biden was declared the winner. Joe Biden would be the next President of the United States.

When Kamala Harris learned the news, she called Joe.

"We did it, Joe." she said with tears in her eyes.

Yes. We all did it.

When Pete dropped out of the primary on March 1, we couldn't see beyond our grief to the hope and success beyond. Now I knew that it was all meant to be. Joe needed Pete to win. Equally so, he needed Pete's army. Team Pete. All those months working on the Pete 2020 campaign were not in vain. In the end, it was worth it.

✈

Epilogue

On December 15, 2020, President-Elect Biden named Pete Buttigieg as his pick for Secretary of Transportation. Pete would be the first openly gay Cabinet member to be confirmed by the Senate, which he was by a vote of 86 to 13. Pete joked that he would no longer be *Mayor Pete*. He'd be *Secretary Pete*. And I knew he'd be taking his Rules of the Road along with him to the Department of Transportation, which was very fitting indeed.

As soon as Pete received the nomination for Secretary of Transportation, Team Pete went wild. We were so proud. We were also energized. Something new to work on—transportation advocacy! Immediately the hashtag #LearnAboutDOT was created, and we set about to learn what this exciting new position entailed. And just like before, rebranding occurred. Julie, *Buttons for Pete*, developed a line of transportation-themed merchandise. Graphic artists made up new Secretary Pete themed images that could be shared. Later on, a transportation education and advocacy organization called *Build the Era* would be formed by a team of grassroots volunteers. Team Pete was on the move. With all of this excitement for Transportation, I thought maybe I could do a series of podcast interviews on transportation issues. Which I did, starting in late December. *Twitter Travels for Pete—Transportation Edition.*

Secretary Pete wasn't going to be like the usual Cabinet secretary and fade into the background. No. He still had the same presence on social media and in news interviews, now as Secretary of Transportation. Just like before, he was everywhere. It was clear the Biden Administration was still in campaign mode, which was smart because all those policy ideas had to be sold. And Pete was a crucial asset to the team in this regard. It was a relief to know that we'd still be seeing him around. I felt like we had won twice.

As I look back over Pete's primary campaign and the time leading up to the election, my first thought is: *What a blast!* What a wild ride I had doing my podcast and working on the campaign. As soon as I trusted my gut to use my skills, what I was good at, things fell into place. I'll never be an accountant or a project manager. What I'm good at is meeting people. Those social butterfly skills sometimes come into good use. Now, I no longer hesitate. I know meeting new people and connecting them with each other is what I'm meant to do.

What was it about Pete that brought so many people from all walks of life together to work so hard to get him the nomination? At first glance, it was his progressive policy ideas. That was the *What*. But many candidates had the same positions. The difference was the *How*, how Pete was going to get it done, the manner in which he would get things done. The *How* was the *Rules of the Road*. That's what sold us. And the *Who*? Pete himself sealed the deal. He made us feel like we all BELONGED.

Photos from the adventure can be found at
travelingthetrailforpete.com

✈

The Rules of the Road

*T*he *Rules of the Road* were developed by the Pete for America campaign as a code of conduct for staff and volunteers to adhere to. Since the campaign, the rules have been adapted for general use by Win the Era Action Fund and are listed on their website, wintheerra.com.

Reprinted with permission from Win the Era Action Fund

Respect

In our thoughts, words, and actions we cultivate a sense of respect. We respect one another on this team, we respect every public office, and we respect every individual we encounter on the campaign trail, including our competitors. The better we hold up this value among ourselves, the better it will reflect outside. It will represent a quiet antidote to the idea that this project is too audacious to be taken seriously.

Belonging

We seek to serve and unify a diverse nation. Let us build a team and a coalition of supporters that kindly embraces and reflects the increasingly diverse country to which we belong. We will honor this value not just in our makeup but in our practices, as we proactively work to include people of different backgrounds and viewpoints in every major decision, and cultivate a sense of welcome to all.

Truth

Honesty is in our nature, and it is one of our greatest means of restoring faith in our democracy among everyday Americans and building a national movement rooted in trust and faith in our country and our beliefs. Internally and externally, our effort will be characterized by fidelity to the truth.

Teamwork

We are all working in service of our country and to elect leaders who will represent our values and make American lives better. In moments of disagreement, the temptations of pride and ego will arise. Rooted in our mission, let our common purpose be a touchstone as we foster a climate of trust and mutual respect.

Boldness

We will not hesitate to take bold stances and to accept risk in the defense of our values. Our respect is reserved for people, not for conventions. We accept no truisms without questioning. The spirit of originality will create the pressure and permission for us to do things not done before, to stand out from the crowd not by waving our arms for attention but by the fact of being different.

Responsibility

The conduct of an organization can be as influential as its outcome. Everyone on this team has a responsibility to live up to our values, and everyone must model this. When there is a mistake, we take ownership, learn, adjust, and move on. Missteps are inevitable, but they should never be repeated. We own our choices and our work.

Substance

There is no point mounting an unorthodox, underdog effort unless it is one of substance. We have the opportunity to bring meaningful ideas forward for debate. We will take questions seriously and answer them directly. We will lay aside the superficial in favor of the meaningful. We embrace complicated challenges and will work to improve the overall dialogue in how policy is debated.

Discipline

A project like ours will require enormous discipline. Through energy and determination, we will handle our resources with the stewardship they deserve, mindful that this effort is fueled by the gift of other people's time, money, relationships, and reputations.

Excellence

A functioning organization is such a marvel that we may at times be amazed simply by the fact of what we are doing. But the standard we should hold ourselves to in every part of our work is not whether it is at the level of any organization, but whether it is at the level we would expect of the best organization of this time.

Joy

Amid the great challenge we face, let us be joyful. We are privileged to be doing this work and. we are assembling a team of wonderful human beings. Along the way, we will all get many opportunities to lift one another up and lift up those we encounter. America itself is one of the greatest experiments in the history of our world. It will shape us but we can shape it too. Let us shape it, partly, by spreading the joy of working for our beliefs.

✈

Acknowledgments

Writing a book does not happen in isolation, and thank God for that! I owe a depth of gratitude to my editing team, which is almost entirely derived from the Team Pete community on Twitter. First of all, thank you to Betsey for advising on everything from editing to publishing, and to Kirin, my fearless copy editor and layout designer. But before the manuscript got to them, I had a team of amazing beta readers giving valuable feedback with each chapter I wrote. Thank you to my beta readers: April, Gina, Jan, Jodi, Laura, Myndee, Patti, Susan, Tracy, and Tulsa, with a special nod to Debra, Jennifer, and Paula, the three who went beyond the call of duty.

A big thank you goes to Michael Yoder, my podcast producer and website designer. So much of this story wouldn't have happened without him. Without Michael, I would have never become a podcast host. *Twitter Travels for Pete* wouldn't have come into existence. And to all my podcast guests from the original series during the campaign to the Rules of the Road series to the Transportation edition– thank you for allowing me to interview you! I valued and cherished your enthusiastic participation.

To Minnesota for Pete—ALL of you—thank you for so many good times. I regret that I couldn't mention more names in the book, but there were just too many names! I apologize in advance for missing anyone, but let me attempt to mention you here: Abby, Anthony, Beth-Ann, Betsy, Caitlin, Chris, Chuck, Craig, Elise, Emily, Eric, Gina, Gloria, Jeff, Jenny, Julie, Karen, Kathy, Katie L, Katie M, Kelly, Kyrstin, Leslie, Linda, Lisa, Lynn, Margy, Mary, Melani, Pam, Peter, Rachel, Sarah, Sarah, Saren, Shelly, Stephanie, Tammy, Tave, Therese, and Tricia.

Thank you to South Bend for welcoming me as an honorary South Bender: AJ, Amanda, Arielle, Breana, Greg, Jackie, Jim, Joy, Julie, Kathy, Marisel, Laura, Lety, Michael, Ryan, and Susan.

To staffers for Pete for America and Win the Era, thank you for being so friendly and welcoming to me. It made all the difference in the world. A special thank you to Stefan Smith, PFA Online Engagement Director, who continues to nurture Team Pete online.

And lastly, I owe a debt of gratitude to my husband, Steve, who put up with my constant coming and going while I was traveling for my podcast and for his encouragement for writing and self-publishing this book.

✈

About the Author

Sue Ann Rawlins loves meeting new people. As an Adult Education ESL teacher, she's met hundreds of students from all over the world. With social energy to spare, she's also met many people online and formed friendships, often traveling to meet them in person. Until the 2020 Democratic presidential primary, this hobby did not include meeting people working on a political campaign. But when she heard Mayor Pete Buttigieg speak about immigration issues from a community perspective—something near and dear to her heart—she was sold. She decided to do all she could to help this remarkable, once-in-a-generation candidate win the nomination.

After getting her feet wet with the *Minnesota for Pete* group, Sue Ann branched out and traveled around interviewing grassroots volunteers she'd met on Twitter for her podcast *Twitter Travels for Pete*. Being a podcast host was so fun she continued doing episodes even after the campaign ended, first with a series on Pete's *Rules of the Road* and then a series on transportation issues once

Pete became Secretary of Transportation. All twenty-eight episodes of the *Twitter Travels for Pete* podcast are still live and can be found on various platforms. Sue Ann continues to support the issues advocated by Pete in the campaign through the Win the Era Action Fund. She has a home with the Team Pete community, especially on Twitter, and still travels to meet those kindred spirits in person.

Before her *Traveling the Trail for Pete* memoir, Sue Ann was no stranger to writing about her travels to meet online friends. Her previous book *Novel Friends: an unexpected journey from online to real life* was of the same vein and is still available on Amazon. To support the book, she wrote more than a hundred blog posts on friendship for her former Susie Young at Heart website. Sue Ann is an experienced speaker and facilitator, having earned the Distinguished Toastmaster distinction through Toastmasters International. Sue Ann lives in Minneapolis with her husband, adult son, and dog Jojo. She can be reached on Twitter @sueannrawlins.

CPSIA information can be obtained
at www.ICGtesting.com
Printed in the USA
LVHW012118130921
697730LV00013B/1255